PURSUING HORIZONTAL

STUDIES IN GOVERNMENT
AND PUBLIC POLICY

PURSUING HORIZONTAL MANAGEMENT

THE POLITICS OF PUBLIC SECTOR COORDINATION

B. Guy Peters

University Press of Kansas

Published by the University Press of Kansas (Lawrence, Kansas 66045), which was organized by the Kansas Board of Regents and is operated and funded by Emporia State University, Fort Hays State University, Kansas State University, Pittsburg State University, the University of Kansas, and Wichita State University

Library of Congress Cataloging-in-Publication Data is available.

Peters, B. Guy.
  Pursuing horizontal management : the politics of public sector
  coordination / B. Guy Peters.
    pages cm
  ISBN 978-0-7006-2093-7 (hardback) — ISBN 978-0-7006-2094-4 (paperback)
  1. Political planning—Case studies. 2. Public administration—Management—
Case studies. 3. Policy sciences—Case studies. I. Title.
  JF1525.P6P47 2015
  352.2'9—dc23
                    2014040570

British Library Cataloguing-in-Publication Data is available.

Printed in the United States of America

10 9 8 7 6 5 4 3 2 1

The paper used in this publication is recycled and contains 30 percent postconsumer waste. It is acid free and meets the minimum requirements of the American National Standard for Permanence of Paper for Printed Library Materials Z39.48–1992.

To Sheryn, who keeps trying to keep me coordinated and coherent.

Contents

Preface and Acknowledgments   ix

1. Introduction: The Coordination Problem   1

2. Barriers to Coordination   26

3. Approaches to Understanding Coordination   45

4. The Instruments of Coordination   74

5. Case Studies in Coordination   103

6. Is Coordination Always the Answer, and Can It Be?   127

Notes   157

References   163

Index   189

Preface and Acknowledgments

This book examines the issue of policy and administrative coordination. Coordination is a problem in everyday life. The water company digs up the street in front of our house and patches the street, then the gas company comes the next day to dig up the same street. The schedules of trains and planes leave us with connection times of only a few minutes, or many hours. Busy friends struggle to find a time they can all meet because of conflicting schedules. In all these cases individuals or organizations are not taking into account adequately the activities and priorities of others, and as a consequence the outcomes for all the actors are less positive than they might otherwise be. As much as these coordination issues may frustrate us in our daily lives, the coordination problems faced by governments are larger and may affect the lives of thousands or even millions of citizens.

Since their inception governments have to contend with the issues of specialization and coordination. On the one hand governments require specialized organizations and programs to deliver services to the public using expertise. In the extreme of Franz Kafka working in his pension office, public servants would perform one specialized function repetitively, with specialization ensuring that the activity is performed as well as possible. On the other hand, however, those same governments have also attempted to coordinate the numerous specialized functions in order to produce more coherent and integrated services to the public, as well as to save money and irritation for those same citizens by eliminating duplication. The assumption has been, as Aaron Wildavsky once commented, that coordination is a "philosopher's stone" for the public sector, capable of transforming ordinary, flawed patterns of governing into more effective and efficient performance.

Governments have tended to concentrate expertise within specialized organizations. The typical collection of organizations within the public sector contains primarily agencies and departments focusing on particular functions or clienteles. This pattern of organization makes political sense by providing services and a clear target for lobbying for clients. It also fosters policy expertise and therefore can promote high-quality public policies.

Yet these specialized structures can also create problems for government. For example, many clients of social assistance programs also require health, labor market, and educational services. The segmentation of programs in most governments, however, makes it difficult to integrate the full range of services required for those clients. Those social service clients may also suffer from the failure to link eligibility criteria with the tax system, thereby creating "poverty traps" that make it more difficult for individuals to work their way out of poverty. These problems are rife in social policy but appear in many other areas of public sector activity.

So, too, are businesses affected by the segmentation of public policies. Contradictory regulations can collide—for instance, back-up horns on construction equipment required for safety reasons may violate antinoise regulations. Entrepreneurs may face duplicative requirements for information if they want to start a new business, causing them to trek from office to office providing officials the same information again and again in order to receive the full array of licenses required. Thus, starting a business in some countries may take months, whereas when there is a "one-stop shop," with its more coordinated response, the process may take only a day or two.

The common reaction of governments to policy problems has been to specialize, and that tendency has been exacerbated by several tendencies in recent governance. Perhaps the most important of these tendencies has been the popularity of the "New Public Management" as a foundation for reform. This approach to public administration has emphasized breaking larger public organizations down into smaller, single-purpose organizations. Because they are expected to be more autonomous and entrepreneurial, they also are more difficult to coordinate. While these more autonomous organizations—usually described as agencies—are assumed to enhance efficiency and accountability, they also make putting programs together more difficult.

The emphasis on performance measurement and performance management in the New Public Management also has posed some challenges for coordination. While shifting the basis of public sector accountability to the actual delivery of services is in many ways positive, it also tends to narrow the vision of public officials. If the budget of an organization, or the salary of an official, is dependent on meeting certain performance targets then the actors involved will be less likely to cooperate with other organizations to reach broader public service goals. Thus, somewhat paradoxically, the performance of individual organizations will be improved while the performance of the public sector as a whole may be diminished.

In addition to the impact of the New Public Management, increased segmentation of government also has resulted from the so-called governance reforms in the public sector that have sought to link organizations more directly to networks of social actors. While these interactions with the private sector may help to improve the implementation of policy, and even in the development of policies, they also tend to segment the public sector. The connection with stakeholders means that those social actors will want to maintain what they consider as "their programs" whereas coordination and policy integration may weaken that attachment.

If coordination is such a problem for the public sector, why hasn't someone done something about it? The answer is that they have, but producing more effective coordination has proven to be difficult. Efforts to integrate policies and create more coherent action within the public sector are likely to produce political opposition from organizations and their clients. Further, the professional training of members of public organizations and their commitments to particular ideas about public policies may limit their willingness to cooperate. Even if they are not committed to particular policy approaches, public organizations and their leaders may want to maintain their independence and power, which would be threatened.

While governments have become more segmented, they have also sought to fight back against these centrifugal tendencies. The New Public Management has emphasized the role of managers in the public sector and in turn has tended to denigrate the role of political leaders in governing. Political leaders have sought to restore the "primacy of politics" through a number of means, including developing more strategic approaches to policy that involve coordination around the major goals of governments. Beginning with the "joined-up government" in the United Kingdom, presidents and prime ministers have been using coordination and coherence as one means of reasserting their primary role in governing.

The typical response of governments to a perceived need for greater coordination is to use hierarchy and authority. Presidents and prime ministers and their staffs can be central to this process, but so, too, are central agencies such as ministries of finance. Further, assigning junior ministers responsible for clientele groups such as women and families, and even mandating simple information sharing among organizations, can enhance the capacity of the political system to act together in order to address public programs.

There are also increasing political pressures to provide more coordinated policies. In addition to the pressures for lower costs and lower taxes, clientele groups demanding cross-cutting services and a wider range of services have also begun to be more relevant politically. Women, children, the elderly, and families are all examples of client groups who require a broad array of public services and would be better served if services and programs were better coordinated. Children, for example, require services from most government departments, and if coherent packages of programs could be developed to serve them, the overall impact of government programs on their lives could be improved.

And finally, although I have been singing hymns of praise to coordination, we must also be conscious of the limits of coordination as a solution for the governance problems encountered in the public sector. The need for specialization is the most obvious of those limitations, but attempting to coordinate may also produce other problems within government. For example, coordinated policies pose problems for accountability because the blending of legal authority and financial resources makes it difficult to monitor those assets. Further, there are instances in which having multiple organizations and redundant programs may actually produce better outcomes for citizens, despite their apparent inefficiency.

My book will examine the concept of coordination, or horizontal management, in the public sector. This term is used in a variety of ways and I will examine not only its meaning but also various ways of achieving a goal of coordination. This conceptual discussion will be supplemented by several mini-cases to illustrate the difficulties of achieving coordination within governments. I hope that this discussion will make the importance, and the difficulties, of coordination clearer to students and practitioners of governance.

This book has been in preparation for a long time—much longer than either I or the University Press of Kansas would have preferred. An earlier version of the manuscript could not pass a careful review, so an almost complete revision was undertaken. Although a great deal of time has been lost in the process, I believe the time was well spent. I have had time to rethink the basic structure of the book, as well as to expand the theoretical and analytic perspectives utilized to attempt to understand coordination.

Governments have been attempting to create higher levels of coordination since there have been governments, but this task appears to have become more rather than less difficult. Governments themselves have become more internally complex, and therefore the demands placed on would-be coordinators (and would-be scholars of coordination) are even more pressing. Perhaps the greatest difference between this volume and the previous version of the book is that the complexity inherent in coordination and policy coherence is more clearly understood and I hope also more clearly explained. Also, the trade-offs between coordination and other important administrative and political values are now more apparent than they were in the earlier draft.

As well as being informed by the academic literature, this study of coordination has been informed by working with governments in the "real world" as they confront challenges to their own capacity to govern. I have been able to work as a consultant on issues of coordination in a number of countries, including Finland, Serbia, Bosnia and Herzegovina, Canada, and Mexico. These consulting opportunities not only helped me understand the processes of coordination but also helped me understand the ways in which academic theories relate (or sometimes do not) to that real world. But practitioners interestingly also found that the theory illuminated what they did on a day-to-day basis and indeed could help them perform their tasks more effectively.

Several people deserve special thanks for helping me complete this book. A very special thank-you goes to Fred Woodward. Fred has been extremely patient and supportive during this long process. I enjoyed working with him on my first book with the University Press of Kansas and continue to have great respect for his professionalism and judgment. Although not directly involved in this project, my previous research with Geert Bouckaert and Koen Verhoest in Belgium helped me in developing my understanding of coordination, especially in comparative context. And a word of thanks also for José Luis Mendez at El Colegio de México, who enabled me to rethink some of the points being raised in this manuscript.

Last, but certainly not least, my colleague and friend Jon Pierre continues to provide support and advice. It has been a blessing to have someone like him to turn to when the words do not come, and when some of the insanity of contemporary academic life threatens to overwhelm me.

PURSUING HORIZONTAL MANAGEMENT

1. Introduction: The Coordination Problem

Coordination is a common problem in everyday life. A plane has to wait for catering, or baggage handlers, before it can leave. The street in front of our house is dug up this week by the city water department, repaved, and then dug up again next week by the power company.[1] Two national organizations in the same field schedule their annual meetings at the same time. Citizens in Ghana have at least six identification numbers because government organizations do not coordinate their programs. Even the spate of serious railroad accidents in Europe has been blamed on the failure to coordinate older and newer equipment and technologies (Carvajal 2013). I am sure any reader could expand this list easily, understanding how much difficulty failures to coordinate can produce for us all (see Conklin 2005).

And it is not just national and subnational governments that encounter problems of fragmentation and an absence of coordination. As international regimes continue to proliferate and to gain increased power over a range of policies in the international arena, the fragmentation and overlap of these regimes has become a significant problem for effective governance (Biermann et al. 2009; Van de Graaf 2013). It seems that wherever there are governments, there will be conflicts between the specialization of organizations and programs and the coordination of all the programs in the policy area.

Coordination is also one of the oldest problems for the public sector. As soon as government was sufficiently differentiated to have several organizations providing different services, or providing the same basic service in different ways (an army and a navy, for example), coordination became an issue. So long as government remained relatively small and under the control of a monarch or other central figure, coordination could be handled relatively easily. A monarch such as Henry VIII, or his Wolsey, might be able to manage the affairs of state himself and might know what was happening in all the relevant policy areas and be able to ensure that there was some degree of coherence in policy.[2] Even in those primitive governing systems, however, there might be problems with coordination, and public offices were created to ensure that there was some common policy throughout the territory governed by the monarch.[3]

As government became involved in an increasing range of activities and attempted to impose its rule over larger geographical spaces, coordination quickly evolved into a "philosopher's stone" for government (Seidman 1998; Jennings and Krane 1994; Webb 1991; Anderson 1996; 6 et al. 2002). That is, the more the public sector has evolved and expanded, the more incoherence and the failure to be capable of encouraging, or coercing, programs to work together have come to be seen as among the more crucial root causes of the numerous perceived failures of government. Governments are inherently multiorganizational. The specialization reflected in that multiorganizational nature is often positive for the quality of decisions (Bouckaert, Peters, and Verhoest 2010). Further, specialization is important politically for government because it provides a clear locus for the identification and activities of client groups within society.

Despite those virtues, the many organizations existing in government create problems of coordination and coherence, and those coordination problems are very troubling to political leaders. As Glyn Davis (1997, 131) argued, in government, "An elective official confronted with a state which simultaneously encompasses internal conflicts, competing external imperatives, contested boundaries, unclear jurisdictions, policy lacunae and interest capture is likely to desire some form of coordination."

Often one organization of the public sector does not appear even to have the most basic information about what other parts are doing, and the individuals involved appear to care little about the actions of their counterparts elsewhere. And even different regional offices of the same organization may not know what other offices are doing, and in their mutual ignorance may produce policy failure. For example, the Boston and New York regional offices of the Securities and Exchange Commission each had part of the needed information to stop the Bernard Madoff Ponzi scheme but neither knew what the other had learned. Therefore, Mr. Madoff was able to continue to cheat investors for another year at least (SEC 2009).

Further, coordination failures are particularly vexing to leaders in the public sector (and also to citizens) because they appear so fundamental (National Commission on Employment Policy 1991). No matter how numerous they may have become, the programs that are not coordinated adequately are all part of the same government and therefore should be capable of working together toward a common public purpose. Everyone appears to know that coordination is fundamental but yet no one appears to be capable of producing an effective working pattern that produces that coordination.

The search for the philosopher's stone was, as we are well aware now, a futile search. This source of inestimable wealth was never found, and never will be. The history of policy coordination in government provides only slightly more reason to be optimistic. There are instances of successful coordination of public programs. These successes, however, tend to arise in special circumstances or because of idiosyncratic factors. For example, despite the numerous and well-known failures more successful coordination is likely to occur in crises such as wars or economic downturns. As another example, strong political leadership may be able to produce coherence even in the face of divisions within government.

Despite some successes, the stories of failure and the significant, and at times even amusing, consequences of those failures are by far more numerous. Governments have invested a great deal of time and energy in generating coordination (Challis et al. 1988; 6 et al. 2002; Bogdanor 2005), but in the end the outcomes are that programs have remained inconsistent, and few citizens actually have received the high-quality, integrated services they might feel entitled to receive. There are numerous very good political and administrative reasons for those failures in governing (see Chapter 2), but they are still very much failures. Indeed, some of the same factors that are argued to create coordination, e.g., crisis, may also produce failures (see Boston 1992).

To some extent the failure of coordination is, like the failure to find the philosopher's stone, made all the more disappointing because of the high expectations for the outcomes. There is some sense among practitioners (see Mountfield 2001, for example) as well as in academic writings about coordination, that if only we can create adequate coordination and coherence then many of our policy problems will be solved. This pursuit of coordination begs the question of whether well-integrated programs that are themselves poorly designed and underfunded can really make life better for citizens. Indeed, one might argue that good coordination among poor programs might only exacerbate the fundamental shortcomings of those programs, just as good coordination among well-designed programs should create some synergy among those same programs.[4] Still, everything else being equal, better coordination can be reasonably assumed to produce benefits for the public sector and for the public and is therefore a goal that continues to be worth pursuing.

THE MEANING OF COORDINATION

We have been discussing coordination as if we know what the term means, and as if there is a single definition and a single type of problem that is undermining the capacity of government to deliver an integrated and effective collection of services to the public. That is not the case, and although coordination has a common-sense meaning, it has a number of facets and complexities that need to be considered for academic investigations. For example, coordination is both a process through which decisions are brought together and an outcome of that process. In addition, a number of other terms are often used as virtual synonyms for coordination—words such as *cooperation, coherence, collaboration,* and *integration.* Therefore, before I can proceed any further I will need to define the term, and the problem, that is central to the analysis, and then discuss the various types of failures in coordination and their possible consequences for government.

Although it is in many ways a common-sense term, there is a need for a clear definition of coordination. One of the most direct and most generally applicable definitions of coordination in the policy and administration literature is "the extent to which organizations attempt to ensure that their activities take into account those of other organizations" (Hall et al. 1976, 459). Another definition holds that "a set of decisions is coordinated if adjustments have been made in it such that the adverse consequences of any one decision for other decisions in the set are to a degree and in some frequency avoided, reduced, counterbalanced, or outweighed" (Lindblom 1965, 154). In many ways both Hall's and Lindblom's definitions are deceptively simple. All governments have to do is have their programs and organizations find means of taking into consideration the actions of other organizations and programs and consider in advance the consequences of decisions. That definition does not take into account explicitly, although it certainly does implicitly, the numerous different causes for coordination problems, and the barriers to effective coordination that exist in almost all political systems. Further, as Metcalfe (1994, see pages 22–23 below) has pointed out, there are various *levels* of coordination that can be achieved through different investments of resources, or simply because some programs are easier to coordinate than are others, and some civil service systems may promote coordination more explicitly than do others. The question then is what level of aspiration the participants in the process have for the coherence of the outcomes (see also Kassim, Peters, and Wright 1999).

Some scholars have focused on "policy integration" as another meaning of coordination, and one with somewhat stronger requirements of the participants. For example, Underdål (1980) argued that a perfectly integrated policy was one where "all significant consequences of policy decisions are recognized as decision premises, where policy options are evaluated on the basis of their effects on some aggregate measure of utility, and where the different policy elements are consistent with each other." In other words, integration requires that each policy choice take into account the effects of that choice on the full range of other organizations and programs, and that as much consistency among the choices as possible be achieved. This level of integration is a difficult standard to achieve but is facilitated by the development of comprehensive policy ideas—such as social inclusion, competitiveness, or sustainability (Lafferty and Hovden 2003)—to guide the actions of a range of policy actors (Hertin and Berkhout 2003).

The term *coherence* also has been used to describe the creation of more compatible forms of policy across organizations and policy areas. To some extent coherence implies greater attempts to write legislation and design interventions in ways that are not inconsistent, rather than an *ex post* process of attempting to get programs and organizations to work today (May, Sapotichne, and Workman 2006; Persson 2004).

While this policy coherence may be more effective in the long run, given that policies would be designed to work together, achieving such coherence *ex ante* may be more difficult politically. Creating coherence involves understanding *ex ante* the possibilities of cooperation and the possible gains. Individuals and organizations may therefore be asked to alter or perhaps even eliminate their current programs in favor of some possible coordinated program in the future. And the legislative or executive officials responsible for designing the coordinated interventions may themselves be committed to particular policy stances.

Given the above somewhat generic definitions of coordination and integration and the various levels of coordination that may exist, there is a need to examine more analytically the conditions under which coordination problems arise in government. As noted, the basic root of coordination problems is specialization and the division of governments along both horizontal and vertical dimensions. Specialization, and the resulting organizational divisions, produces numerous benefits for government as well as many for the clients of government programs. It enables governments to concentrate expertise and gives public organizations, and public employees, clearer missions (see Goodsell 2010).

Specialization, however, is also the source of numerous problems within the public sector. At the same time that specialization focuses expertise on a public problem or the needs of clients, it tends to segment (often artificially) those problems and those clients rather than presenting a more integrated conception of the causes and possible remedies for the difficulties. The benefits of specialization in public tasks must be balanced against the benefits that could be obtained from a more unified and holistic approach to governing. This more unified conception of governing and of service delivery can provide services to the "whole client," while potentially also saving government money by eliminating redundant and conflicting programs.

More integrated conceptions of governing might also have a greater prospect of identifying, and even resolving, underlying program design difficulties in public programs. These design difficulties often arise in the classification and categorization of the targets of public programs. For example, means-tested social programs, or aids to small businesses, have arbitrary cutoff points for income or receipts above which the client is no longer eligible for assistance. These threshold values tend to create difficulties for clients in themselves, but their problems become even more apparent when several of them interact to place clients or potential clients in situations that are worse than either of them alone would have produced.

Coordination is a familiar term, but a number of other terms are being applied to the same general question in the literature on public management. One of the earliest differentiations made in the organizational literature (Schermerhorn 1975) was between cooperation and coordination. The former was deemed to be a more temporary and informal means of creating relationships among organizations for mutual benefit, while the latter is conceptualized as creating more formal structures and procedures designed to impose greater coordination among individuals and organizations. Similarly, Janet Weiss (1989) argued that problem definition and framing enhance cooperative solutions to problems while formal methods and structures emphasize power and control over actions. Thus, in that view, coordination involves formalizing patterns of interactions among the organizations.

The literature on the management of social programs in particular has been discussing "collaboration" as a mode of positive interaction among organizations. For example, Eugene Bardach (1996; Bardach and Lesser 1996) has written a great deal on collaboration and the deceptively simple aspects of "managerial craftsmanship" required to get agencies to work together. More recently there has been a burgeoning literature on collaborative management in both the public and private sectors (Skelcher and Sullivan 2008; Agranoff and McGuire 2003). In the management literature on collaboration there is a greater emphasis on the role of boundary-spanning agents whose task—mandated or self-assigned—is to work across the boundaries of different organizations to generate greater cooperation (Davies 2009).

In this book I will be dealing with collaboration as a subset of coordination, in which the cooperation and "working together" is voluntary and based on normative agreements. This approach to collaboration is valuable but as noted above and as will become increasingly evident throughout this book, a good deal of coordination is not produced by agreement but rather is the result of either coercion[5] or the use of incentives. It is certainly more pleasant if the coordination can be based on common norms, but we do not have to wait for that agreement to coordinate.

Common norms can also be generated through political processes if there is not sufficient *ex ante* agreement. Bardach (1996) emphasizes the need to find common agreement among agencies in order to facilitate their working together. Schön and Rein (1994) consider how to resolve "intractable policy disputes" and argue for a process of reframing in which the participants develop a common frame for the policy issues from their competing frames. Earlier, Lindblom (1965) discussed this process as "partisan analysis," in which one actor attempts to define his or her policy preferences in a way that conforms with those of another actor. In all of these versions of collaboration the emphasis is on finding common definitions of the problem and common understandings about modes of intervention.

Jan Kooiman has discussed collaboration and cooperation in a somewhat different manner. He argued (2003) for a difference between these two terms, with the former representing something more fleeting in terms of agreements among organizations to work together, while the latter represented more enduring patterns of working together, and perhaps (although Kooiman is far from clear on this point) something approaching the level of policy integration previously mentioned above. Thus, Kooiman's distinction between coordination and collaboration tends to mirror that of Weiss mentioned above.

Kooiman is interested in all these forms of interorganizational working as the means for achieving his more general goal of "governance." In that perspective governance means a substantial level of coordination not only within the public sector but also between the public and private sectors. Governance in this view is providing steering for the society through complex interactions of multiple actors across multiple areas of policy. This interactive conception of governing (see Torfing et al. 2012) assumes that hierarchical control through governments will be less effective in generating coordination than will more collaborative interactions among social actors, with or without the public sector being involved.

Practitioners, especially those in the United Kingdom, have also been using terms such as *joined-up government* and *holistic governance* to address the fundamental issue of coordination and coherence in governing (Mountfield 2001; 6 2003; 2004; Pollitt 2003; Bogdanor 2005). These terms were designed to be political terms as much as or more than they were intended to provide analytic leverage for scholars, but they do describe tasks and styles of coordination within the political system. The Blair government began early in its time in office to talk about creating joined-up government (Cabinet Office 2000), reflecting in part the fragmented government they had inherited from the previous Tory administration.[6] That government had decentralized government substantially, but even without that decentralization there would have been more general problems of coordination that are endemic to all governments. The Blair government's drive to create "joined-up government" was, however, superseded by a concern among at least some of the individuals involved with creating a "holistic" government, meaning that not only is there an attempt to get programs to work together effectively, there is a further ambition that programs have more consistent goals and that there be greater coherence across the public sector. Attaining that level of integration would, in turn, require reframing of policies and using common ideas about the causes of policy problems and the possible remedies for those problems (see Chapter 4).

When dealing with definitions and alternative meanings of coordination, we should be clear about some other terminology to be used. Throughout, I will have to discuss "policy areas" or "policy domains," meaning policies defined in terms of familiar functional categories such as agriculture, defense, or whatever. These are the familiar "silos" or "stovepipes" that for centuries have plagued people working in government when they confronted the need to create greater coordination. Despite the disdain that many public sector employees have expressed toward these policy structures, they have been able to perpetuate themselves in part because of the felt need for expertise and specialization (Bouckaert, Peters, and Verhoest 2010), and in part because of the power of the clientele groups, and the professional groups of service providers who support them (Wilkinson and Appelbee 1999). At times the policy domain question becomes even more narrowly defined, as some types of social work programs find it difficult to coordinate with others presumably providing similar services.[7]

WHY WORRY ABOUT COORDINATION?

Why do governments worry about coordination, and especially why do they seemingly worry more about this issue in the first several decades of the new millennium than they have in the past? I have already argued that governments have been concerned about coordination virtually as long as there have been governments, but why more so now?

Cost. The first answer to the question of why worry about coordination is that poor coordination wastes public money, and does so now in an era in which the public budget has become a major political concern. In the clear cases of redundancy documenting and actually counting up those costs is possible, but in other cases the issue may be more opportunity costs than manifested costs. How much money have we wasted (in terms of future production, etc.) because education, labor market, and social policy programs are not more coherent?

Contradictions. As well as duplicating one another, poorly coordinated public programs may actually contradict one another. In the United States the federal government spends large sums of money to prevent smoking while it also spends large sums of money supporting tobacco farmers. While this is good politics—programs in different departments serving different constituents—it may be bad policy. And to some extent also bad politics because it gives the public an impression of a government that cannot decide on a single policy and one that is willing to squander resources.

Success of Vertical Management. During the era of the New Public Management the management of individual public programs improved. Much of this improvement was, however, bought at the expense of greater integrity within the public sector. The emphasis on single-purpose agencies and on performance management—emphasizing the success of individual programs and their managers—tended to disaggregate public action. As will be noted later, this movement in public management provoked reactions from governments (see pages 98–100) but there have been continuing effects of this movement on the public sector (Christensen and Laegreid 2007).

Legitimation. As well as being faced with financial problems, contemporary governments are also faced with significant problems of legitimation (Norris 2011). As the public sector has faced pressures from perceived poor performance, excessive taxes, and bureaucratization, the need to legitimate its existence has become more central to politics and policymaking. This has become true even for the countries of

Northern Europe that have enjoyed a great deal of trust and respect from their citizens. The seeming disorganization and lack of coordination within the public sector is one of numerous factors that have been undermining the legitimacy of government.

Availability of Means. Greater supply of the means for coordination to some extent has created greater demand. The development of information technology in particular has made coordination, information sharing, and collaborative working of all sorts more possible in the public sector (see Cabinet Office 2000). The question of why government cannot be better coordinated therefore becomes even more a question of the lack of will rather than the lack of readily available mechanisms.

Globalization and Regionalization. Finally, globalization has tended to force together policy areas that might otherwise be more separated. One clear example is the role of education in "competitiveness policies." As economic policy becomes more defined in terms of global competition in an information age, education policy-makers are more driven to coordinate with their colleagues in the conventionally defined economic ministries. Likewise, as foreign trade is a larger component of economic well-being, other ministries such as agriculture also become connected more closely to economics. Although this discussion is in terms of the economic effects of transnational action, some of the same could be said for other policy domains, especially within the European Union.

DIMENSIONS OF COORDINATION

Having some sense of the meaning of coordination, it should be clear that this one term covers a number of different, if related, problems in the public sector. Each of these problems involves the interaction or absence of interaction of multiple public organizations. The roots of the problems we observe are political, administrative, and organizational. Individuals and organizations may be pursuing specific policy and political goals and may not want to cooperate for fear of reducing their chances of reaching those goals. Likewise, administrative routines and even legal mandates for implementation may be undermined by attempting to achieve greater coherence in governing; and finally, organizations (whether public or private) tend to maintain their own patterns and not to cooperate whether out of self-interest or simply routine. In short, there are any number of ways of thinking about the problem of coordination in government, and no shortage of villains for this story.

Positive and Negative

Implied in the definition of coordination given above is the notion that programs and organizations should work together to achieve ends that are not attainable through their individual actions. That is a reasonable reading of ideas of coordination, but a minimalist version of coordination could be attained without even that very basic degree of collaboration. *Negative coordination* involves only the agreement, even if tacit, of the actors that they will not harm each other's programs or operations. Fritz Scharpf (1997), for example, has discussed negative coordination as one component of his discussion of governance, noting that it was a minimum condition of governing. This principle is often enshrined in law and practice, as in the *Ressortsprinzip* in German government that each minister has the right to control policy and administration in his or her own area.

Although this negative conception of coordination appears limited, it can actually be a significant contribution to governing in situations in which programs often bump into one another as they attempt to reach their goals. In particular, negative coordination is often crucial for nonhierarchical forms of coordination in which actors negotiate bilaterally to find ways of not affecting each other negatively—so-called "clearance negotiations" (Scharpf 1997, 39). Further, the bilateral nature of negative coordination reduces the complexity that often arises in multilateral negotiations characteristic of positive coordination.

The major focus of this book will be on the *positive* aspects of coordination, and how coordination can generate coherence, rather than just minimize conflict, across policies and organizations. This positive conception of coordination is much more difficult to achieve than is negative coordination. Positive coordination may require the actors involved to give up some of their own policy goals, and almost certainly some of their preferred ways of achieving those goals, in order to attain greater overall performance of government (Thomson, Stockman, and Torenvlied 2003).

Asking for that self-denial may be asking a great deal of organizations that have developed their goals and procedures in the sincere belief that what they are doing serves the public. If these organizations are correct in that belief, as they generally are, then expecting them to give up some aspects of those programs in favor of some vague benefits achieved through coordination is asking a great deal. This request for pursuing the greater good is all the more true given that contemporary managerialism in the public sector tends to focus on the performance of single organizations (see below) and perhaps more basically the need that organizations have to preserve themselves, their budgets, and their programs.

Process or Outcome

The discussion of positive and negative coordination leads to the question of whether we should consider coordination as a process or as an outcome. The answer is obviously that we need to consider both of these dimensions when we think of coordination. There is a political and administrative process directed toward improving levels of coordination, and we need to assess the extent to which coordination has been achieved.[8] The answer to the above question is also that we will be concerned with different aspects of coordination and coherence depending upon whether we focus on process or outcomes.

The majority of the discussion within this book will be of the success or failure of political systems in generating coordination. But we will also be considering some aspects of the political process that may or may not be able to produce that level of desired coherence (Nowlin 2011). For example, the literature on collaboration emphasizes process and the means through which individuals and organizations work together (Bryson and Crosby 2006). Further, the processes of framing and reframing are central to understanding how policies can be made more coherent and consistent. We therefore need to consider how to design policy processes that can facilitate coordination and also understand the elements of those processes than can inhibit coordination.

Vertical and Horizontal

The bulk of the discussion of coordination in this book will be of the horizontal dimension of interaction among programs, but we should not forget that there is a crucial vertical dimension as well. Even in a government that intends to be highly centralized and unitary there must be some freedom for subnational governments to make decisions of their own (see Duran and Thoenig 1996; Desage 2013). This latitude, in turn, means that there must be some means of producing a desirable level of coherence among the decisions taken in these levels of government. The notion of a desirable level of coherence is important, because that level will vary among countries, and perhaps across different policy areas.

Federal political systems, for example, will generally permit greater diversity in programs as delivered than will unitary political systems. To a great extent the intention of a federal design is that local conditions and local preferences may be expressed more clearly in policy choices, and hence vertical coordination is less of a concern. Differences in local climates will require different standards for housing or road construction, and differences in religion may produce different styles of delivering education or social services. Even in a federal system there may attempts to create some uniformity across a country for fundamental rights and responsibilities of citizens, but the general reaction to policy questions will be to permit diversity. Further, some federal systems (Germany) will demand higher levels of coordination than will others (the United States or Canada [Hueglin and Fenna 2006]).

Although the vertical dimension of coordination is usually considered in terms of multilevel government and federalism, unitary regimes may have some of the same problems. Not only do some unitary regimes grant substantial autonomy to their subnational governments, but even departments within national governments are not designed in ways that facilitate cooperation in delivering policies. Hogwood (1995), for example, found that regional structures of departments in England were not aligned, making cooperation less likely.

Also, some policies may require greater uniformity and coherence than do others. Policies that affect the basic civil rights of citizens should, everything else being equal, be uniform throughout a country, while policies about parks and recreation may vary considerably without creating any substantial injustice. Countries differ, however, in the range and types of services that they consider essential and therefore that must be provided equally. The French concept of *services publics,* for example, considers a range of social services, including education, to be essential to the citizen and therefore requiring uniformity (see Fauroux and Spitz 2002), with that uniformity being enforced by the central government. In contrast, however, education is the one service that citizens in the Anglo-Saxon world tend to consider the most important for local control and opportunities for innovation.

Issues of vertical coordination are becoming more important as "multi-level governance" (Szczerski 2005; Bolleyer and Börzel 2010) becomes a more common challenge for contemporary governments. This issue is most clearly defined in Europe as the addition of another tier of government within the European Union has increased problems of vertical coordination, and even horizontal coordination. This is perhaps especially so given that the more loosely structured pattern of decision making emerging as a result of multilevel governance has tended to enhance the capacities of some subnational governments to bargain directly with Brussels and escape vertical coordination at the national level. Some regions within Europe, such as Scotland and Catalonia, have been especially effective in making their own connections with Brussels and being able to maximize their own benefits through those connections.

In addition to the opportunities that multilevel governments create for subnational governments, segments of government (especially bureaucracies) can generate control over a policy area throughout several levels of government and create vertical integration. This capacity for integration is especially evident for bureaucratic actors such as the Directorates General in the European Union (Rhinard and Vaccari 2005). The policy integration created through these processes is perhaps even more resistant to horizontal coordination than is the sectoral politics within a single level of government.[9] These vertical "stovepipes" are the product of bargaining among the levels of government so that any attempt to alter their patterns of making and implementing policy would open up a new round of negotiation. Further, these structures tend to be supported by epistemic communities that shield them from external interference (Miller 2003).

The final point emerging from thinking about coordination through multilevel governance is that coordination as a process can be used to produce substantive policy change. The Open Method of Coordination (Buchs 2007) has been used to produce greater uniformity in policy areas that the European Union might not otherwise be able to address. I will be examining this process as one of the principal examples of coordination in Chapter 5, but the possibilities of making policy through coordination in multilevel systems (Bolleyer and Börzel 2010) also demonstrate the general relevance of coordination for policymaking as well as for policy implementation.

Policy and Administration

One of the most fundamental issues in the analysis of coordination is the strategic question of whether the strategic policymaker should focus on policy or administration if coordination is the goal. Like most interesting and important questions about governing the answer to this question is not easy, and there are good reasons for choosing either answer. This debate to some extent mirrors the "top-down" versus "bottom-up" issues in implementation (Sabatier 1986; Linder and Peters 1987; Winter 2012). The fundamental question in that literature is whether it is possible to design policies sufficiently well at the top of government to produce the desired outcomes in the field or whether the policymaker needs to depend more upon the local knowledge of the implementers at the bottom to produce viable programs and coordination.

The first option is to coordinate from the top and be sure that the policy is coherent and integrated, with the assumption that if the underlying policies are consistent then their implementation will by necessity also be compatible. The argument supporting this view of coordination is that if policies are fundamentally compatible then administration can proceed along normal functional lines and still produce outcomes that will be coherent (De Jong 1996). Further, this style of coordination, if it can actually be achieved, is likely to be more efficient than one that depends upon local bargaining. This is especially true if there is a strong desire for uniformity of implementation in the field. Relying on coordination in the field means that there will be numerous local bargains and hence potentially broad differences in the policies as implemented.

The alternative approach would be to argue that so many aspects of policy can go amiss between the center of government and the field staff and that even the most compatible policies in the center may well diverge once they are implemented. Phrased in more economic language, there is a danger of loss of agency (Huber and Shipan 2002), with administrators making their own decisions about good policy and the intention of legislation that will be different from the intentions of the "formators" (see Lane 1981). Further, the investment of political effort and time in policymaking may not be an efficient means of producing coherence when difficult issues, and individual cases, will still have to be worked out at the level of implementation. Therefore, in this view, the better approach is to focus on making the bottom of government, and the administrative process, better coordinated and then there will be a better chance of getting the policies right.

Attempts at preventing the abuse of children offer an important example of the contrast between top-down and bottom-up conceptions of coordination. In several fatal cases of child abuse in the United Kingdom there appeared to have been *ex ante* agreement among the organizations involved, such as police and social work. These arrangements failed, however, because the lower levels of the organizations did not know about them or did not follow through on them (Marinetto 2011; Laming 2009). In this view coordination at the top is likely to be relatively ineffective unless the "joining up" pervades the organizations.

The choice between those two strategies often is political, given that the design of policies may be the result of political decisions in a legislature or the political executive. At times those political leaders may not wish to face the political battles necessary to coordinate effectively (see below) and will simply leave it up to their officials to confront the problems in the field. That choice, in turn, provides the political leaders the opportunity to blame any resulting failures in coordination on the failings of the infamous "bureaucracy." This abdication of responsibility is by far the easiest political strategy, but it is one that obviously may produce suboptimal results for citizens and for the bureaucrats.

Political and Administrative

This dimension of coordination is closely related to the previous dimension of policy and administration. In both cases one option is to emphasize resolving coordination difficulties through the capacity to make programs work together once they have been adopted and begin to be implemented. This bottom-up approach to coordination obviously emphasizes the role that administrators can play in producing effective coordination. The alternative is to focus on the decisions of the political actors responsible for the formulation and management of programs, rather than to focus on the actions of the administrators who are involved in the day-to-day process of implementation.

The logic of approaching coordination as a political rather than an administrative activity is that the legitimacy and political power necessary to push and prod organizations out of their established patterns of delivering policies through "silos" or "stovepipes" may be vested in political leaders rather than in administrators. Producing effective, coordinated policy action requires making government go against many of their ingrained patterns of making decisions and managing programs, and most administrative officials will have few incentives to engage in that type of battle with their fellow public servants. Therefore, it may be up to political leaders to utilize their legitimate power in government to change the ingrained patterns.

The political leadership will, however, almost certainly have to be at the very top of government (Peters 2004a; Dahlström, Peters, and Pierre 2010). Relying even on politicians with responsibilities for a particular ministry may not be effective in producing the type of horizontal coordination that may be required for effective governance. To be effective as the leaders of an individual ministry or agency the political officials will need to defend that organization and its programs against threats at the cabinet table, in budget hearings, and in other settings in which the resources and political power of organizations are tested against each other. Presidents and prime ministers, however, do have some incentive to produce coordination and more effective management of government as a whole.

Administrative officials also may be committed to their organizations, and perhaps even more strongly than are their ministers. Civil servants may have no place else to go, whereas political leaders' ambitions may be better served by being cooperative with their colleagues in cabinet. That having been said, however, senior civil servants are often professionals in governing, in addition to being members of a particular organization, and may have ideas and commitments that extend beyond the narrow interests of one ministry (see Wright and Page 1999). If indeed those civil servants are committed to the process of governance they may be more natural entrepreneurs for effective coordination than are politicians.

Administrative coordination can be brought about in a number of different ways. Perhaps the simplest way is to have a number of different programs administered through a single office—the "one-stop shop" that has become a common strategy for increasing efficiency and citizen satisfaction with government (Pollitt and Bouckaert 2004, 81–82). This administrative solution may be a relatively minimal form of coordination, given that the policies being administered may themselves not be compatible with one another. This places the onus of coordination on administrators involved to make decisions about which set of regulations to adhere to most closely when coping with citizens. But for those citizens this level of coordination may be the most important because it shapes the policies delivered to them.

Inside and Outside

The bulk of the discussion of coordination in public administration and public policy is concerned with the behaviors of multiple public sector organizations. This is reasonable, given that these organizations might be expected to be playing on the same team and cooperating to produce better services for citizens. That having been said, however, there is also a clear and growing need for organizations in the public sector to coordinate with organizations in society, whether those be for-profit or not-for-profit organizations. This need for working across the boundary of state and society has always been there but is becoming more clearly defined as "governance" begins to become a paradigm for the public sector and public sector management (see Pierre and Peters 2000; Tiihonen 2004). As Salamon (2000) and others (Kettl 2002) have pointed out, many if not most major initiatives of government now involve some elements of partnerships between the public and private sectors, and therefore thinking about coordination across that permeable boundary between state and society becomes all the more important.

The same issues about collaboration that arise within government itself will arise between government and the private sector. Both sets of organizations (and their members) may have individual goals that they are pursuing and will find that they may have to give away something to achieve the possible gains through cooperation (see Stokman and Van Oosteen 1994). Likewise, when negotiations over collaboration begin the organizations may find that their goals are not as compatible as they may have appeared when the differences did not have to be confronted directly. In the area of social policy, for example, private sector organizations may now not be as anxious as public sector organizations to move clients into the workplace, whereas the orientation to "workfare" motivates the public sector to think primarily about employment options.

Further, as argued above concerning coordination through implementation, the public sector may be able to coordinate internally by going outside. That is, the potential conflicts between organizations within the public sector over resources, or their narrow vision of the needs of their clients, or the complexity of a policy area, may lead to lower levels of cooperation within government itself. The clients of various programs, or the participants in various policy networks, may understand better the interaction of programs. Thus, when those client groups can articulate their needs and goals effectively they may be able to generate more coordination among official actors.

Similar or Complementary Goals

Yet another general issue to be raised about the politics of coordination, within and across policy sectors, is whether coordination is more feasible within individual policy domains or across those sectors. One could hypothesize that coordination is more likely to be effective within a single policy domain. The actors within that domain should share a common set of goals and values and should be able to communicate more effectively with their common professional language or organizational jargon. These numerous similarities among allied programs should make coordination a natural outcome of interaction among organizations and individuals.

On the other hand, however, when programs and organizations are operating within a single policy area they may think of themselves as competitors for the same clients and the same resources. While coordination might make a great deal of sense from the perspective of the client or the disinterested academic analyst, for the participants in the process that cooperation might be conceptualized as threatening to established resource bases and standard operating procedures. For public programs, and perhaps especially for social service programs, clients are a major resource; losing one's client base may be followed very quickly by losing budgets and other resources. Therefore, public organizations tend to be very protective of their clienteles and to be unwilling to engage in high levels of sharing and program consolidation.

Organizations with complementary goals may therefore have an easier time coordinating than those with more similar goals. For example, in the case of the Open Method of Coordination in the European Union (Chapter 5) labor market organizations and social policy organizations both have goals of improving the life chances of members of workers and the socially excluded. Those two sets of organizations would go about those tasks rather differently and would have different short-term goals, but they would not be in competition with one another and therefore may be able to work together effectively (see Maas 1951). On the other hand, organizations with very similar goals—for example, serving disabled populations—but who do it in rather different ways, may find coordination more challenging (USGAO 2004a).

Policy-Specific or Systemic Goals

Most of the discussion to this point has been about the coordination of specific policies and problems, but some coordination efforts are directed at the policies and behavior of the political system more broadly. Two of the more prominent of these coordination dimensions have been environmental and gender issues, but other issues such as the protection of aboriginal populations and energy also have been relevant (Malloy 2003). These dimensions of policies have supplemented the financial and budgetary considerations that have long been systemic issues that have guided policymaking in government. As mobilization around environmental issues became more important politically, governments attached environmental reviews to most policymaking and ministries of the environment and their equivalents became new versions of central agencies (Doern 1993; Nilsson and Persson 2003).[10] At the most extreme, environmental concerns can trump other considerations.

More recently gender issues have been treated much the same as have been environmental issues, at least in some countries with strong agendas for equality. That is, the implications of all policy decisions for gender equality, and in some cases racial equality, are included as a part of the consideration of those issues. For example, in a survey of its member countries, the Organization for Economic Cooperation and Development (2005) has shown that most of the countries now examine the gender implications of policy choices and attempt to implement programs in ways that will maximize the opportunities for women to receive equal treatment. Those reviews by no means assure equal treatment, but they do indicate some commitment to the issue and an attempt to make this meta-policy consistent across programs.

What these concerns with both environment and race and gender equality issues do is to impose additional cross-cutting criteria on programs, ensuring that they are coordinated not only among themselves but also with other government-wide priorities. While these criteria have obvious social benefits they also have internal decision-making costs for government. Decisions must take that many more steps, and must meet that many more criteria, when these criteria are included. Further, these social goals may interfere with other goals of programs, so that the decisions that ultimately must be made will require choosing to maximize one set of goals or another. Thus, as I will point out at much greater length below, as I assess the importance of coordination, coordination is important, but how important? Is it better to achieve the individual program goals, even if inconsistent, and to pay the price in redundancy or even conflicting outcomes, or is coordination a more important outcome of the policy process that should be emphasized?

Further, thinking about cross-cutting goals need not imply only pursuing social goals. For example, competitiveness has become a central goal for many governments (Oughton 1997). This term may be defined in a number of ways but it does tend to emphasize the integration of a range of educational, social policy, and labor market policy concerns with more traditional institutions and instruments of economic policy. In a contemporary knowledge-based economy, it is not sufficient to get the economics right to be competitive; a range of other policy areas must also be involved.

At some points the attempt to infuse policy concerns throughout the full range of public sector activity can only really be done through the use of information. For example, advocates for children have developed children's budgets in a number of settings to attempt to demonstrate what is being done, and what needs to be done, for children through the public budget (Tsegaye and Mekonen 2010; HAQ 2013). In these cases demonstrating the overall budgetary allocation for this segment of the society demonstrates the range of services required by this clientele group and the need to consider them across the policy process.

Short or Long Term?

Yet another consideration in thinking about the problems of coordination in the public sector is the length of time the cooperation is expected to occur. In many cases the cooperation will be only for a specific project, or even for a specific problem that can be solved, and then the two organizations go back to being blissfully ignorant of each other. For example, organizations may coordinate around a construction project, or perhaps around a disaster, but once the work is completed they can return to their normal patterns of doing business in isolation from one another. Crisis situations, such as the hurricane disaster in the southern United States, produce short-term needs for massive levels of coordination vertically as well as horizontally, but those needs may become reduced significantly after the crisis has passed.

The more important cases for coordination, however, require continuing cooperation and the creation of some sort of institutionalized pattern of interaction. By *institutionalized* in this context I do not necessarily mean that formal structures have to be created and formal rules have to be written (see Chisholm 1989). Rather, I mean that there needs to be some routinization of the interactions and that common problem solving becomes valued by the individuals involved. Philip Selznick (1957, 27) defined institutionalization as "infusing a structure with value greater than that needed for the mechanical achievement of its tasks." In other words, being involved in a relationship with other organizations and individuals in order to provide better services has to come to mean something to the individuals involved if the structure is to persist and be effective.

IF COORDINATION IS EVERYTHING, THEN MAYBE IT'S NOTHING?

Aaron Wildavsky's (1973) famous question about planning has been paraphrased any number of times, but it continues to be a useful question. We have discussed a number of alternative dimensions of coordination that appear to capture questions about policymaking taken more generally. For example, I have pointed to the possibilities of the failure of programs to cover the range of needs for citizens in areas such as social policy as possibly a problem of coordination. It may well be, but it may also simply be a poor policy design, or a conscious acceptance that government cannot, or will not, solve all problems. The holes in this social safety net may be genuine policy choices rather than the somewhat more technical question of a failure to coordinate.

If coordination is to be useful analytically, and even practically, it will require some interpretation of both intentions and outcomes. The above discussion of alternative meanings has been concerned primarily with the outcomes of the process, but intentions are also important and need to be a part of the calculation when we attribute problems to a failure to coordinate. Some actors in government may not have the ambition to coordinate their actions but prefer to maintain their dominance in a particular policy area, or not be willing to invest money and other resources in cooperating with other programs. That is, if there is an intention to address a broad problem area effectively, or to provide comprehensive services to a target population, and major gaps remain in those services, then there is indeed a failure to coordinate effectively. Likewise, some redundancy in public programs may be designed and desirable, so that these should not be considered coordination failures.

Multiple Meanings

The coordination problem is actually several problems, each resulting from failures to align one public program with others. Government programs sometimes overlap and duplicate, or even contradict, each other. Reporting, inspection, and licensing requirements are often cited as examples of public sector programs that overlap and duplicate each other. For example, the Canadian government in the late 1990s and early part of the twenty-first century engaged in an effort to eliminate the duplications found in food inspections and licensing. Prior to that time inspections were done by both the federal and provincial governments and by several organizations within each. The creation of the Canadian Food Inspection System has helped to minimize these duplications, and therefore has reduced costs to food producers and ultimately to consumers (see www.cfis.agr.ca for a description). Similarly, in the United States the General Accountability Office found there were twenty-three federal programs that had special provisions for the elderly, some of which almost inevitably duplicated one another (USGAO 2005).

Ordinary citizens also feel the impact of poor coordination when they must cope with government. The emphasis in management reforms on the "one-stop shop" for social services and for small businesses is one indication of the demands of the public for reduced duplication of requirements and forms (Hagen and Kubicel 2000). Even then, however, the individual may have to fill out multiple forms containing the same information to obtain the range of services desired—the only difference will be the ability to do so at a single location. The more desirable outcome of a coordination process would be to have common forms for a range of allied services or licenses so that so much redundancy would not be required.[11] Centrelink in Australia (Halligan and Wills 2008) is an attempt to produce coordination of that sort for the clients of social services and labor market programs, but this is but one of numerous attempts to produce institutions for integrated services.

Although the duplication of programs does demonstrate problems in coordination, coordination problems leading to direct contradictions are even more troublesome. One of the more commonly cited examples of programs that contradict each other is the tobacco policy, or policies, of the United States. On the one hand the

US Department of Health and Human Services spends millions of dollars attempting to reduce or eliminate smoking in the United States. At the same time the US Department of Agriculture spends millions of dollars subsidizing tobacco growers. Likewise, it spends money supporting the export of tobacco to many parts of the world. Even a more rationalist government such as that in France finds that on the one hand it is promoting the consumption of (French) wine but also extremely concerned about the level of drunk driving (Sciolino 2004). These different policy emphases are explicable from the commitment of different departments and ministries to particular constituencies and to their own policy missions, but the outcome is nonetheless inconsistent and wasteful of public money.

The above example of inconsistency and conflict among program goals is costly but produces little direct harm to citizens, except in their capacity as taxpayers. Other examples of inconsistency and incompatibility of programs may have more tangible negative consequences for citizens. One such set of inconsistencies has been the "poverty trap" that existed in the United Kingdom and other countries for years, as a result of the failure to coordinate means-tested social benefits and taxation (Harkness, Gregg, and MacMillan 2012; Barling 1984). This lack of effective coordination meant that as low-income individuals earned more money there would be points along the earnings scale at which their net income would reduce for the marginal pound earned, given that benefits were lost or taxes began to be charged.[12] While the most extreme cases of this problem have been eliminated, tax and benefit programs are rarely well coordinated and low-income families tend to bear the burden of those programmatic inconsistencies.

In other instances government programs may have major gaps so that necessary services are not available to the public, or to specific segments of the population. These service gaps often occur in social services where certain categories of people with particular characteristics are excluded from receiving services. For example, failures to coordinate Medicare programs for the elderly with public pensions and other services often produces the need for the elderly to become legally bankrupt in order to receive medical benefits available only to the indigent. And the services in question may be those most needed by the elderly, such as skilled nursing care. Some of the more egregious cases of coordination failures producing service gaps have come to light as a result of the events of September 11, 2001. It became clear as the causes of that disaster were considered that there were massive coordination failures that played no small part in permitting the disaster to occur (see Chapter 4). Each of the major security services in the United States—the Central Intelligence Agency, the Federal Bureau of Investigation, and the National Security Agency—as well as other organizations such as the Immigration and Naturalization Service and the Federal Aviation Administration, had a part of the picture, but no one had been able to "connect the dots."[13]

The lack of adequate policy coordination may also result in something as simple as lost opportunities for effective cooperation among programs and organizations charged with delivering public services. Very few public services can be as effective as they might be without the involvement of other services, but coordination is more often seen as a real cost to the organization rather than a potential benefit. The calculus in which organizations and their leaders engage is rather predictable. The benefits of cooperation and coordination are uncertain and remote while the costs are clear and immediate. Further, it is not clear to what extent each organization involved in a cooperative effort would be rewarded for their involvement. In such a situation the rational manager or political leader might well decline to participate.

Measurement and Degrees

Any concept in the social sciences must be able to be measured if it is to be useful in advancing our understanding of the phenomena in question, and coordination is no different. There is a tendency when discussing coordination to speak as if this were a simple dichotomy—coordination exists or it does not. The world of governing is, however, much more complex, and there are certainly degrees of coordination. Indeed, establishing the threshold at which coordination can be said to exist involves making judgments about where the policy area or areas in question stand relative to some underlying scale of coordination (see Sartori 1991 on "degreeism"). Saying that a policy area is "coordinated" usually means it is sufficiently coordinated in the mind of the evaluator, but that evaluation often varies among observers.

One way to think about the measurement of coordination is to consider the degrees of coordination that may be achieved. For example, Les Metcalfe (1994; see Table 1.1) has presented a scale of coordination that extends from independent decisions by organizations as the lowest level of coordination (or in this case almost total absence of coordination) of activities among public programs to a very high level of cooperation and coherence indicated by a coherent government

Table 1.1 Metcalfe's Policy Coordination Scale

9. Government Strategy
8. Establishing Central Priorities
7. Setting Limits on Ministerial Action
6. Arbitration of Policy Differences
5. Search for Agreement among Ministers
4. Avoiding Divergences among Ministers
3. Consultation with Other Ministers (Feedback)
2. Communication with Other Ministers (Information Exchange)
1. Independent Decision Making by Ministers

strategy encompassing all areas of the public sector. The nine levels of coordination presented in Metcalfe's analysis each will require greater specification, and some criteria for having been achieved, but they do represent the beginnings of a metric for coordination (see Matei and Gogaru 2012).

If we attempt to move beyond the ordinal measures presented by Metcalfe, attempting to measure coordination and the degree to which it has been achieved is substantially more difficult. One of the earliest efforts to assess coordination on a more continuous scale was developed by Ostrom, Parks, and Whitaker (1974). They were interested in the delivery of police services at the local level in fragmented jurisdictions and the extent to which there was joint use of facilities and joint patrolling. Their primary method of determining coordination was observation and interviewing, and they also looked at the levels of coordination relative to the opportunities for joint action.

The measures of coordination used by Ostrom, Parks, and Whitaker depended largely on evidence about attempts to coordinate and on formal patterns of linkage among organizations. The attempts of the OECD (2005) to understand building coherence in development policy employed a rather similar method. This study identified a number of institutional processes that are directed toward creating greater coherence but did not provide any clear measures of the success or failure of these efforts. Helen Briassoulis (2005) considered numerous dimensions of possibilities for measuring policy integration (especially in the context of the European Union) and also developed numerous possible measures, most depending upon efforts to achieve integration rather than actual levels of success (see Table 1.2).

Another of the important attempts to assess levels of coordination focused on social welfare and jobs training rather than on policing. Jennings and Krane (1994) were not able to assess actual levels of coordination in these policy areas in the American states but they focused more on the attempts of the actors involved to coordinate. They utilized a set of questions to the participants, asking both about their attempts to coordinate with other programs and to some extent about their success in doing so. The evidence on activity is more compelling than the

Table 1.2 Briassoulis's Dimensions of Policy Integration

| Institutional Criteria |
| Legislative Criteria |
| Administrative Criteria |
| Financial Measures |
| Market Measures |
| Technical Measures |
| Communication Measures |
| Hybrid Measures |

information on success and failure, but this constitutes more movement ahead in attempting to measure actual coordination in governing.

Finally, there have been a number of efforts to measure interaction in networks of organizations in general, and particularly in networks of actors responsible for public policies (Kriesi, Adam, and Jochum 2006). In one of the earliest studies of coordination in public administration Chisholm (1989) enumerated linkages among the many organizations responsible for public transportation. Although important for studying interactions, this literature is perhaps less useful for studying coordination per se. We know who talks to whom in these delivery systems, but not necessarily about what topics. Nor does it tell us much about whether these interactions actually produce effective policy coordination. Again, the emphasis is on measuring the *process* of coordination more than on the success or failure of that process.

In summary, while all these efforts at measurement do indeed help to advance the study of coordination, they do not provide definitive measures of coordination that would allow us to say that one policy area is coordinated and another is not. This failure is in part a result of lacking any meaningful standard of what is enough coordination, and in part a function of the weakness of indicators, other than process-based indicators, of the success of coordination efforts. We tend to be able to identify coordinated programs within the public sector but not to develop an effective metric for that coordination.

SUMMARY AND CONCLUSIONS

This chapter has provided an introduction to the study of policy coordination. This term, and its synonyms or near synonyms such as *coherence, collaboration,* and *integration,* has been a continuing concern for governments. Despite the long history of concern and attempts to coordinate, there has been very little success in generating effective coordination in most governments. And the search for coordination becomes increasingly difficult with the greater levels of involvement of nongovernmental actors in the policy process and the decentralization and disaggregation of contemporary political systems.

Academics, practitioners, and the informed public all tend to treat coordination as an undifferentiated whole. There are, however, a number of questions about what this concept means and the best ways of conceptualizing it. While these differences may appear academic, in the worst sense of the term, they actually have significance for both understanding and practice. Perhaps most importantly, understanding the alternatives for intervention can assist in strategic choices by governments.

Knowing that there is a problem with coordination is only the beginning of the political and administrative action necessary to address that problem. Therefore, the remainder of this volume will attempt to expand the understanding of the causes and remedies for the coordination problem. This elaboration of the issues will involve detailing the reasons that coordination so often is wanting, and also something of the theoretical and analytical approaches to coordination. There is also a rather fully stocked tool chest of instruments that can be used to generate enhanced coordination, and I will detail and evaluate those. Finally, several short case studies will illustrate the ways in which governments have attempted, and often failed, to address coordination.

2. Barriers to Coordination

I have now advanced what I believe to be a *prima facie* case for the virtues of co-ordination of policy and administration in the public sector. Given all the virtues that can be identified that arise from enhanced coordination and coherence in the public sector, why are there so many poorly coordinated programs? Further, why do so many political and administrative leaders appear to tolerate these coordination failures and invest little effort in improving that coordination? The answers to those questions should to some extent already be obvious from the previous discussions of coordination failures, but it is still useful to present some description and analysis of the barriers to effective coordination. That discussion can serve as a foundation for thinking about the theoretical perspectives on coordination in the following chapter, as well as thinking about the remedies that have been proposed for coordination problems that will be presented in Chapter 4.

Unlike the approaches to coordination in the following chapter, there are no encompassing theoretical justifications for the failure to coordinate. The failures to coordinate to some extent replicate the familiar problems identified in public organizations and may be related to the connotative meaning of bureaucracy as routinized, rigid, and conservative (Wilson 1989). Very much as Graham Allison (1971) described the "organizational process" model of bureaucracy, the organizations seek to maintain their routines, even if doing so reduces their capacity to coordinate effectively with other organizations in order to achieve their formal goals.

From a more rational perspective there are few incentives for an organization or an individual to pursue a path of coordination with others. Most of the rewards available within the public sector—for politicians and especially for civil servants—arise from working within a particular policy silo, rather than being more creative and finding ways to create linkages with others. Coordination in the public sector often becomes a collective action problem (Ostrom 1990). Government as a whole will be better off if there is greater coordination, but the incentives for individual actors—individuals and organizations—are to maintain the status quo and not to invest in coordination.

As well as the absence of more rational motivations for collaboration, the ideational foundations of governing also tend not to emphasize coordination. Most organizations within the public sector operate with a set of ideas, and those ideas may be used to justify the self-interest of the organization or individuals within it (Hay 2011). The tendency to maintain the silos within government also emphasizes the importance, and the positive contributions, of specialization within the public sector, a virtue that may be undermined by an excessive emphasis on coordination (Bouckaert, Peters, and Verhoest 2010).

SIMPLE PIGHEADEDNESS

Perhaps the most vexing problem for would-be coordinators in government is that many participants in the process are simply not interested in coordinating. This lack of interest in cooperation is generally the product of some of the other factors to be mentioned below. In some instances, however, it may be simple inertia or simple unwillingness on the part of individuals to take the time and trouble to consider what can be gained by working with other organizations. Coordination requires some flexibility and some willingness to think about policy and administration in less conventional manners, and hence individuals and organizations operating in the stereotypical, path-dependent manner usually ascribed to "bureaucracy" may be unwilling to shake out of the existing patterns.

Even if the leaders of organizations may have some interest in producing more innovative and coordinated styles of making and managing policy, they are confronted with organizations that have established routines that would be upset by those changes. Likewise, if coordination may indeed be easier to generate at the bottom of organizations than at the top, then these actions by street-level bureaucrats may be perceived as undermining the authority of the leadership and perhaps the integrity of the organization. Few employees can afford to be perceived as traitors within their own organizations.

As we will point out below, however, what appears from the outside to be sheer obstinacy or protectiveness may be quite rational on the part of managers in the public sector. From the perspective of historical institutionalism, the simplest logic undergirding persistence in an established path is that it has worked in the past, and the positive feedback has reinforced the behavior (Pierson 2000). Further, all the political supports for an organization and its programs tend to be tied to persistence rather than to creative solutions to problems that cut across boundaries. Finally, the leaders of the organization may not be interested in moving the organization ahead, but simply in preserving their own careers and their own comfort (Downs 1967; but see Huxham and Vangen 2003), and if coordination involves risk then perhaps it is not a clever investment of resources.

PIG IGNORANCE

Not to belabor the porcine phrases, but pig ignorance is one of the major problems in creating effective coordination. Information may be the most important prerequisite for effective coordination. It is difficult for organizations to work together if they are not aware of what each other is doing; but such information on other parts of government is not widely available nor widely sought out. Organizations naturally tend to think of their own priorities first and do not naturally spread around information to other organizations, even if they perceive no particular reason not to cooperate through sharing information. For much the same reason those organizations will not invest much time and effort in finding out about the other programs in government, even if they may perform similar functions.

This lack of interest in sharing and acquiring information generally reflects poor understanding of the programs of other agencies in government and the possible benefits of the closely held information to other organizations. Although the consequences of this lack of understanding of other organizations may not particularly damage the organization it can obviously have negative consequences for clients, as well as for the public at large. If clients have their initial or primary contact with one organization, and that organization does little to link that client with other relevant services, then the true needs of the clients will not be met (see, for example, Dubois 2010).

This tendency of organizations, and the individuals within them, not to be concerned with sharing information also reflects the search of public organizations for greater autonomy. The discussion of autonomy for public organizations is usually expressed more vertically than horizontally, as organizations seek freedom from political control (Carpenter 2001; Yesilkagit and Christensen 2010). That said, however, organizations may not want to be too entangled with other organizations, nor too dependent on those organizations for fulfilling their own missions. The logic of collaboration is powerful, but so too is the logic of autonomy and the desire of an organization to control its own agenda and activities. And if autonomy is perceived to be crucial for the success of the organization then searching out information on other organizations is unlikely.

The ignorance of other programs may be overcome by individuals within organizations, especially those who attempt to play a boundary-spanning role. This choice to play a boundary-spanning role is more likely to be a personal choice for the individuals, rather than an organizational role sanctioned by the leadership. There are some discussions of the presence of "orthogonal cultures" (Boisnier and Chatman 2002) in organizations populated with individuals who may be less committed to the dominant culture of the organization. These individuals may be more capable of working with other organizations and other policy priorities.

In summary, the members of many public organizations remain largely uninformed about the programs of other organizations in government. That ignorance may be the result of the simple lack of inquisitiveness about what else happens in government, but ignorance may also represent a reasoned strategy to protect themselves from too much involvement with those other actors. In terms of defending their programs and existence ignorance is perhaps a reasonable strategy, but in terms of providing better and even less expensive services to citizens, ignoring what other organizations are doing is far from reasonable.

SECRECY

In addition to the absence of common information about policies that may be natural in a complex governing system, there are often strong incentives for maintaining secrecy—hence poor coordination—in government. Information is power for organizations (public or private), and organizations are often reluctant to share information because they will lose their bargaining position with other organizations or political leaders. One standard bargaining scenario in governing is that organizations are willing to trade the information they have for that held by others, or more commonly exchange it for budgets or programmatic latitude with politicians or with central agencies such as ministries of finance.[1]

One of the more recent and serious examples of this root of poor coordination comes from the events leading up to September 11, 2001. The three major intelligence organizations in the US government each had some parts of the story about the threats to the United States, but none found it desirable to share what they had with the others (Posner 2007). Some of the evidence emerging after those events showed that these three organizations were often purposive in not giving information to other organizations that were in many ways their natural competitors for funding and for positive publicity. In the end, of course, all the organizations received severely negative publicity from their failure to coordinate. Unfortunately, information and communications problems were also at the heart of some of the difficulties that the various authorities encountered in responding to Hurricane Katrina in the Gulf Coast states (Block and Cooper 2007).

At times organizational secrecy is very intentional and perhaps necessary for the primary purpose of a program, but that also can produce significant coordination failures. For example, when government agencies employ undercover agents to infiltrate criminal or terrorist organizations, they obviously do not notify other organizations of the names and activities of those agents. At times, several law enforcement agencies will infiltrate the same organization, and the agents of one organization will at times spend their time reporting on the activities of the agents from other public organizations. While this secrecy is understandable, and perhaps necessary, it can be a major impediment to efficiency and to the actual pursuit of the real suspects.[2]

A somewhat less glaring, but potentially more destructive, result of secrecy comes from the impact of data protection laws and government protection of privacy. These personal protections are, of course, crucial issues for individual civil liberties (see

Chapter 6), but at the same time present manifest problems for effective admin-istration. For example, in some data protection systems one social service agency might be prohibited from sharing information with other organizations delivering complementary services to the public. Likewise, police and social service agencies often are incapable of sharing information even on vulnerable populations, such as children who are potential objects of abuse by parents or guardians (see Chapter 5). And many governments legally and constitutionally prevent sharing information across policy areas, even if that sharing may make government programs perform more efficiently, as when tax information and social service assessments of clients cannot be linked, or correlating tax and expenditure data may help to reduce tax evasion.

As concern about terrorism has grown, governments have relaxed their restric-tions against data sharing and have begun to use information in multiple databases to attempt to identify possible threats (Bignami 2007; USGAO 2013a). Although barriers to data sharing in security areas have been reduced, in some areas of social policy they have actually been increasing as concerns over privacy and data shar-ing have increased (see Erkkilä 2011). Thus, in making domestic policies, the view that government may have of clients remains segmented, and therefore the policies adopted are also likely to remain segmented.

MANAGEMENT AND THE NEW PUBLIC MANAGEMENT

One of the barriers to coordinating policies is the success of administrative reforms during the past several decades, which have stressed values of decentralization, or-ganizational autonomy, and greater independence for public sector managers. The "New Public Management" (NPM—see Pollitt and Bouckaert 2004) has produced increases, often substantial increases, in the efficiency of the public sector, but it has focused on the efficiency of individual programs rather than the performance of the policymaking system as a whole. For example, one of the central programs derived from the NPM approach has been the creation of autonomous and quasi-autonomous organizations (Pollitt and Talbot 2003) and emphasis on the need for those organizations to act with minimal control from the center of government or even from the political leadership in the sponsoring ministries.

Performance management is another central element of NPM and it, too, em-phasizes the efficiency and effectiveness of individual programs. This emphasis on measuring the performance of individual programs implies that managers of those programs have little incentive to utilize scarce time and resources to cooperate with other programs to fulfill collective goals. Some attempts have been made to develop government-wide performance goals[3] but these tend to be less influential than the goals established for the individual programs. The assumption appears to be that if government can make the individual programs more efficient then government as a whole may work better, but that assumption may not be sustainable in reality. Rather, the continuing decentralization of public programs has created sufficient control problems to force some strengthening of central agencies (Dahlström, Peters, and Pierre 2010).

Although it may be convenient to place the blame for the disaggregation of the public sector and coordination problems on the NPM, strong management may in general tend to reduce the willingness of organizations to cooperate. To the extent that managers are successful in creating strong internal cohesion and an integrated organizational culture, as advised by many organizational gurus, then the organization and its participants may be less interested in cooperating with others (Lynn, Heinrich, and Hill 2000). At the same time that some strands of management thinking stress collaboration (see Chapter 1), other management theory may stress creating strong, autonomous organizations.

In fairness, however, NPM reforms may have had some positive effects on the capacity of governments to coordinate public services. For example, the emphasis on "one-stop shops" and the capacity to deliver a range of services through a single location or even a single window has provided an important focus for coordination among organizations delivering complementary services. Organizations such as Centrelink in Australia have been created to institutionalize coordination of this type. This style of service delivery facilitates coordination of the implementation of the programs involved but may not add appreciably to the compatibility of the programs themselves. In addition, the emphasis on efficiency in government has tended to integrate "back office" activities such as purchasing and personnel management to force some greater coordination through those activities (Bakvis and Juillet 2004).

RISK AVOIDANCE

The stereotypical view of public bureaucracies and of public bureaucrats is that they are risk averse. Although this is an often-repeated negative perception, it also contains a good deal of truth (Hood 2011). The aversion to risk that is often easy to observe in public organizations is rarely the fault of personal failings or character flaws, but rather tends to be a function of the fundamental nature of the public sector and the manner in which it is managed. The emphasis on rules, hierarchy, and accountability in traditional public administration has been alleviated little by the more market-oriented styles of management associated with the NPM or with the empowerment of employees through other styles of reform (see Burgess and Ratto 2003).

Attempting to collaborate and coordinate with other organizations involves a certain degree of risk for any established organization.[4] Any organization has a policy "heartland" that it seeks to protect from incursions by other organizations in the budget process and in policymaking (see Downs 1967).[5] Collaborating with other organizations and programs may imperil that heartland and open the organization up to unwanted changes. Thus, potential collaboration presents an organization with the classic collective action problem. Its self-interest (at least in the short run) can easily conflict with the public interest of (perhaps in the long run) lower costs and better public services.

The formality of rules within the public sector tends to exacerbate the risk aversion within the public sector. Despite attempts to make the public sector more flexible, rules remain important for structuring the behavior of members of public organizations (and private organizations). The rules that emerge in most organizations to guide the behavior of members are almost entirely concerned with internal management rather than external relations with other organizations. Therefore, to the extent that the individual administrator is risk averse he or she will act in areas in which there is clear guidance and avoid fuzzy areas without guidance.

TURF

Politics at an organizational level is about defending the organization's "turf." Turf in the language of Washington and other governments represents the things that the organization holds dear and may perceive as threatened by other organizations, such as money, space, and time (Bardach 1996). In the federal government Miles's law—where you stand depends upon where you sit—is an often-cited adage to define the importance of the organizational basis of politics and the need to defend that base with the greatest possible vigor (Seidman 1998). Coordination may involve ceding some turf to other organizations, mainly in the form of using some of the hard-won budgetary resources from individual organizations to achieve more collective goals (Althaus and Yarwood 1993). Likewise, coordination may involve sharing clients and perhaps being willing to accept that one's own organization and its programs are not the only, or even best, means of addressing the needs of the clients.

The turf wars inherent in organizational politics are reinforced by the preferences of clients. While it may be that the clients will be better served by a more coherent and coordinated manner of delivering public services, they may be reluctant to change their existing relationships with one organization. Those relationships provide the clients with access and influence that they believe they have gained through the existing organizational focus for their services, and their political pressures, and that is more desirable than some uncertain future. Most groups of clients want to maintain their "own" organization in government, and further, this one organization must rely heavily politically upon the support of the particular interest group concerned with the organization. For example, during the Carter administration the president thought that government would work better if the education programs in the then Veterans Administration were transferred to the Department of Education, the housing activities in the VA to the Department of Housing and Urban Development, and the health activities to the Department of Health and Human Services. Veterans' organizations did not think that greater coherence in government should be purchased at the loss of their power and their organization and mobilized their political base. The president quickly changed his mind.

A more recent example gives an indication of the extent to which organizations who should in principle be allies will go to defend their organizational "turf." In late 2002 the Federal Bureau of Investigation (FBI) circulated a memo within the law enforcement community attacking the proposed movement of the Bureau of Alcohol, Tobacco and Firearms (BATF) from the Department of the Treasury to the Department of Justice (Lichtblau 2002). The apparent purpose of the FBI's opposition was to maintain its own monopoly over the investigation of domestic terrorism. The BATF has substantial expertise in tracking explosives and weapons, and if it were in a law enforcement department rather than in Treasury it could well challenge the FBI's supremacy in investigating terrorism, which in turn could challenge the FBI's prestige and budget.

The FBI lost this battle over reorganization and the BATF was moved into the Department of Justice in 2003. That movement has not, however, lessened the competition among the organizations.[6] They have refused to share data on bombs and bomb threats and the FBI began to train its own sniffer dogs, something not really needed since the BATF has been in that business for some years (Markon 2008). As well as simply being wasteful, the competition for this particular piece of turf has been argued to reduce the overall effectiveness of the fight against terrorism, the ostensible purpose of moving the BATF in the first instance.

Changes in public sector management ideologies have been reinforcing by changes in the management regimens in government. Even before the development of the NPM and its emphasis on private-sector styles, changes in practices within the public sector tended to make turf barriers more significant. As implementation came to include multiple organizations and multiple goals the capacity to protect turf has been threatened (Radin 1996), but at the same time this stretching tended to reinforce the need to maintain organizational identity and integrity (Albert, Ashforth, and Dulton 2000).

With the adoption of the ideas of the NPM, the increasing use of performance management to assess the success of organizations and managers and to allocate resources among organizations (Halligan and Bouckaert 2007) provides strong incentives for those individuals and organizations not to cooperate with other organizations. The only exception would be if there were demonstrable benefits for any organization that could arise from the cooperative behaviors. No manager will be anxious to allocate resources to purposes that are not directly related to improving ratings on the indicators on which his or her performance is being assessed and his or her future career depends. Thus, performance management may enhance the performance of each program but paradoxically may not contribute as much to the performance of the administrative system as a whole.

REAL COSTS

I began this discussion of barriers to coordination with an almost flippant discussion of the "pigheadedness" of individuals and organizations within the public sector when faced with coordination possibilities. That discussion made the decision makers in public organizations appear almost totally devoid of concern for the public interest. Most literature on leadership in public organizations, however, tends to argue quite the opposite (Perry 2000), emphasizing the commitment of most people in government to serving the public and delivering the best possible programs for citizens.

Several of the other sections concerning the barriers to coordination also may appear to emphasize the irrational and the defensive behavior of individuals and organizations in the public sector. While those negative stereotypes may have some truth, they can also mask the reality of the potential costs to organizations from engaging in coordination and collaboration with other organizations. Some of the sections in the discussion above have noted the costs that coordination may impose on organizations, but it is important to emphasize those costs and the rationality of the behavior of decision makers when confronting those costs. We have tended to emphasize the costs of the failure to coordinate, but there are costs of coordinating as well (see Lanzalco 2011).

Organizations may face a variety of costs if they engage in collaborative activities. At the extreme they can be put out of business. If in cooperating with other organizations it becomes apparent that their programs are redundant or can be done better by another organization, then they may simply be terminated. Terminations are relatively rare in the public sector, albeit not so rare as the critics of the public sector would like to believe (see Hogwood and Peters 1986; Boin, Kuipers, and Steenbergen 2010), but they do occur. Especially in a time of poor public finance an organization can be quite correct in sensing threats from too much cooperation.

Even if the organization is not terminated it can still incur political costs from attempts at coordination. Organizations in the public sector depend upon political support from their clients if they are to be successful, and organizations are often more successful if they have a close, symbiotic relationship with their clientele. By cooperating with other programs they may lose their identity to the client base; even if they are in fact delivering better services, it may not appear that way and in politics perceptions may be more important than reality.

PARTISAN POLITICS

I will point out below that politics can serve as an important means of integrating policies and enhancing coordination among programs. On the other hand, however, politics also can present major barriers for policy entrepreneurs seeking to achieve needed coordination. Those political problems often appear in coalition governments when there are ministers from different political parties responsible for different policy areas (Döring 1995). Those political differences within a government may produce different policy priorities that will make creating policy coherence difficult. In addition, the political differences may simply make cooperation less likely among the participants in cabinet, with each minister potentially being unwilling to help the other, whether for ideological reasons or simply for possible partisan gains in a coming election. Further, the tendency to have broader coalitions in many European countries means that achieving cooperation may be even more difficult.[7]

Although almost by definition coalition governments may present difficulties for policy coordination, there are significant differences among countries in the ways in which they manage coalitions. In most coalition governments the political parties that become members of the coalition must sign a formal agreement among themselves to support the coalition so that there should be some greater capacity to ensure compliance and coordination across ministries. At the other extreme (Denmark; see Knudsen 2000) there is almost no formal agreement on policy within a coalition, and each minister may have to create individual coalitions around each bill. Even in the more formalized coalitions, however, the inevitable policy differences and political ambitions of the participants will make for problems.

As well as the problems created for horizontal coordination within each level of government, partisan politics can create problems for vertical coordination among the levels of government. This problem of vertical coordination is especially important in federal countries in which the different levels of the political system have substantial policy autonomy and there are often subnational governments with governments from political parties other than that in control of the central government. Those political problems can be managed but are indeed a problem (Scharpf, Reissert, and Schnabel 1976). Even in unitary regimes, however, subnational governments may be granted sufficient autonomy to resist attempts by the center to coordinate their actions and to create common patterns of policy across the political system (Gremion 1976).

Partisan politics also can be a major barrier to the intertemporal consistency that could also be considered a dimension of coordination. The natural tendency of one party or coalition upon replacing another is to undo or at least deemphasize the policy initiatives of the preceding regime. For example, the second Bush administration deemphasized the administrative reforms of the Clinton administration (Kettl 2002) even though those reforms promoted many characteristics that should have appealed to the market ideology of the incoming Republican administration. In the place of the Clinton reforms came a new series of administrative programs directed at not dissimilar targets as the previous programs' (Bruel 2007). Partisanship is important in itself but may be more important when it coincides with strongly held ideologies that create "stop-go" approaches to economic policy and other significant policy areas.

GROUP-BASED POLITICS

Partisan politics are one major source of low levels of coordination among programs and levels of government, but group-based politics may be even more significant. By group-based politics I mean the importance of linkages between interest groups, and other social actors, and public organizations. These linkages are present in all types of political systems, even nondemocratic regimes (Fewsmith 2012), but they are perhaps most significant in pluralist regimes. These linkages tend to flow in both directions, with the social actors attempting to influence government while government also attempts to influence and to utilize the social actors.

These connections between interest groups and government organizations create the greatest difficulties for coordination when the organizations depend directly on a single group, or a limited number of groups, for their political support. As noted, in pluralist regimes symbiotic relationships exist between the groups and they depend on those groups for political support. In turn the groups tend to demand direct access and services from "their" agency. This mutual dependence tends to focus the agency on a narrow range of concerns and makes cooperation with other programs less feasible politically.

BELIEFS AND PROFESSIONALISM

The commitment of individuals and organizations to beliefs about what constitutes good policy in their area of concern is one of the more difficult barriers to effective coordination to overcome. In addition to the partisan ideologies mentioned above, organizations have ideologies, or more exactly the members of organizations have ideologies about policy, and those belief patterns shape their approach to the policy (Chan and Clegg 2002; Campbell 2001). Further, the organizational ideologies often make it difficult for organizations to cooperate. They begin with fundamentally different conceptions of a problem and find it difficult to work together, as in the failure of police and social services to cooperate effectively in helping children discussed in Chapter 5.

Organizational ideologies operate in two ways to make coordination difficult. The first is that these ideologies define the policy problems, as noted above, and more significantly the ideologies attach greater importance to one dimension of a broad socioeconomic issue. Why are people poor? Is it because of poor health, or inadequate education, or some weaknesses in the culture?[8] Different organizations will tend to give different answers, as we have seen in several comprehensive attempts to solve poverty. Further, the ideology defines what an appropriate response is, based upon that ideology. Coordination does not happen readily simply because each program believes that it is doing the best possible things to alleviate a problem and therefore any attempt to coordinate will probably decrease rather than increase the probabilities of dealing with the policy problem effectively.

One of principal sources of beliefs in public sector organizations is professional training. One of the characteristics of professional training is that it provides the recipient of that training with a set of concepts and beliefs that help define the policy situation and also points the individual professional toward a range of acceptable remedies to the problems identified (see Willumsen and Hallberg 2003). For example, in the United States, there are two organizations in the federal government that have some jurisdiction over antitrust issues. One, the Antitrust Division of the Department of Justice, is dominated by lawyers, while the other—the Federal Trade Commission—tends to be populated more by economists (Fox and Sullivan 1987). Not surprisingly, the two organizations approach the issues in economic regulation differently, tend to pursue different types of cases, and tend to produce rather different regulatory outcomes. Thus, rather than having a single approach to antitrust enforcement, the United States has (at least) two that are to some extent based upon different professional perspectives on the nature of economic regulation.[9]

The impact of professionalism on coordination is perhaps more pervasive in social service programs, in which different approaches to providing services to clients and different definitions of the needs of clients may hamper cooperation and coordination. Most clients who present themselves to social services providers have multiple needs (Meyerson, Choi, and Mills 2003) and would benefit from multiple types of assistance. The benefit would be even greater if that assistance could be provided in an integrated and coordinated manner. Professionalism may, however, limit the extent to which service providers are willing to provide those more integrated services or, perhaps more fundamentally, may limit the extent to which the service providers would conceptualize the needs of the client in the more inclusive manner. That tendency may be further enhanced by the tendency of organizations to reproduce themselves and to continue to hire staff with particular types of expertise and to provide the same types of services.

The negative impact of professional differences on coordination may be manifested in large part through the framing of issues and policy problems. For example, as the European Union has attempted to manage its development policies for Africa (and for other parts of the world as well), the competing frames of security and development, embodied in different pillars of EU activity, have made creating coherence difficult (Sicurelli 2008). The different frames available for policies such as drugs or mental illness tend to promote competition among organizations rather than cooperation, with those frames being defined at least in part through the professions involved and their beliefs (see Payan 2006; Kall 2010). These frames are closely analogous to the organizational ideologies mentioned above, but here we are emphasizing the role that professions and their perspectives play in creating these frames.

I should point out here that the professions can also make an important contribution to successful coordination under the proper circumstances. When professionals of the same training are distributed across a number of organizations they may constitute a network that enables those organizations to work together more effectively (Gargan 1993). These "epistemic communities" within the public sector (Zito 2001) share common languages and common approaches to policy problems, and their agreement on the fundamentals within the area will facilitate their cooperation.

Further, as Eliot Freidson (1986, 63) points out, members of the same profession tend to have common economic interests that go along with their commitment to a particular intellectual viewpoint on policy issues.[10] Thus, the task for the would-be coordinator in health care and other policy areas dominated by professions becomes finding means of making professionalism serve the ends of coordination, rather than remaining the barrier to cooperation. Producing this cooperation may require reframing the issues involved away from particular policy domains or professional expertise and more in the direction of common professional standards such as service to the client. For example, medical professionals in the US federal government are distributed across a range of organizations—the National Institutes of Health (DHHS), veterans' hospitals (DVA), and the Native American Health Service (DOI) among others. They may have different organizational allegiances but their common allegiance to the profession can help them work together more effectively.

TIME

Most of the discussion of coordination involves differences among programs and the need to make programs cooperate as they deliver services at a single point in time. Indeed, one rather mechanistic view of coordination might stress the need to have all components of a program available at the same time. While coordinating programs at those single points in time is certainly an important issue for public management, and is the most common format of cooperation among organizations, there are also problems that emerge as organizations and programs must work together across broader spans of time. Governments often make successive decisions about an issue, and those decisions must be compatible if the desired outcomes for the society are to be produced. This coordination problem extending across time may be even more difficult to manage than the conventional issues because the organizations involved may not be in immediate contact with each other, and hence they may not recognize the manner in which decisions interact.

One of the most compelling examples of the issue of time in coordination is food safety and regulation. Citizens in industrialized countries have come to expect a safe food supply but numerous incidents during the 1990s and the early part of the twenty-first century—dioxin in cola drinks in Belgium, *listeria* in cheese in Britain, salmonella in eggs in any number of countries, and *E. coli* in ground beef in the United States, to name some of the more notable cases—have made it clear that guaranteeing that safety is difficult. The process by which animals and plants move from farms to the consumers' shopping carts and then to their tables is a long and complex one and often involves a number of government departments, often at different levels of government (Dyckman 2004), that regulate food production, food processing, and the distribution of food. That regulatory process has become all the more difficult, given the amount of food that now moves across international borders (Coleman 2005), and there is a need to track and regulate those foodstuffs at all stages of the process.[11]

Food regulation involves multiple actors over a limited amount of time, given that it is perishable, but many categories of regulation may extend over substantial periods of time, and some consistency may be necessary for that coordination to be successful. For example, environmental regulation in the United States is often seen as a federal responsibility housed in the Environmental Protection Agency implementing laws made by Congress. In reality, however, much of the implementation is done by subnational governments that have some latitude in implementation, including the ability to set standards that are more stringent than the federal standards and to write some of their own regulations for enforcement (Hoornbeek 2004). As well as being geographically dispersed, this class of regulation may take some years to be put into effect, with additional opportunities for drift away from the original intentions, and difficulties for the regulated to match their actions to changing standards. In this instance there are also questions of vertical coordination among a number of different political jurisdictions, as well as the problem of maintaining consistency across time and classes of pollution.

Time is also relevant for coordination because effective coordination often involves developing long-term relationships among the actors involved. As I will point out below relative to the network approach to coordination, trust is often a central factor required to make networks, and therefore coordination, perform well. Trust does not develop overnight but arises through interactions over time. Building trust in these situations may be analogous to the tit-for-tat building of cooperation in game theory (Axelrod 1997).

Thus, the absence of time for continuing interactions and building confidence among the actors involved may inhibit coordination. Many attempts to create coordination will be one-time or short-term, perhaps responding to a crisis or pressure from a political leader. These attempts to produce effective coordination are unlikely to succeed, other than perhaps in a symbolic manner of being capable of saying that meetings have been held and the issues have been discussed. And any coordination that is actually produced may be as short-term as the interactions that produced it.

ACCOUNTABILITY

The final barrier to effective policy coordination to be discussed here is far from the least important. Accountability is always a crucial question in a democratic government, and it can also constitute a major barrier to coordination among public organizations. In order for administrative accountability to function effectively there must be clear patterns of responsibility for action and identifiable purposes for which public funds are spent. Coordination can cloud some of these authoritative relationships and make it more difficult to trace the sources of legal power and uses of public money. For example, at one point the Department of the Environment designed urban programs in the United Kingdom that required merging funds from several ministries and from several programs within the same ministry. These urban programs soon ran afoul of the Treasury, which wanted to be certain that it could trace all the money being spent and provide a full accounting of those funds.

It is not just financial accountability that can be threatened by attempts to coordinate programs. As already noted, performance management programs attempt to hold managers and their organizations accountable for meeting predetermined performance targets. There can be performance systems that work across departments and programs and even develop government-wide systems of performance indicators,[12] but since no organization really "owns" these indicators or can be directly responsible for the outcomes on the indicator, then none of them is really accountable for the outcomes. Achieving these system-wide goals may be desirable, especially for the center of government (presidents and prime ministers), but the level of commitment of any individual program manager to achieving those broad goals is likely to be less than for the individual programs for which he or she, and the associated organization, is responsible. The manager is being judged on the basis of, and his or her career may be depend upon, the performance of the single program and hence there may be little real interest in the performance of the cross-cutting programs.

Finally, coordination may present problems for clients and citizens as they attempt to hold government accountable for the services they are receiving, or not receiving. The logic of accountability, at least in its traditional forms, has been the ability to identify where incorrect decisions are made and to hold the individual or individuals accountable. In more coordinated service delivery systems there is the problem of "many hands," and it becomes difficult to identify who is in fact accountable for the decisions that have been made (Thompson 1980; Sullivan 2003).

Accountability is an absolutely central issue in any democratic government, and the demand by financial overseers and political leaders to be able to follow money and lines of responsibility generally reinforces the stovepipes that exist naturally in government. Simple, functional structures and simple means of administering programs make tracking money and responsibility easier. Although most citizens and politicians prize accountability, they must be aware that pursuing this one value may also prevent cooperation that might otherwise be undertaken by programs and organizations. As noted above, ministerial and administrative efforts at improving coordination have been undermined once the weakened lines of authority and accountability have been better understood by the participants in the process. Further, performance management, with an emphasis on quantifiable indicators and targets, is becoming central to accountability as well as to management of individual programs, and this shift reinforces the existence of the policy stovepipes even more.

PRIVACY

The protection of privacy within the public sector is in some ways the antithesis of accountability, given that it depends upon maintaining secrecy, while accountability depends upon transparency (see Erkkilä 2011). I demonstrated above that organizations attempting to control their own information can produce coordination problems, and this is also true when organizations are attempting to protect the privacy of their citizens. There are good legal and moral reasons to prevent organizations in the public sector from sharing information about citizens, but those protections, laudable as they may be, do affect coordination.

The impact of privacy on policy coordination can be seen most clearly in the absence of connections between tax policy and other areas of policy. For example, tax policy and social policy could be more effective if they were more closely connected but laws often forbid sharing information at an individual level across agencies. For example, if social service agencies were able to access tax and income data readily they might be able to better monitor welfare fraud and also match the needs of individuals more effectively with benefits. If nothing else, these organizations might be able to perform their jobs without asking citizens again and again for the same information.

The political controversy in the United States over the widespread data collection by the National Security Agency (NSA) has led to a number of questions about the use of this information by other organizations in government, most of which have complementary purposes to the NSA. For example, the same phone and internet logs that might help catch terrorists might also help catch hackers and money laundering (Lichtblau and Schmidt 2013). Privacy remains the principal barrier to this data sharing, but the requests also point to other problems in defining coordination. Would such sharing be coordination in fighting crime in general, or should the information (and the policy area) be defined narrowly?

SUMMARY

Although it has been discussed by virtually every government since there have been formal governments, coordination remains a central problem for political and administrative leaders. There are any number of reasons why a government organization may choose not to cooperate with other organizations, and some of those reasons may be valid even to a disinterested analyst. Still, it is also apparent to most analysts, and many practitioners, that government can perform its tasks better if the organizations and individuals involved in the process of governing act more cooperatively. The task for the public sector manager, and his or her political masters, therefore is to find the means of cajoling, enticing, or threatening actors in the public sector to coordinate their actions.

Although coordination has long been an important issue for government, the issue is becoming more important and more complex, as it involves now many actors in the private sector as well as the public. The emerging "governance" style in public administration and public policy (Papadopolous 1999; Peters 2004a) leads to involving large numbers of private sector actors in the formulation and implementation of policy. That involvement, in turn, creates even greater coordination problems for the public sector, as well as problems in reconciling a range of diverse interests in the initial formulation of policy.

This chapter has done a better job of specifying why coordination failures can occur than of specifying the possible remedies for those failures. Much the same has been true for the implementation literature in public administration that has been relatively strong in identifying failures (see Winter 2012). The failure stories about implementation, and about policy more generally, seem more interesting than stories of success (see Bovens and 't Hart 1996; Bovens, 't Hart, and Peters 2000), but understanding cause and effect in these settings requires information about both success and failure. If we have only failure stories then the very same factors we can identify as being present in policy failures may actually also appear in successes, meaning that we need to look for other causes for the observations.[13]

Also like the implementation literature, coordination failure can be instructive. By understanding how attempts to achieve greater coordination and coherence have failed to reach their targets we can understand, with some good fortune and perseverance, how to come closer to attaining those targets the next time coordination is required. Learning effectively, however, requires careful attention to understanding the particular circumstances associated with success and failure and being sure to understand the contingent factors in those situations that may have influenced the observed success and failure. In the cases of coordination that will be discussed in this book there are a large number of contingent factors, and I will not be able to eliminate all the sources of extraneous variance in the "data" being used. Still, by careful consideration of the circumstances, and an understanding of organizational dynamics in the public sector, I can at a minimum make some preliminary judgments about the efficacy of the various possible strategies for coordination in different contexts.

Attempts by governments to create better coordination in government are too numerous to even mention in this one book, much less to analyze systematically. I will, however, attempt to cover a range of cases. These cases are drawn from a number of political systems and policy areas and were selected primarily to illustrate the use of a variety of alternative instruments for achieving better coordination. In particular, I will look at one major attempt (the Department of Homeland Security in the United States) to use organizational change to create coordination, and another (Finland) that focuses more on procedures. Dealing with child care issues in the United Kingdom has been approached largely through the use of "czars," while the Open Method of Coordination in the European Union tends to use more of a network solution to the problem.

The attempt in this volume is to shed some new light on one of the oldest problems of governing. Although the issue by now appears rather hoary, it is nonetheless important and is appearing on the desks of political and administrative leaders every day. Governments are under pressure as perhaps never before to perform their tasks efficiently and effectively, and a failure to communicate will not make these systems appear better managed. As important as coordination is, however, it must also be considered in the range of goals and values that affect the public sector, so decisions must be made about how much effort to invest in making government more coherent and coordinated. I hope that if this book does not provide a definitive answer to that question—and if it will not—at least it can advance the understanding of this classic question of governance.

3. Approaches to Understanding Coordination

Coordination is not a simple political and administrative problem. It can reflect a wide range of problems within the public sector, and the need for improved cooperation may arise for a variety of administrative and political reasons. It is not surprising, therefore, that scholars have advanced a variety of theoretical approaches to understanding this subject, nor is it surprising that practitioners have tried a variety of methods to achieve coordination. The theoretical approaches to the range of coordination problems already identified are in most instances the same as those utilized in many other areas of inquiry in political science. Probing the applicability of these approaches for understanding coordination, however, enables us to understand better how enhanced coherence among programs and organizations can be brought about, as well as the range of possible solutions to the common problem of achieving cooperation.

As is true for other areas of organizational and institutional analysis, the study of coordination has some difficulty in identifying the relevant actors and with the anthropomorphizing of the organizations involved in the process. Thus, discussions of coordination often describe decisions being taken by *organizations,* and argue that organizations are pursuing their own political interests. This language is a useful shorthand for describing the political dynamics involved in coordination, but it does not describe adequately the incentives and actions of the decision makers within those organizations. We can identify objectively the interests of organizations, but those organizational interests must be identified and actually put into action by the members of the organizations.[1]

In addition to the four dominant theoretical approaches identified in this chapter—hierarchy, markets, networks, and collaboration—I will attempt to identify the fundamental social processes that are involved in making coordination work within and among organizations (Thompson et al. 1991). The underlying argument here (see Hedstrom and Swedborg 1998; Mayntz 2003) is that to understand social and political dynamics it is necessary to identify the basic mechanisms—such as bargaining, authority, cooptation, and coercion—that are required to make coordination (or other organizational processes) function effectively. These mechanisms involve utilizing the resources implied by the various theories and help to understand how these theories actually are placed into effect.

In this chapter I will discuss four alternative theoretical approaches to coordination in the public sector. Each of these approaches has something to contribute to understanding the causes of coordination problems, the gains to be achieved through coordination, and the mechanisms through which better coordination can be achieved. Although each approach has its own self-contained explanations and conceptions of coordination, none of them by itself appears capable of providing a complete picture of the political and administrative dynamics of behavior involved in coordinating programs. Therefore, while attempting to provide a reasonable account of the strengths and weaknesses of each of the approaches, a more complete analysis is possible through the application of several approaches. This use of multiple theories, or triangulation, is a means of providing alternative lenses (see Allison 1971; Wolf 2010) through which the phenomena in question can be approached.

In the triangulation of a social phenomenon, it is also important to consider approaches that are more macro and depend upon social structure versus those that are more micro and depend upon individual behavior. Most approaches to coordination have depended upon building structures and assuming that these structures will remedy the problems. As already noted, however, we need to be sure that the structures created will provide sufficient incentives or sanctions to ensure that the members of the structures will comply. Individual administrators or politicians may still receive most of their rewards as a function of belonging to their "home" organization, and therefore may find little reason to cooperate with others. Therefore, as we think about structure we need to think about behavior, and vice versa.

Likewise, researchers can use multiple methodologies to gather information about the same phenomenon and thus elaborate the analysis. Triangulation with different methodologies is especially useful when quantitative and qualitative approaches are used, or obtrusive and nonobtrusive instruments are combined (Webb, Campbell, Sechrest, and Schwartz 1981; Wolf 2010). That is, most of the methodologies used in political science and public administration involve the researcher being directly involved with the subject, and therefore creating a somewhat artificial social situation that will affect the behavior of the subject. Research on policy coordination, for example, often involves interviewing participants in the process and asking for their assessments of the processes and the success or failure of coordination. These actors usually have a stake in the outcome of coordination and want to make themselves, and their organizations, appear in as positive a light as possible, so the results of this interviewing contains a good deal of extraneous variance (see Peters 2013a).

HIERARCHY

The most familiar approach applied to understanding organizations in the public sector is hierarchy. For management and control within public organizations the use of hierarchy can have two aspects. The first, and dominant, approach using hierarchy is based on the assumption that public organizations remain at their most basic bureaucracies that are controlled by rules and internal authority. While the numerous administrative reforms of the past decade might easily lead one to question this assumption about public administration (Pollitt and Bouckaert 2004; Christensen and Laegreid 2001), there is still a pronounced element of legalism and formalism in government. To some extent the nature of the public sector is that there must be some formal rules that guide the behavior of participants in the governing process and specify the rights and obligations of citizens and administrators.

The alternative conception of hierarchy in the public sector that is relevant for the coordination issues being discussed is a more political conception of hierarchy. In this conception public sector organizations, and their behaviors, ultimately are, or at least should be, controlled by political leaders. The control exercised by those politicians is often imperfect, and delegation to bureaucracies lessens both the workload of the political leaders and their control (Huber and Shipan 2002). The bureaucratic elements within the hierarchy may actually dominate policy (see Page 2012), but politicians continue to attempt to exert control. Likewise, many of the hierarchical methods of control discussed here and in the next chapter depend heavily upon the willingness of the politicians to assert their formal powers. Further, even within the political structures themselves, there may be hierarchies that also strive for control over other aspects of government structure.

Bureaucracy as Hierarchy

Although Max Weber argued that bureaucracy and hierarchy were sources of coordination (see Derlien 1999), that optimistic perspective has found little support in the actual practice of public bureaucracies. Indeed, the familiar hierarchical model of government might be seen as the *locus classicus* of coordination problems. This characterization of bureaucracy as the source of many coordination problems can be defended easily, given the numerous ways in which bureaucratic, formal organizational structures contribute to the apparent incapability of organizations to work together effectively in government (see, among others, Moe 1984). Perhaps the dominant source of these coordination problems is specialization (see Harmon and Mayer 1986), especially specialization on the basis of *purpose,* following the familiar classification scheme for organizations developed by Luther Gulick (1937).[2]

Specialization provides a number of important benefits to government, but it also creates a number of problems. Organizations that are structured around particular purposes, and that have clearly defined policy goals, will tend to organize in a rather linear, top-down manner that will focus attention on the delivery of that service. In the simplest form this organizational format would lead to a clear, hierarchical focus on achieving the purpose within the department that limits weighing other considerations when making decisions. The manifest purpose of the organization[3] may constitute a set of blinders that will make it difficult for members of the organization to find common cause with other organizations and with other policy purposes.

But few organizations in the public sector have a single purpose, and tradeoffs typically must be made among the range of goals that they are pursuing. This tradeoff is especially evident given that at least some among the goals of any but the most altruistic of organizations will be *reflexive* (Mohr 1982; Merton 1957, 199) and oriented toward maintaining the organization and its place in government, rather than toward the achievement of the purposive, public goals for which it was created. Organizational leaders and employees may still have to choose among the purposive goals of the organization, and different levels of an organization may have different interpretations of those goals. In the political setting in which public sector organizations function, the legislature or other formulator of policies may create a range of goals and priorities without guidance on how the members of the organizations who are charged with implementation must select and interpret the conflicts or inconsistencies.

Organizations structured on the basis of clientele will encounter many of the same types of coordination problems as those structured on the basis of purpose. If anything, clientele-based organizations will have their natural specialization reinforced by the political power of the clientele and their demands for continued services. The extent to which the clientele basis for organization does decrease the capacity to coordinate will be in part a function of the breadth of service considered within a single organization. For example, the US Department of Agriculture is able to supply a rather broad array of services to their clients, the farmers, including crop supports, insurance, farm credit, marketing assistance, advice for farm families, and a range of other services. Given the full services being provided, these clients may have fewer needs to seek services outside that single department.[4]

Both process and area, the other two dimensions identified by Gulick for organization in the public sector, may provide some greater hope for coordination, within the organization itself if not necessarily across other organizations. Area-based structures have responsibility for services, and perhaps a wide variety of programs, within a geographical area and hence may have a greater tendency to coordinate the full range of services available within the organization and provide them to citizens. The above example of a department serving farmers could easily be translated into an organization serving rural areas, and could still provide the same range of services, or perhaps even a wider range. The farmers might lose some claims on the department, with rural merchants gaining some greater political advantages, but the net effects need not be dissimilar.[5]

Most organizations, no matter what their dominant basis of organization is, will have substructuring based on some or all of the other elements already described. For example, almost all organizations will have some process organizations such as personnel and budgeting that manage across the entire organization. This substructuring may provide for some greater internal coordination of the organizations, especially when there are service delivery units based on area or clientele that must pull together some of the activities of the organization and actually provide services to real clients, although paradoxically perhaps having structures within the organization that are more collaborative may actually reduce the capacity to coordinate across. That is, having well-organized programs within the one organization may lessen the internal appeal of cooperation, both from a sense of already doing the job well and also perhaps from a concern about upsetting an internal equilibrium. If there have been extensive negotiations within the organization to coordinate its own programs, the participants will not want to have to open those agreements again after bargaining with external actors.

The internal structuring of organizations may merely enhance the illusion of control within bureaucratic organizations. For example, the Securities and Exchange Commission in the United States, like many organizations, has a substructure based on area, assuming (probably correctly) that regional offices will enhance delivery of services in different regions of the country. However, these regional offices often exhibit some of the same pathological behaviors in dealing with each other as does any other set of organizations. In this case the New York and Boston regional offices both had substantial information on the Bernard Madoff Ponzi scheme in 2008 but did not share the information because each wanted the glory of prosecuting the case individually (SEC 2009).

Even in the decentralized, reformed versions of contemporary governance that have become central formats for governing in many contemporary political systems, there are important hierarchical elements that may contribute to problems of coordination. For example, even those reforms such as the creation of autonomous and quasi-autonomous organizations within government (Pollitt and Talbot 2003) tend to retain some forms of hierarchical control for leaders in the public sector. Indeed, the notion of autonomy in the public sector is generally argued to exist more than it appears to in reality, in both analytic and practical terms. The real question in understanding autonomy and control is: what forms of control remain and how are they imposed on the presumably autonomous organizations? Further, it would be irresponsible for governments not to continue to maintain some controls (accountability) over organizations responsible for delivering public services.

The same logic that applies to organizations applies even more clearly to the control of individuals within the public sector. The ideas of New Public Management (NPM) may shift the form of control over employees from formal rules to market-based incentives and sanctions, but those controls are, if anything, more pervasive and powerful than those in traditional public management systems. In particular, protections that once were available to civil servants, for example, tenure, are now largely abolished, and public employees are exposed to greater pressures to perform or lose their jobs or certainly not be rewarded in the way that they might have expected. Given that hierarchical superiors in government are setting the rules by which the personnel are managed it is still reasonable to assume that hierarchical control remains a central element in the control of government personnel, and hence of government management as a whole.

Politics and Hierarchical Control

The alternative form of hierarchical control over organizations in the public sector is politics, emphasizing the role of political leaders to control the other actors within the public sector. The nominal authority in any political system, democratic or not, derives from political office, and the bureaucracy is expected to follow the lead of those officials in making its own decisions and in implementing policy. Politicians often complain that once they are put into office they find that they have responsibility for the policies that are being implemented but actually have relatively few powers over those policies. Whatever the reality, the responsibility and accountability for what occurs within government are certainly lodged with the politicians.

Richard Rose (1974) some thirty years ago presented a clear and compelling analysis of why political leaders have great difficulty in actually making this hierarchy work. The political apex of the public sector has, in most instances, the legitimacy to create action in government but often lacks the organizational and managerial capacity to do so. Further, the political leaders may face many of the same divisions based on specialization that have produced coordination in the first instance. Ministers have responsibility for a particular, specialized aspect of the total public sector and are responsible for making that set of programs work. Further, they often face strong pressures from below to defend the budgets and other resources of the ministry—its turf—against other ministers, and against the prime minister, who may have fiscal policy goals that call for less spending and less policy action (Blick and Jones 2010).

Faced with these divisions within their own cabinets, presidents and prime ministers often have fewer tools of hierarchical control than they might like. These powers vary (see Chapter 4) but in general collegiality as a political norm makes the imposition of hierarchical control by prime ministers or ministers of finance over other ministers rather difficult. This power of collegiality is especially evident in coalition governments in which individual ministers not only have their own organizational power but also carry the banner for a political partner within the coalition (Andeweg 2000).[6] Prime ministers in such situations can expect to exercise little authoritative control over the participants in their governments and to engage more in political bargaining than in imposing authority.

Perhaps the most important aspect of the hierarchical elements of political control over organizations and their capacity to generate coordination is the interface between the political and the administrative leaders. This interface is crucial for making government work in more general terms (Peters 1987; Peters and Pierre 2001; Page 2012) and is also directly relevant for coordination issues. If the conventional analysis of bureaucracies presented above is at all correct then political leaders will experience a substantial control deficit when they attempt to impose their own priorities on senior civil servants. The same barriers face the political leaders when they attempt to control the organizations over which they nominally have control, and they often report themselves extremely frustrated in attempting to exercise their managerial functions. In these settings the formal power and authority coming from hierarchy often is confronted with other bases of power that make coordination difficult. Organizations and their top civil servants have substantial reservoirs of information and have other sources of authority coming from the closer connections of organizations with clients and from their direct relationships with legislative organizations in divided governments such as the United States.

Summary

Hierarchy remains a central element in the understanding of the public sector, and especially the coordination activities in government. The traditional assumption within government is that authority and hierarchical power can be used to impose coordination on organizations and individuals. Governments certainly attempt to use their authority, but are often confronted by the political power of interest groups that may make a public organization reluctant to cooperate with others. Studies of the public bureaucracy make it abundantly clear that organizations can find ways to avoid compliance, or ways to delay compliance, so that authority is not a certain means of producing coordination. The networks of public and private organizations discussed below as a possible means for coordination also have been powerful mechanisms to reduce coordination.

In addition to the general limitations of hierarchy in coordination, changes in thinking about the best ways to manage in government have tended to reduce the capacity of authority to produce the type of control desired. Advocates of the NPM have argued that the quality of governance in contemporary societies will be enhanced by permitting skilled public managers heading individual organizations to make more of their own policy and implementation decisions. This approach has particularly tended to denigrate the capacity of the political leaders in government to make effective policy and administrative choices (see Peters and Pierre 2001). Given that perceived weakness in political control, the bureaucracy may be left to make more of its own decisions on coordination. And given that the emphasis within the NPM tends to be on the autonomy of organizations, there will be less pressure on the organizations involved to comply with requests for coordination. Even if organizations are operating with delegated powers, however, they are operating "in the shadow of hierarchy" (Scharpf 1997), and governments can find ways to impose greater hierarchical control as needed.

Finally, we have to consider the aspirations of political leaders to control their bureaucracies and especially to coordinate the public sector. The assumption here, and in most of the literature, is that political leaders want to exercise close control. But they may be willing to delegate to their bureaucracies, in part to be able to avoid blame for failures (Hood 2011). Even when prime ministers and presidents appear to exercise almost obsessive control over their governments, the emphasis tends to be on controlling communications and their external image rather than controlling policy (Thomas 2012).

MARKETS AND RATIONAL CHOICE

Markets are inherently mechanisms for coordination between buyers and sellers. Without the creation of market institutions, through laws establishing property rights and providing for the enforcement of contracts, buying and selling would be very difficult and expensive, rather than a part of normal life. Once established and functioning properly, markets are able to rather effortlessly coordinate the actions of the buyers and sellers who participate in the market, using the price mechanism as a means of finding an appropriate level at which the buyers and sellers can both be satisfied (see Dahl and Lindblom 1953, 239). Rather than having to impose controls over the participants in this coordination process, market-based mechanisms depend upon the self-interest of those participants, and relatively simple signaling devices such as price.

The market may not, however, be as obvious a mechanism for coordinating policies and programs in the public sector as it is for coordinating buyers and sellers. Most importantly, the actors who need to be coordinated in the public sector tend to be competitive, while those in the typical market setting are more complementary. If programs and program managers conceptualize their actions as complementary and not as being in competition for scarce funds, then market mechanisms may be extremely effective, but if the actors thought of their programs that way then almost anything would be an effective coordination device. In the real world of competitive politics, or at best indifference between programs, markets may not exist and may be created with difficulty. Thus, from the economic perspective, policy coordination may be a classic collective action problem in which all the actors may be better off if the good is produced, but no one has an immediate incentive to produce it (Peters 2013b).

Markets are based on exchange, and another question that arises for the use of markets as coordination devices in the public sector is what will be exchanged. The most obvious answers are money and services, but there may be other answers as well. As noted already, clients are a valuable resource for programs, especially programs in the human and social services (for a classic statement, see Litwak and Hylton 1962). By having clients programs have a claim on the public purse and can bargain for the other things they may want from their "sponsors" in the legislature or the political executive.[7] Those clients generally are not politically quiescent either, and will mobilize political support for "their" agency when budgets are being considered, or new program authority is being sought.

In the public sector some significant questions about how to establish the mechanisms for interactions among autonomous actors arise. One mode of thinking about the market logic of policy coordination, therefore, comes from thinking of the political system as composed of a series of autonomous firms and individuals who seek to maximize their own utility. In most cases these organizations are likely to believe that the utility can be maximized through more autonomous action, rather than through more collaboration with other organizations. Just as individual firms may see profits as being zero-sum games with other firms in the same industry, so, too, do agencies consider the opportunities for increasing budgets to be zero-sum (see Nicholson-Crotty 2005). In such a setting, cooperation is unlikely.

If we take the discussion of political markets as populated by teams and firms seriously, then coordination actually may be an even more difficult process from a political or administrative perspective, and the barriers from that perspective are more than sufficient to make good coordination problematic. The most obvious point is that firms as utility maximizers may not see much utility gain from cooperation. While there may be gains for clients and for other external actors, it may be difficult for the "firm" to internalize these "profits." Rather, they are likely to see their advantage coming from differentiating their "product" from that of the other firms in the market and doing the best job possible in delivering that good or service.

Herbert Simon (1947) has argued that collections of programs and organizations should be designed in ways that minimize their interdependency. If the public sector can achieve that target then the coordination and collaboration problem may be minimized or even eliminated. If one public organization can achieve its ends without reference to another then coordination will simply not be an issue. The problem is that it is almost impossible to think of a public program or organization that does not to some extent depend upon others in order to be successful. A large organization such as the US Department of Defense may attempt to provide for many of its own needs—it has its own health care, its own educational apparatus, etc.—but even then will find that it will need some outside assistance. Defense, for example, depends to some extent upon the Central Intelligence Agency and the National Security Agency to supplement its own efforts at collecting and interpreting intelligence about potential adversaries, and it relies heavily upon the Department of Energy for research and development of atomic weapons.[8] Further, the Department of Defense and the Department of State are closely linked in the design and implementation of national security policy.

Leaving the obvious difficulties aside for the moment, if we begin with that conceptualization of autonomous firms attempting to maximize their own utilities in a complex political and administrative market, we can begin to apply various models developed to understand the games that actors play in a number of decision situations (Lam 2005; see also Cooper 1998). Lam, for example, conceptualized the policy coordination process in Hong Kong using several different, if well-known, games. The most obvious example of a game that can be used for understanding coordination is the Prisoner's Dilemma. In this game two actors, conceptualized as prisoners being interrogated separately, are attempting to maximize their utilities when they do not know the behavior of the other player. The payoffs for the actors are best when they both refuse to "rat" on the other, but if one defects and the other does not then the one who had continued to resist comes out poorly. If they do choose to "rat" on each other the outcomes are of course negative for both.

If we convert this to a game for policy coordination then the actors (agencies and their leaders as the designers of the strategies) may both be better off if they cooperate and coordinate their actions. If, however, one agency attempts to be cooperative and gives up some resources and the other does not then the noncooperative actor is far better off. Likewise, if they both do not cooperate they may perhaps be no worse off, given the absence in most political systems of strong enforcement of coordination initiatives. Politically, they may be better off given that they will continue to serve their own clientele well and will not divert resources to other purposes that are not directly related to their particular mission.

The obviously superior strategy for organizations to follow in this setting is to cooperate, but how to get to that strategy, given all the reasons that organizations have advanced for their failures to coordinate (see Chapter 1)? The Prisoner's Dilemma game depends upon a mechanism for enforcement that can impose costs on defectors—those who choose not to cooperate with each other in this coordination game. Coordination is basically a public good so that any losses from a failure to coordinate will not be highly visible to clients, and hence political mechanisms for enforcing cooperation are not likely to be effective. Thus, this rational, economic model for thinking about coordination may not work without a hierarchical mechanism—strengthening Fritz Scharpf's (1997) basic point that a great deal of the seemingly autonomous action in the public sector is occurring in the shadow of hierarchy.

As well as the more individualistic approach of game theory, transaction cost analysis represents another economic approach to the problem of coordination. The assumption of the classical model of economics, as noted above, is that there are multiple autonomous actors, each acting rationally. The logic of transaction cost analysis, on the other hand, is more that of bounded rationality. Further, in transaction cost analysis information is costly, so that working in an unconstrained market is expensive and excessively uncertain. Rational action from this perspective then minimizes costs through finding mechanisms for reducing costs and maximizing the possibilities for effective interaction. If costs are sufficiently high the logic is to construct hierarchical institutions rather than attempt to coordinate through less direct means. For example, merging ministries or programs may be seen as a means of reducing transaction costs and thus improving the probabilities of coordination.

Transaction cost analysis leads one to think about contracting as a mechanism for coordination. Contracts enable potential participants in a coordinated group of organizations to stipulate their participation in the collective activities of the group and the prices at which they will buy and sell certain products and services. For example, Itoh (1992) discusses the possibilities for designing contracts within single organizations that reward agents for their contributions to collective outcomes, as well as to the outcomes of a more constrained agent providing a single product or service to the organization. The same logic may be applied to groups of organizations so that a "grand contracting approach" can manipulate incentives to induce greater cooperation among the members of groups of organizations providing public services.

Another option for using contracts is to think about "relational contracting" as a complement to other forms of contracting (Brown, Potoski, and Van Slyke 2006). The stereotype of the market as a series of one-time, formal, relatively impersonal contacts between buyers and sellers seriously underestimates the institutionalized and persistent elements of market relationships in a mature economy. Working in the public sector is much more analogous to this continuing pattern of relationships than it is to the atomistic market of neoclassical theory. Most of the participants in the public sector—individuals but especially organizations—have much less to gain from a short-term deal, even if advantageous, than they do from developing stable working relationships with other participants. Those relationships are in many ways the fundamental basis for coordination and cooperation across programs.

Contracts at their simplest are an agreement between two or more individuals for some sort of exchange. We sign contracts with our employer to work, I signed a contract with the publisher for this book,[9] and firms and government departments sign contracts to purchase a range of goods and services. For the purposes of understanding coordination, we can think of organizations in the public sector entering into agreements with one another to exchange information, or to exchange clients who need different types of services, or for one organization to provide assistance in delivering a program through its field structure when another does not want to open a whole range of branch offices. These contracts may be formalized, or they may be informal arrangements among organizations that see that their common purposes can be better achieved through collaboration than through competition or through ignoring one another.

Contracts bridge the theoretical space between market models of governing and the next approach to coordination that I will discuss—networks. This linkage is especially evident when we think of relational contracting (Williamson 1995). In a strictly market conception of policy each "deal" would be struck *de nouveau*, but in practice a great deal of contracting is repetitive, and the participants minimize their decision-making costs rather than maximize possible economic gains.[10] Relational contracts also emphasize the crucial role of trust in coordination and indeed in other matters of public management.

A particular model of rationality and exchange in the process of coordination is usually discussed as dependency or resource dependency (Oliver 1990). The assumption is that many organizations in the public sector depend upon each other in order to be effective in achieving their ends. That interdependence can be manifested through the possession of different resources—money that comes from the central organizations and political support from the line agencies, for example. The game of institutional politics, therefore, is one of developing strategies to maximize the resources that an actor is seeking while expending a minimum of one's own resources.

This process of resource dependency has been conceptualized as a set of games by some political theorists working from a rational choice perspective. In particular, scholars of federalism have attempted to understand how actors can reach decisions in complex bargaining arrangements. Fritz Scharpf (1988), as mentioned above, has argued that the coordination outcomes in these settings are likely to be disappointing. If the actors involved do act rationally then they will block actions that do not correspond to their own preferences, and the result is often the lowest common denominator as the outcome of the bargaining process.

All these economic approaches to coordination highlight the fundamental problem of collective action. Individual organizations generally believe that they have strong incentives to deliver their own programs and not to cooperate with others. Some of the economic arguments presented above demonstrate that these perceptions can be short-sighted and there may be long-term gains if organizations cooperate. The political difficulty, however, is to integrate that type of thinking into the motivational structures of organizations and to find ways of achieving coordination without the imposition of hierarchy.

NETWORKS

The third of the usual suspects who are rounded up when discussing fundamental modes of explanation in the public sector is networks. In many ways thinking about the utilization of networks in the public sector should be a natural approach for dealing with coordination; the very existence of a network may be evidence that a certain amount of coordination is occurring with or without conscious design by government officials. Within the existing literature on coordination through informal interorganizational systems there has been a gradual evolution of conceptual models. Initially the interorganizational literature that developed within the sociology and management literatures identified the interdependency of organizations and the need to structure their interaction (Oliver 1990; Provan and Lemaire 2012). As the literature has evolved the more contemporary network literature provides a development and to some extent a complementary perspective on the interaction of multiple organizations as a means of reaching collective goals.

Before I discuss this evolution of thinking, and the general importance of network analysis, I should first point out that less formal theorizing, and less formal action, may also be important for producing coordination. A common political or corporate culture that may exist among a set of actors may produce coordination with minimal formal interaction. One description of the logic of cartels has been that rather than formal collusion there may simply be a "corpsgeist" held by the executives resulting in similar behavior (see Alexander 1995, 74). Further, professionals in different organizations may well respond in similar manners when confronted with a particular policy challenge, and therefore the organizations in which those professionals work may appear more coordinated than they actually are simply through the structure of their personnel. Finally, the public sector itself may have a sufficient management culture to produce relatively common behavior across a wide range of organizations.

I should also point out that much of the literature on public sector organizations within networks tends to focus on the individual organization and its placement in a web of interconnections with the other organizations operating in its "field" (see Dimaggio and Powell 1983). Inevitably this approach involves some of the logic of networks of organizations, but it primarily emphasizes the individual organization and its capacity to perform its tasks in that complex environment. The connections among the organizations within that theory involve mutual resource dependency, often arranged voluntarily (see Marsh and Rhodes 1992). Further, those organizations are engaged in mutual adjustment and potentially in joint decision making produced through cooperation among participants.

In public administration the literature on interorganizational analysis grew out of the study of policy implementation. Beginning with Pressman and Wildavsky (1974), students of implementation recognized that public programs rarely were implemented by the "single, lonely organization" (Peters 2013b) but rather were put into effect by "formally autonomous, functionally interdependent, organizations" (Metcalfe 1979). Although the analysis approach does depend heavily upon the interaction of multiple organizations, the implementation approach often begins with a focus on a single program, and with that often a single organization. That focus is more conducive to be able to track through the deviations of policy from the stated intentions of the "formators" (Lane 1981) of the policy.

One important early analysis of interorganizational relations involved in coordination (Whetten 1982) argued that there were three alternative strategies for managing coordination, all within this broader approach to interagency relations. Interestingly, those three approaches are analogous to the broader approaches developed here. For example, the "mutual adjustment" model in the interorganizational approach looks very much like the collaborative approach to be discussed below (pages 65–69). That is, these interactions are loosely structured and depend upon creating informal norms and modifying agency goals. On the other end of the spectrum the corporate strategy was argued to be a highly formalized and centralized pattern of interactions among the participants that regulates the interactions of the actors involved through formal rules. As the name implies, this approach is considered to be very much in the vein of traditional management within private sector corporations.

The intermediate level in this taxonomy of interorganizational relations is described as the "alliance model," in which there are negotiated rules and a mixture of collective and agency (organizational) goals (for an original presentation see Benson 1975). This model is the closest to what we now consider to be network analysis of government action. This alliance model implies that organizations are at once pursuing their own goals and using the interorganizational environment in which they function as a means of pursuing those goals. At the same time they must recognize that they are members of the collectivity of organizations and that there are some collective goals (if only inchoate at times) that can only be achieved through cooperation. The negotiation among the various organizations will define the extent to which those collective goals actually become operational, and the extent to which individual organizations can develop means of achieving their own ends through the pursuit of the common goals.

Network Analysis

Networks have evolved as an approach that concentrates on explaining policy and administrative coordination from a multiorganizational perspective. After all, the inherent nature of networks is to promote groups of social and political actors working together to solve common problems (Kickert, Klijn, and Koopenjan 1997; Milward and Provan 1998). The typical representation of networks is one of cooperative arrangements among relatively autonomous social actors, with the result being some form of governance within a particular societal sector. In the study of public administration, this network mode of thinking has come to be characterized as *governance* (Kooiman 2003; Frederickson 2005), in contrast to *government* and traditional public administration with their greater reliance on hierarchy (see Pierre and Peters 2000; Peters 2004a). The network approach differs primarily in degree from the interorganizational literature, emphasizing more the collectivity of organizations and their interactions, and especially their role in creating governance, rather than the individual organizations.

Although networks may appear to be a natural form of coordination for government, there is a need to think carefully about the impacts of the increasingly important governance style in the public sector. In particular, we will need to consider the differential impacts of networks within government from those based primarily in the civil society. The governance notions mentioned above focus on the role of networks that bridge the divide between state and society (Torfing et al. 2012). Those networks are, however, supplemented by strong networks within government itself that may supplement those in society, or in some cases may be used to overcome the difficulties created by excessively strong links with society.

The first task required when conceptualizing the role of networks in policy coordination is to differentiate among different types of networks and policy communities that surround almost all policy areas in the public sector. On the one hand one can identify closed, rather exclusive, policy communities that tend to restrict membership based on acceptance of particular views of the policy in question. Marsh and Rhodes (1992), for example, argue that, among other things, policy communities or networks in the public sector (1) restrict access to policymaking; (2) decide which issues are included; and (3) privilege certain interests. This conceptualization also implies that the members of the network will share many common orientations toward policy and would tend to differentiate themselves from other possible groups who might be concerned with some of the same or similar policy issues.

Even more exclusive, epistemic communities (Haas 1992; Miller and Fox 2001) assume specialized knowledge bases are held by all members of the network. These knowledge bases make membership in the network difficult for clients, or for the general public, and may leave control over policy in the hands of those experts.

While expertise defines membership in these communities, once created they have the capacity to govern in their own self-interest and can make control by the public sector by either political actors or by client groups more difficult. Further, the logic of the community may simply not be compatible with broader social interests. For example, much of the foundation of medicine is acute care in institutions, while for social purposes preventative medical care offered closer to the homes of the citizens (patients) would be more desirable. It is, however, generally difficult for the public sector or patients to transform the manner in which health care services are delivered, and even in countries with more extensive state involvement in health care, the acute care model tends to dominate.

At the other end of the dimension of exclusivity, issue networks are open to a more diverse group of actors and permit a range of interests and actors to be involved in policymaking. Although a good deal of network theory is vague concerning the criteria for membership, it appears as if networks can include whomever they wish to include, with membership being a function of interaction, rather than vice versa. When networks begin to interact with public programs the definitions of membership may require clarification, given that public organizations may be using these networks as means of legitimating public action. If policies or administrative actions are being justified through the involvement of a network, there is always the danger that inadequate representativeness of the group can backfire and make the policy appear illegitimate.[11]

While the openness of networks, as compared to communities, is apparently admirable from the perspective of democracy and inclusion, that openness and the range of interests that can be involved in the networks potentially presents severe difficulties in making decisions in a timely and effective manner.[12] The participants in networks may not agree on even the fundamental premises about the policy, and hence agreement, and therefore coordination, among the participants may be difficult to achieve. Continued interactions among the members of the network may facilitate making decisions in a more timely manner, but if these structures are open and the membership is relatively fluid then they find making decisions more difficult. Thus, although networks appear open and democratic, and to some extent they are, the absence of legitimate mechanisms for making decisions in the face of conflict, e.g., *ex ante* rules such as majority rule, may make them less effective as policymaking structures. This difficulty is not dissimilar to that noted by Scharpf (1988) for making decisions in political systems that require unanimity.

On the more positive side of the ledger, networks may link actors that have different interests and that have different types of policy expertise. Further, given that the clients who receive a variety of benefits from government organizations may be involved in different policy networks, coordination may emerge from the bottom up, coming through the clients themselves. Part of the logic of coordination, especially for social services, is that government programs should serve "the whole client," rather than just the health needs or the income needs, or whatever other particular needs an individual program may address. Governments have been built up on the basis of expertise and specialization but find that specialization can be a major barrier to effectiveness, especially in providing the range of services required by clients with multiple needs.

As well as these extreme versions of definitions of networks, there are also extremes in the roles that are assigned to networks in governance. A good deal of the network literature assigns these relatively informal structures a strong, or even dominant, role in governing (see Kickert, Klijn, and Koopenjan 1997; see also Helmke and Levitsky 2003). The assumptions undergirding these analyses are that governments are incapable of governing because of their rigidities, their self-interest, and their inadequate connections with their society. On the other hand, networks of social actors are argued to be capable of responding to changes in their own priorities and to attempts by government to control them and can do so without the bureaucratic rigidities of the public sector. This role for networks can be contrasted with a more descriptive version of network analysis that notes that these structures do indeed exist and influence government but are largely subordinate to the formal institutions of government.

Given that political demands on government often are incorporated directly into policy, using client-based organizations as the initial locus for many of the pressures for coordination may be an effective strategy for pressuring governments to achieve greater policy integration. Working from a perspective of principal agent models coming from economics, Dixit and his colleagues (Dixit, Grossman, and Helpman 1997; see also Bertelli and Lynn 2004) have argued that the "common agency" model implied by multiple groups placing pressures on government can in fact contribute to policy coordination, although the contending forces may limit the gains for any one group from their involvement in the policymaking process.

The above having been said, however, it may be inappropriate and inefficient to place the burden of coordination on the recipients of public services. For certain types of programs this locus of pressure may perform well, given that the clients have some social and political capabilities and are able to mobilize the political and organizational resources needed to get what they want from government. On the other hand, however, the clients who would most need more, and more integrated, service are those who would be least capable of advocating for their benefits on their own. However, somewhat paradoxically, the logical advocates for the interests of the socially excluded often are among the most likely to segment their clients and to focus on a particular type of problem that affects those clients (for the public sector see Denhardt and Denhardt 2011). This pattern of service provision reflects the patterns of training and the competition within the not-for-profit sector, and the professional blinders that both professionalism and organizational boundaries place on employees.

There is some risk, however, that networks linking state and society may exacerbate, rather than remedy, problems of coordination for the public sector. Surrounding all the major policy areas are aggregations of interest groups, non-governmental organizations of all types, and generally also a range of other public sector organizations as well. The nature of these aggregations of organizations is that the participants interact with one another, and through processes of bargaining and mutual adjustment, are able to reconcile differences and make decisions about public policy.[13] Given the significant amount of negotiation that may be required to produce decisions within a network, any subsequent attempts to coordinate with other networks, or with other institutions responsible for public policies, would be difficult. In more theoretical language, networks can reduce the transaction costs among their own members, but in the process increase transaction costs with other actors, including other networks.

In political and democratic terms reliance on networks as a means of coordination also means reliance on groups and organizations and may therefore tend to exclude individuals and interests who are not sufficiently organized to participate effectively. Networks therefore may become a means of capture of the policies of government by organized interests rather than the open and inclusive model their advocates assume they are. The capture argument is especially relevant given that each policy area will be dominated by the groups that are interested in it, rather than by any more general sense of the public interest. Further, when the nature of the network involved is more of an exclusive community then the exclusivity of that sort of relationship among actors tends to exclude the public interest even more.[14] In addition to the democratic control issues involved in the power of policy communities over policy, these structures will further exacerbate difficulties in coordination encountered by political elites.

Although the network model is usually discussed in terms of interactions between state and society, networks can also exist within the public sector itself. The informal contacts among organizations and individuals within government have many of the same characteristics that are used to describe the state-society linkages. Thus, the ongoing informal structures that often supplement the formal structures of government may be crucial for the success of management and policy in government. Most leaders in public organizations understand that they are not the "single, lonely organizations" that have dominated a good deal of the thinking about policy implementation (see Hjern and Porter 1981; Pressman and Wildavsky 1974). Although they may understand that simple fact, their behavior often does not reflect that understanding and they focus excessively on their own organization and its needs.

Donald Chisholm (1989) has argued that although most analyses of coordination are based on hierarchy and the use of formal powers, effective coordination can be achieved by relying upon more informal mechanisms. There is a long and important literature (see Gouldner 1954; Crozier 1964) on informal organization within individual organizations, and some of the same logic can be applied to the study of groups of organizations within the public sector. Just as informal patterns of interaction within an organization can facilitate the performance of that organization by supplementing and bypassing the formal structure, the same may be true of the role of informal interactions as a means of coping with rigidities in the interactions among organizations in the public sector.

The civil service itself is one of the most important informal structures in government. Although the civil service can be conceptualized as an institution in its own right, it can also be seen as a network of individuals who occupy crucial roles within the apparatus of governance. Perhaps most importantly, the majority of civil servants experience a long career in government and may work with one another, and with politicians, over decades. The civil service is especially viable as a coordination network in civil service systems such as the United Kingdom, in which civil servants continue to occupy positions in a number of government ministries in the course of their careers. Given those diverse careers, the civil servants are more likely to have some understanding of the full range of government activity than those in more specialized civil services such as the United States with its correspondingly more specialized career patterns. Even in the specialized systems, however, the civil service may be a natural source of coordination for government given that they are charged with implementing policy and need to find means of working with one another to make that happen (see pages 81–82).

Given the potential importance of the public service as a source of coordination, the opening of these personnel systems to outsiders as part of the agenda of NPM to make them more subject to market forces is perhaps particularly damaging. Even if there may be some efficiency gains from bringing in managers from the outside (an assumption with relatively little supporting evidence), the losses from lost coordination are likely to offset those gains. One of the best natural networks for coordination appears to have been undermined through the search for managerial efficiencies.

Measuring Networks

Networks may have an additional advantage in the study of coordination in that they provide some opportunities for measurement that help to supplement measures that are focused directly on the policy choices. The advantage of these measures (see Provan and Sydow 2011) is that they provide a quantitative assessment of how organizations interact. For example, we could measure the density of interactions, or the multiplicity of linkages that exist among organizations, and individuals within them, that may be associated with the particular policy domain under consideration. And likewise, this type of analysis, assessing the interactions among organizations, can help to identify the holes in the patterns of interaction. While these measurements concerning the nature of networks can be valuable mappings of the relationships among organizations and individuals, they are not necessarily adequate measures of coordination. While we may know that organizations do interact with each other, we do not know what the contents of those interactions are. The assumption may be that if organizations are interacting then they must be doing something positive, but the reality may be quite different. They may merely be justifying their own positions on why they do *not* cooperate with other organizations and why the policies of those other organizations are misguided. This may be a coordination of a sort, but certainly not one that could move a common policy agenda forward.

Summary

In summary, networks can be a significant mechanism for coordinating public activity. The coordination capacity built into networks is based upon rather different social instruments than those undergirding either hierarchies or marketized arrangements. To a great extent the logic of networks is *communication* rather than either authority or incentives. Coordination in the network model results from individuals and organizations being in contact with one another and finding some common interests through their interactions (Tomlinson 2010). At a minimum the simple act of communication among the participants in a network may be sufficient to produce some form of coordination among the participants, if only the negative coordination coming from being aware of what each other is doing. That communication will help the participants in the network define the policy questions and create the cognitive structures needed for effective coordination (Toke 2000). The model therefore also assumes that the participants in the networks are interested in producing better coordination, or at least are not opposed to cooperating with one another to make programs work more effectively.

Network models of coordination also assume that the act of communicating and generating good will can overcome some of the inherent barriers to coordination that exist in the specialized world of public organizations and their continuing commitments to often rather greedy clientele groups. This reliance on communications is perhaps an excessively optimistic perspective on the way in which interactions may be capable of changing attitudes and values, given that these communicative actions must confront the entrenched interests of organizational employees, as well as those of their clients. Indeed, attempts to coordinate may only strengthen entrenched client groups, who will identify the pressures for change as an immediate challenge to their existing benefits and political influence, and therefore mobilize politically to a greater extent than they might have seen without the overt attempts to coordinate.

The network model for coordination need not, however, be based entirely upon communications, trust, and good will among the organizations and individuals involved. It can also be conceptualized in terms of resource dependency among the participants, and especially the mutual resource dependency that exists among different levels of government (see Duran 1999; Rhodes 2002). In such a model of organizational interactions coordination is likely to result from the needs of each actor to maintain at least a minimal working relationship with others on which they may be dependent for some crucial resource. In some sense this resource dependency conceptualization of networks approaches the market model discussed above, in that it assumes that there are crucial exchanges among the relevant actors that coordinate their activities and force some mutual agreement on goals. This network or even discursive perspective on interactions among actors attempting to coordinate differs little from the market approaches, given that to some extent the actors are pursuing rational strategies to maximize their utilities. It differs, however, in that the basic logic is one of maintaining interactions rather than maximizing any particular budgetary or personnel benefits.

Although the advocates of the network approach can point to some successes in coordination and collaboration, it is also important to consider that they can be too successful. Network collaboration is based on the autonomy of the actors and their ability to make deals among themselves. Those arrangements may be successful for the clients and the organizations, but the outcomes may not conform with those intended by the officials designing the policy and funding the networks. Thus, there is the danger that the network may be well coordinated internally and have high levels of trust among the actors but be isolated from other policies and policymakers (including other networks) that may be important for its success.

COLLABORATION

The final approach to coordination is the least developed theoretically of the group, yet still has the potential to explain some behaviors in the policy process. Further, the more psychological roots of collaboration as an approach is a useful complement to the more political and economic bases of the other means of understanding coordination. Collaboration can, as I will point out below, also have substantial structural and political manifestations, but it depends largely upon building other types of interconnections among programs and perhaps more importantly among individuals. Thus, this model of coordination has some affinity with the network model discussed above but is based more on the attitudes of the participants in the process than it is on the structural relationships among the organizations or individuals. Of course, if the attitudes of the participants in the process of coordination are changed then the interaction and the networking will almost certainly develop, but in this model the change of attitudes precedes the change in behavior.[15]

Eugene Bardach (1998) developed the concept of collaboration based on his research on the coordination of social programs in the American states. Bardach (1998, 8) defines collaboration as "any joint activity by two or more agencies that is intended to increase public value by their working together rather than working separately." This definition is close to those provided for more positive forms of coordination, in contrast to the negative conceptions of coordination in which organizations simply avoid conflicts with each other's programs. Thus, when using collaboration, there is an effort to move the policymaking and policy delivery capacity of government as a whole forward, rather than focusing entirely on a single range of issues and concerns.

To some extent Bardach's notion of collaboration also can be seen as an approach to enhancing creativity within the public sector, and collaboration becomes a mechanism for thinking about options for policy design (on design see Linder and Peters 1987; Howlett and Lejano 2013). The dynamic term that Bardach gives to the practice of collaboration is *craftsmanship* (1998, 19ff). That is, the role of the public manager when thinking about designing programs, or managing his or her own programs, is to craft solutions that can produce greater public value than might otherwise be possible through less well-designed programs. That enhancement would result largely from opportunities that consider the ways in which organizations can be encouraged to develop their own cooperative solutions to policy problems. This conception is actually similar to the idea of coordination developed in the interorganizational literature, stressing the development of new norms of collective action and new means of achieving collective goals.

The notion of craftsmanship as a mechanism for collaboration to some extent bridges the policy versus administration divide in the study of coordination. On the one hand, collaboration is primarily an administrative device for producing greater cooperation among organizations, relying upon agencies and agency managers to produce changes in their own behavior in order to create that "public value."[16] On the other hand, the target of these collaborative activities is primarily to change policy, rather than simply improving the implementation of programs through coordination. There is certainly a great deal of virtue in coordinating programs and eliminating duplication and conflicts, but the purpose of collaboration is somewhat more ambitious. Certainly some of the activities described by Bardach might be seen as administrative, but most of those activities would put a very creative and entrepreneurial cast on the role of the administrator in the public sector.

Bardach's conception of collaboration also links more formal and hierarchical approaches to coordination with those perspectives emphasizing the integration of policy ideas (see Lanzalco 2011). Much of the discussion of craftsmanship involves reframing policy ideas in ways that make them agreeable, or even appealing, to all the organizations involved. Although not addressed in great detail, however, the concept of craftsmanship also implies utilizing other mechanisms to create collaboration among the participants.

Collaboration as an approach to coordination depends upon the willingness of public managers to invest heavily in the process of coordination. Managers obviously must work within a legal and institutional framework but also can be seen as exercising some personal skills and initiative in changing their behaviors and the behaviors of their organizations and in improving policy outcomes as a result of those changes. The skills for creating organizational change involve mobilizing resources, financial and otherwise, motivating staff, working with the stakeholders, and a host of other relatively ordinary managerial activities. What differentiates craftsmanship from normal administration, then, is the specific purposes toward which those activities are directed. Further, craftsmanship requires a more activist form of administration than might be expected in many administrative systems.

This approach to coordination assigns the public manager a central role in the process of managing the interaction of public organizations. What it does not explain so well are the strategies that the manager may undertake in order to mobilize sources of motivation for a different form of the desirable behaviors on the part of these managers. Page (2003) has focused on the entrepreneurial role of managers in promoting coordination in government, pointing out the extent to which the success of collaborative efforts in government depends upon the actions of individual leaders in public organizations. Further, those leaders need not be in formal leadership positions but may instead be found at much lower levels in the bureaucracy where substantial amounts of policy are actually constructed.

I have already pointed to a number of barriers to managers adopting a collaborative perspective on their tasks, and indeed if anything the pressures toward maintaining a greater commitment to the particular organization and its programs have been increasing during the past several years (Skelcher and Sullivan 2008). We can all agree that greater collaboration and coordination are desirable, but what may be missing are motivations for the manager that are sufficient to overcome the managerialist pressures to emphasize performance by the one organization. Some forms of performance management have developed government-wide goals and can assess managers according to the extent to which they and their organizations contribute to achieving those goals as well as individual organizational goals. Those tend to be the exceptions, however, and the dominant approaches to performance, and managerialist approaches to government in general, do not concern themselves much with coordination but rather only with the performance of one organization and its leadership.

The logic of the collaboration approach to coordination is in many ways similar to that of the normative institutionalism developed by James March and Johan P. Olsen (1984; 1987). The group of organizations involved in coordination can be conceptualized as an institution in its own right, and the normative institutionalism of March and Olsen depends upon building a "logic of appropriateness" among the members of the institution (see also Peters 2010). Having a logic of appropriateness implies that participants in public organizations will alter the manner in which they think about and perform their tasks. Further, March and Olsen (and to some extent Bardach) place a great deal of emphasis on the necessity of managers and other leaders in the organization shaping those collective values for the organization or institution. Bardach's collaboration model relies more on lower-level officials in the organizations than does the normative institutionalism, but that collaboration may be dependent upon the leadership of the organization establishing a climate conducive to that collaborative behavior. Thus, these approaches both assume that the best way to produce action within or among organizations is to create normative agreement among the actors involved that there is an "appropriate" way of addressing the policy problem in question.

The collaboration approach to coordination also has very close similarities with the framing literature used in the study of policy agendas (Schön and Rein 1994; Callaghan and Schnell 2005) and social problems (Best 1989). Policy problems can be defined in a variety of ways, and that initial definition may be crucial for the final solution of the policy problem (see Entman 1993). If a problem is defined in a way that may make it amenable to joint solutions rather than solution through individual programs and organization, then the collaborative approach would be more likely to be adopted. The tendency identified in most of the examples of framing are those in which those individual organizations attempt to define the policy problem they are confronting in a manner that enables the organization to capture the problem for its own benefit. For example, debates over framing the issue of the control of illegal drugs have been primarily a conflict over which organizations (and definition of the problem) would prevail, and the debate over viable energy programs has been extremely contentious because of fundamentally different perspectives held by the protagonists (Temkin 1983).[17] Framing these and other policy problems in a more cooperative manner, however, could facilitate cooperation but also would require something other than the usual manner of behavior within the public sector.

As well as framing in the first instance, when issues are first working their way through the policy process, the logic of collaboration is perhaps most closely linked to the need to "reframe" issues once conflicts among different conceptions of the problem, or different programs delivering related services to the public, become apparent. Schön and Rein (1994) discuss this as a means of resolving disputes, but the same logic can be applied to coordinated complementary programs that can gain from collaboration. The difference may be that the need for reframing may not be as great when there is not the overt conflict (see also Hisschemöller and Hoppe 1995).

Framing an issue is usually considered a component of the formulation stage of policy, and hence the focus is on the initial design of a program rather than on its implementation. The collaborative approach to coordination, on the other hand, tends to stress the need to create cooperation among the officials responsible for implementing programs and especially on the lower-level administrators in the organizations involved. That bottom-up perspective in collaboration, however, does not obviate the possibilities of using framing to enhance coordination. Framing may work much as Charles Lindblom (1974) once described partisan analysis, with each actor attempting to "sell" their programs in terms of the interests and ideas of the advocates of the other program. This role for framing is also related to the view of coordination that stresses the integration of policies rather than more mechanistic conceptions of coordination though administrative action (Jordan and Lenschow 2010).

If we return to the interorganizational literature on coordination, the interpretive versions of interorganizational relations (see Halpert 1982) are closely associated with the collaboration approach as developed by Bardach. Henry Kissinger (see Stuart and Starr 1981) argued that "when the other party is viewed within the framework of an 'inherent bad faith model' the image of the enemy is self-perpetuating." In other words, if relationships among the actors in a set of organizations can be constructed more positively, then the virtuous spiral of action can also be self-perpetuating. The task of the leaders in agencies, and in interagency relationships, is therefore to construct a pattern of interaction that is conducive to improved coordination. That will involve framing the issues in more positive ways and also putting the gains from cooperation in the minds of the members of their organizations.

Collaboration is an approach to coordination that was developed as a specific intellectual mechanism for dealing with the problems of getting organizations, and the members of organizations, to work together. Its own framing of the issue of coordination is largely in terms of advice to would-be coordinators and is an attempt to provide the mechanisms needed to encourage agencies to work together. At the same time, however, it has a number of points of tangency with theoretical approaches to political behavior and especially to the constructivist approaches to policy analysis (see Fischer 2003). That is, the collaborative approach argues that the most effective way of obtaining coordination is to construct issues and interactions among organizations in ways that create a common understanding among the participants in the potential coordination exercise. It is, however, perhaps easier to argue for the need to change policy perspectives held by individuals than to produce those changes.

TRIANGULATION AND BRINGING
MULTIPLE MODELS TOGETHER

The above discussion of four patterns of explanation for coordination has kept the approaches to coordination in rather discrete, watertight boxes. Unfortunately, or perhaps fortunately, real-world governments do not always read the theoretical literature and may develop approaches to coordination that contain several of the four approaches mentioned above. In addition to the hybrids developed by governments, we need also to consider the ways in which the use of multiple analytic perspectives—triangulation—can illuminate the coordination problem and generate more insights into the issues involved.

Perhaps the one conceptual category of coordination that most cuts across the conventional categories is the idea of "holistic governance" (6 et al. 2002). The assumption of holistic models of governing is that somehow all the elements are related and can be encouraged to work together. This appears a wonderful target but is not the best of all worlds, and some mechanisms need to be found to focus on more proximate targets for governance. Further, as will be pointed out in the final chapter, holism may undermine the important virtue of specialization in government programs.

I noted at the beginning of this chapter that no single model of coordination may be able to provide the level of explanation and implicit policy advice that might be required for effective policy coordination. The idea presented there was that some combination of these approaches could provide different lenses through which to understand the same political processes, and the same policy problems. Although triangulation may be a good idea in practice, in reality it is difficult to implement. Scholars tend to be committed to one perspective or another and therefore use their favorite intellectual tools to hammer almost any analytic problem they encounter. Further, having a single and clearly articulated analytic approach to an issue should sharpen the analysis and enable others to understand the weaknesses of the approach and perhaps falsify the hypotheses that were the foundation for analysis. Still, in areas such as public administration and public policy, in which there are so many contending ideas, attempting to synthesize may be useful.

So what might a combination of these approaches, as some form of triangulation of theories and ideas about coordination, look like? First, hierarchy would have to play a central role and almost all coordination would occur "in the shadow of hierarchy" (Scharpf 1997). Even collaboration, as perhaps the least hierarchical of the approaches, is more likely to be effective if government actors have some capacity to invoke sanctions against actors who are unwilling to cooperate in the process of reframing difficult policy disputes. Thus, we can conceptualize hierarchy as an overarching framework within which other forms of action occur, with government always having the capacity to invoke its legitimate authority (assuming it has any) to produce the outcomes desired.

Finding the place for markets in a composite model of coordination is somewhat more difficult. Although the use of market instruments is a major part of the contemporary prescription for improving the quality of governance (see Peters and Pierre 2005), markets do not appear to be particularly useful coordinating devices in most policy areas. Once quasi-markets are established (through law or some other hierarchical means) then some aspects of policy implementation may be achieved through these devices. Further, contracting among public organizations can be a market device that provides some coordination among programs, although again law and hierarchy may be required for the effective enforcement of the contracts. Still, markets often appear to engender competition for resources rather than helping public managers find ways of using those resources in a more cooperative manner. But if well-structured bargaining among market actors can also generate some means of overcoming the conflict over resources then they can facilitate coordination.

The nature of contemporary government, especially given the prevalence of information technology and other means for communication, is to some extent inherently that of a social network. Although many of the connections are in government, many are also outside, so that social actors are also key players in these network structures. Given the presence of these by now natural structures, a certain amount of coordination occurs almost automatically as members of one organization talk with others or with the interest groups with whom they regularly interact. Some coordination through networks may be pursued more consciously, and the involvement of the social partners may be sought as a means of elaborating the issues that confront their members and perhaps proposing solutions. Again, however, this activity may all be done in the context of a system of governing that is based on hierarchy.

Finally, the collaborative approach developed by Eugene Bardach may also be seen in operation at the same time as are the other approaches. To some extent any political process involves framing and reframing the issues that are being considered, and therefore any attempt at coordination will also involve some element of collaboration. What may be most important for understanding the opportunities for reframing is the set of hierarchical constraints operating on any one public sector organization and its members. That is, the opportunities for restating goals and means for achieving goals will be constrained by the nature of formal organizations, with lower-level workers in some organizations (the police, for example) being severely constrained while those in others (social service agencies) may have greater latitude. The differences between those types of organizations become especially important (and apparent) when they must work together, as in the case of child protection (see Chapter 5). The variation in latitude for action may be even more pronounced when public and private sector organizations attempt collaboration.

The analytic problem with having so many different approaches to coordination all being implemented in various ways at the same time is: how does one ascribe relative levels of influence to them? If all the approaches are useful, as indeed they appear to be, and they may all have some effect on outcomes of attempts to coordinate, then determining the relative influence of the approaches and clarifying the relative utility of various approaches to coordination is difficult. This problem is far from unusual in the social sciences, especially when dealing with complex realities such as coordination, but that familiarity does not make resolving the analytic issues any easier. The research strategy in this book, selecting cases that appear to rely primarily on one form of coordination or another, may help assess the relative utility of the approaches, but the accumulation of more cases and bringing them together in a systematic fashion may be required before we can come close to resolving this basic theoretical issue.

SUMMARY

Coordination is a particular form of administrative and political behavior, but it remains yet one of many components of the governing process. Three of the four approaches applicable to coordination (collaboration is the odd one out, being concerned almost entirely with coordination) that have been discussed in this chapter are more generally applicable to understanding policymaking and indeed are the "usual suspects" that are rounded up when behavior within the public sector is discussed (see Thompson et al. 1991). Each of these approaches can illuminate some aspects of the politics of coordination, but each also has some important deficiencies. When taken together the approaches provide a more complete picture of that complex reality, but at the same time a failure to provide more singular explanations for this phenomenon makes developing the needed understanding perhaps even more difficult. Thus, the inevitable task of the social scientist is to seek parsimony but then distrust it.

As well as providing an intellectual understanding of policy coordination, these four approaches are also closely related to a set of more practical instruments that can be used to provide the improved coordination among policies that is being sought by the participants in the political process. If policymakers understand coordination, and the barriers to coordination that exist, in one of the four frames used in this chapter, then it is only natural that the responses to the perceived need to make government better coordinated will be based on those understandings. Although hierarchy remains the overwhelming understanding of most actors, and therefore the most common response when faced with a coordination problem, the presence of the three alternative solutions does demonstrate the intellectual, as well as practical, possibilities of other ways of coping with the problem and perhaps mitigating if not solving it. Further, hierarchy itself had a large variety of different specific instruments available to governments, so this particular resource will have to be specified more exactly to be useful analytically.

Although I have discussed these approaches as alternatives to one another, in reality many attempts on the part of government to enhance coordination will involve more than one of these approaches. Even attempts to impose direct hierarchical control over an organization or set of organizations will perform better if the coordinators can build a more cooperative network among the organizations involved or devise means of collaboration among lower-level employees in those organizations. Conversely, attempts to coordinate more from the bottom up will work better if hierarchy is casting a very deep, dark shadow on the participants. We will now turn to a more careful examination of the usual remedies advanced for solving coordination problems in government. This discussion will be organized within the same four categories as those used in this chapter, but throughout I will be cognizant of the interconnections among the alternative approaches to the question.

4. The Instruments of Coordination

The preceding chapter has presented several alternative theoretical views of coordination but has only implied the range of specific instruments that may be used to achieve the goals of greater coordination and coherence. This chapter specifies more precisely the options available to the would-be coordinator to achieve those desired ends. The majority of the tools that have been developed rely upon hierarchy as the principal instrument, but there are also instruments that will rely more on markets and networks, as well as some instruments that blend the various alternatives available. Indeed, although I will be discussing most instruments as relying on one basic style of coordination, most real-world instruments are blends, especially given that most do operate "in the shadow of hierarchy" (Scharpf 1997), with government always having the possibility of imposing, or attempting to impose, its authority over the actors involved.

As well as cataloging the instruments available for coordination, this chapter will evaluate the likely success of those instruments. Many of these mechanisms for creating greater coordination have been utilized by governments for decades, if not centuries, and there is a reasonable body of evidence about how they perform. More importantly, however, I will be attempting, largely on the basis of the evidence that exists and some limited range of theory available, to make some statements about the relative utility of the various approaches and the various instruments in different settings. The contingencies that will be developed at this stage are at best preliminary, but they may serve as the basis for more testing and theory development in the area of coordination.

As already noted, public administration has long talked about coordination as a goal, but there is remarkably little theory to guide the actor in his or her search for appropriate responses to the problems being faced. The so-called scientific management literature was dismissed by Simon (1947) as merely a set of proverbs, and there has been no paradigm to replace it, although New Public Management, or NPM (see Frederickson and Smith 2003), would like to make that claim. Also, models of public administration based on rational choice perspectives have become central to public administration. This discussion may therefore be the start of building a larger body of theory that can be used for improving practice, as well as for enhancing the academic understanding of public administration and especially the coordination among public programs.

HIERARCHY

The typical response of governments when faced with a coordination problem is to use the conventional hierarchical methods of control to address the problem. This response continues to be dominant even after the paradigm for public management in many countries has shifted toward greater reliance on market and network devices to deliver public services (Pollitt and Bouckaert 2004; Peters 2003; 2004b). In some ways the logic implied in that reliance on hierarchy to cope with coordination problems is valid, given that many such problems in the contemporary public sector are the products of using the less conventional forms of public management that have tended to reduce central control within the public sector. Once the difficulties created by more decentralizing forms of management are recognized governments often jump back into the situations with greater vigor, reverting to their ultimate weapons in the control of public organizations—hierarchy and legal authority.

The Core Executive

The principal locus for horizontal policy coordination and the management of horizontal issues is usually assumed to be at the very center of government—the chief executive and the central agencies that serve that executive. This aggregation of political and programmatic power is now commonly referred to as the "core executive," although there may be divisions within that overall structure (Smith 1999; Hayward and Wright 2002). The ultimate responsibility for policies, and the coordination of those policies, lies with prime ministers in parliamentary regimes, although in many systems the prime minister and minister of finance work as a team to attempt to control government (see Savoie 2008).

The situation of the American president is somewhat more complex, with the Congress also having substantial responsibility for policy (see Oleszek 2007). Even in American government, however, the president bears ultimate responsibility for the execution of policy and therefore for the coordination of implementation even if not for the initial policy choices themselves. Congress itself is a highly fragmented institution with few processes for bringing together the policy work of the numerous committees and subcommittees (see the discussion of budget processes below), and hence the president will almost certainly be faced with having to make coordination more of an executive task, undertaken after Congress has acted.

In other presidential systems, such as those of Latin America, the role of the president in policy coordination is somewhat varied although in general presidents tend to have somewhat more control over policy than does the president of the United States (Cox and Morgenstern 2001). Legislatures generally have the capacity to block policy coming from the president, and presidents also are more likely to govern by decree. That power, however, does not necessarily mean there is more capacity to coordinate given the multiparty nature of most cabinets and the need to exert control within the potentially fractious cabinet (Martinez-Gallardo 2011; but see Amorim Neto 2006).

Finally, semi-presidential regimes such as France constitute a particular case of coordination. In this case there must first be coordination between the president and the prime minister and then coordination among ministers and the bureaucracy (see Fournier 1987). That said, the variance in forms among semi-presidentialist regimes tends to make generalizations difficult. For example, in some, such as Finland and Portugal, the president is relatively weak while in others, such as Poland, the president is a more powerful figure with substantial influence over policy (including coordination). The only real generalization possible is that semi-presidential systems tend to add another veto-player in the policy process and with that, greater probabilities for coordination failures (Tsebelis 1995).

Chief executives in almost all political systems are now attempting to provide themselves with greater means for promoting coordination, whether it is done primarily by the executive him/herself or through the use of cabinet and powerful administrative agencies supporting the summit of government (see Peters, Rhodes, and Wright 2000). This trend is often described as presidentialization (Poguntke and Webb 2005), but in parliamentary regimes the prime minister may actually become a more powerful player than a president because of the absence of separation of powers. These executives have always confronted coordination problems resulting from the divisions of governments into numerous specialized organizations but now face even greater problems as a result of the last several decades of decentralization and deconcentration (see Peters 2004b), as well as performance management programs that emphasize the outputs of individual organizations, often resulting in ignoring the sum of the outputs of government.

Chief Executive Staff

By themselves prime ministers and presidents do not possess much capacity to produce effective coordination. These executives tend to be extremely overworked and have little time to spend on coordinating the activities of the numerous ministries under their overall control. This personal incapacity in coordination is true even though the chief executive may be the individual with the greatest legitimacy in examining the full range of activities of government and making suggestions, or giving orders, about how to make the system more coherent. The complexity of contemporary government, the wide range of issues, and the increasing politicization of the role of chief executives, however, make it difficult for those executives to actually be effective coordinators.[1]

These chief executives can, however, develop staffs and organizations that can assist them in coordination. The most developed organizations of this type are found in the Executive Office of the President in the United States, which in 2011 employed over 4,000 people whose purpose was to ensure the implementation of the president's program in the rest of government. This office contains not only the personal staff of the president (the White House Office) but a number of monitoring and coordinating organizations such as the Office of Management and Budget, the Council of Economic Advisors, and the National Security Council as well. All recent presidents also have had some organization in the White House for coordinating domestic policy, although the names and responsibilities of those organizations have varied.

These organizations within the Executive Office of the President provide the president with the capacity to supervise line departments in a way that can create greater coherence. For example, the National Security Council (NSC) can attempt to bring together the Departments of State and Defense and their often opposing views of foreign and security policy and place a presidential stamp on that policy area. The NSC staff often will have their own views of what good policy is, and there may be conflicts within what is nominally the president's policy team, but it is still the president's team (Hammond 1960; Newmann 2003). Having this coordinating organization enhances the probabilities of a more integrated perspective on policy when compared to a process in which individual organizations dominate their own domains with little reference to one another. Likewise, in economic policy, the Council of Economic Advisors (CEA) can help to integrate the views of the Departments of Treasury, Commerce, Labor, and Energy, as well as independent executive organizations such as the Small Business Administration.[2] This integration is all the more likely because the CEA also has some influence in the budget process (see below).

The development of policy "czars" within the Executive Office of the President represents another major attempt on the part of presidents to exert more direct control over policy and to achieve greater levels of coordination. These czars are responsible personally for coordination in areas such as drug policy (Conley 2006) and serve to some extent as the president's enforcer in these policy areas. The economic crisis following 2008 led to President Obama's appointing more than a dozen new czars to coordinate in areas such as consumer finance.[3]

Although similar offices exist in other governments—e.g., the Bundeskanzleramt in Germany and in Austria (Mueller-Rommel 2000), the Kansli in Sweden (Larsson 1988; Dahlström and Pierre 2012), and the Department of Prime Minister and Cabinet in Australia (Hamburger and Weller 2012)—none has become as fully articulated as the Executive Office of the President in the United States. Organizations serving the primary executive in government appear to fit less comfortably in parliamentary regimes than in presidential regimes, given that the usual rubric for a prime minister is *primus inter pares,* as opposed to the chief executive role that presidents may have in directing the entire executive branch. Despite that formal rubric, the offices serving prime ministers have tended to expand and the role of prime ministers has tended to become more than just one member of a collective executive (Allen 2003; O'Malley 2007). The expansion of the role of prime minister may be as much political as it is administrative, but the creation of larger staffs does give these executives greater capacity to generate coordination among programs, if they have the political will to do so.

One virtue of these organizations directly serving chief executives as a means of managing cross-cutting policy issues is that they tend to be flexible and do not have to be concerned with delivering services to existing clients (other than advice to the chief executive). These organizations can therefore create internal task forces or temporary structures to cope with changing issues and interpretations of issues. Further, they do not have as much policy "turf" to defend as do line agencies.[4] On the other hand, relying on this level of government for coordination is likely to be highly centralizing and may alienate both ministers and clients. In addition, relying on the office of the chief executive to mediate and coordinate policy disputes can overload that office at a time when the prevailing ethos of governance is decentralization and improving the performance of individual organizations. Those problems can be compounded if sources of conflict over issues and policies can be more clearly identified at the lower echelons of government. If that is the case then there can be a significant loss of information by the time the issues bubble up to the top of government, with consequent loss of capacity to understand the real issues involved, or to solve the real coordination problems that have arisen. Thus, the "top-down" approach common to coordination may often not match the "bottom-up" reality of the problems, but only reflect the habitual response of government to coordination problems.

Central Agencies

A more general strategy for achieving coordination from the center of government is to rely upon central agencies. By this term we refer to budgetary, policy, and personnel management organizations that report directly to the chief executive or that are assigned principal responsibility for policy coordination and central management of issues (Campbell and Szablowski 1979; Savoie 1999). Examples of central agencies are H. M. Treasury in the United Kingdom, the Treasury Board Secretariat in Canada, and Departments of the Public Service and Ministries of Finance in a number of countries (see Table 4.1). These organizations often are utilized to enforce the policy priorities of the chief executive, but they also tend to

Table 4.1 Examples of Central Agencies

United States	Office of Management and Budget
	White House Office
	Office of Personnel Management
United Kingdom	Cabinet Office
	H. M. Treasury
Canada	Privy Council Office
	Treasury Board Secretariat
	Ministry of Finance
Mexico	Secretaría de Gobernación
	Officina de la Presidencia
	Secretaría de Hacienda y Crédito Público

develop priorities and managerial styles of their own and to develop substantial power over policy. If nothing else their power of the purse gives these organizations one central lever with which to monitor and control what happens in the rest of government, and even prime ministers enter into conflict with these organizations with some apprehension.

Central agencies can play a significant role in creating coordination, but they also can generate substantial conflict with the line organizations that are actually providing public services. These frictions reflect the conflicts between "line" and "staff" organizations that are typical of interorganizational politics within the public sector (Peters 2004b). This conflict between line and staff is as old as formal organization itself and can be found in private sector organizations as well as the public sector. The former type of organization resents the power exercised by control organizations that do not directly serve the public and which, it is argued, know little about the programs being delivered, nor the demands being placed on those delivery organizations. Staff organizations (including central agencies) tend to believe, on the other hand, that line agencies have extremely narrow views on policy and do not understand the need to impose overall priorities on government. And in an era of fiscal constraint central agencies tend to see line agencies as spendthrifts with little regard for the public purse.

The role of central agencies has been increasing in most contemporary political systems, despite the general zeitgeist of decentralization and deconcentration. The political dynamic producing such apparently contradictory patterns has been that as most public programs are decentralized, the conventional mechanisms of political control have been devalued. Organizations have been made responsible for their own actions, with parliament and the core executive monitoring what has happened after the fact (see Verhoest et al. 2004). The one major control instrument that remains in place is the budget, so that ministries of finance in particular become crucial in the process of controlling administration (see especially Jensen 2003a; Krause 2012). Further, as performance management becomes a central component of managing the public sector then ministries of finance become even more central to processes of control and accountability.

Although they have a number of potential instruments at their disposal, to be fully effective the central agencies must be strongly supported by the prime minister (see Savoie 2008). Central agencies must have the confidence, and the backing, of the chief executive if other organizations in the public sector are going to take their direction seriously, and even then there will be resistance when the budgetary priorities of a minister of finance go against the spending desires of a minister in a line department. In some cabinet systems there are formal or informal rules that if the prime minister and finance minister agree, they cannot be overridden by the rest of cabinet, although an effective prime minister might want to prevent the issue coming to a vote, so as not to underscore any divisions within the government.

Central agencies are usually discussed in terms of the control they exercise over other parts of government, but they can also help to facilitate coordination and collaboration. By definition these organizations are in the center of government and have a very broad perspective on what government is doing. The difficulty in relying on them for effective coordination is that they also have a tremendous range of responsibilities and may find it difficult to engage in the detailed analysis of opportunities for coordination. Especially in times of budget crisis the short-term firefighting tends to drive out longer-term strategic analysis.

Cabinet Itself, Especially with Strong Prime Minister or Minister of Finance

Cabinet itself is another locus for the management of cross-cutting policy issues. In some ways it is the most logical institution to perform this task; all the principal actors in policymaking and service provision are represented. On the other hand, cabinet may be a place in which the ministers must protect the interests of their departments (Di Francesco 2001). Those interests may well not be best served (in the short term at least) by excessive cooperation with other agencies or by examining the broader implications of groups of policies. For the individual cabinet minister, the usual means to gain the respect and confidence of his or her staff is not to make concessions in cabinet but rather to "fight his corner" and defend the department against all comers for budgets and for policy authority. The members of the department may not be expected to have broader conceptions of governing so that this combative and defensive position is to be expected, and to some extent must be honored by the minister.

The cabinet can serve as the locus for the examination of cross-cutting issues if there is adequate leadership, both from the prime minister and from the civil service that serves the cabinet. With that leadership there can be a capacity to redirect the discussion of issues and enhance policy coordination. Even with a strong prime minister, a close link with the minister of finance appears to be crucial in creating coherent government, so that as Donald Savoie (1999) said with reference to Canadian government, there is a need to ensure that "no light shines between them." If the prime minster and the minister of finance are in agreement they can usually manage to control cabinet, and in some cases formally these two can outvote the rest of the cabinet. Indeed, the danger may be that the prime minister may dominate cabinet too much and prevent the type of discussion and bargaining needed for generating coherence (Bakvis and Jarvis 2012).

While the development of staffs in the prime minister's office may be one means of coordination, developing similar staffs for the entire cabinet could be a more effective means of achieving coordination. A common cabinet staff would be especially useful if procedures are developed that can provide, at a minimum, early warning of proposals in cabinet so that each minister is informed and can understand the implications of the proposal for his or her department (for Australia, see Weller 2007). Even in the absence of such procedures a common staff would provide a means of working across the programs and ideas of different departments to produce greater coherence in policy.

All the above having been said, cabinets are busy, political organizations in which it may be too much to expect effective and thoughtful coordination of complex policies to occur. The ability of cabinet to function as a coordinating institution is weakened even more in coalition governments with each minister cognizant of political as well as organizational differences with the colleagues. In some countries cabinet meetings are mere formalities, with each minister primarily responsible for running a fiefdom. The minister and his staff generally are capable of making decisions on their own within that fiefdom, with ministers tending to respect each other's autonomy. In such a system there are many fiefdoms but little serious thought of how all those fiefdoms may make up a single realm. In the extreme, the other ministers may not even be expected to vote with their colleagues on policy measures, leaving it up to each minister to build coalitions around each piece of legislation.[5]

Cabinets can be made more effective as coordination institutions through the use of procedures that require ministers to work more closely with one another. At a minimum, procedures can be used to force ministers to inform each other of planned legislation. For example, in Australia "cabinet comments" are used to give ministers at least forty-eight hours' warning of issues to be tabled at a cabinet meeting. Similarly, the European Union requires directors general to notify others when they are planning to introduce new directives, in order to ensure that all affected organizations are able to participate.

Cabinet Committees

A cabinet may be too large an organization to coordinate programs effectively. This is especially true given that each minister usually will feel compelled to defend the interests of his or her own department, and this need may make the necessary cooperation difficult to obtain. Many cabinets have been reduced drastically in size (Bouckaert, Ormond, and Peters 2000), but may still be too large to function effectively as a single decision-making entity. In the case of problems that are not well defined and that cut across a range of ministries, ministers may feel compelled to defend the claims of their department over control of the issue, with some loss of necessary cooperation across departments (see Table 4.2).

Most cabinet systems therefore have developed working "inner cabinet" systems, or some committees within cabinet that can establish collective priorities and coordinate policies across portfolios (Mackie and Hogwood 1985). One approach to achieving this goal is to create an overarching "priorities and planning committee" within cabinet, as in Canada. This approach can coordinate policies across the entire range of public programs but often will push too many decisions upward to a few senior officials of government (Martin 2004). The alternative approach is to develop a series of cabinet committees, each responsible for a particular segment of policy (Andeweg 2000). This approach has the advantage of bringing the relevant departmental ministers to the table to coordinate their own activities. This capacity

Table 4.2 Ministers[1] with Cross-Cutting Responsibilities

Children and Youth	Australia, France, Germany, Ireland, Latvia, Luxembourg, New Zealand
Disabled	Belgium, France, New Zealand
Elderly	France, Germany, New Zealand, Sweden
Family	Australia, Belgium
Middle Class	Belgium, Luxembourg
Minority Groups	Canada, New Zealand, Sweden
Policy Coordination	Sweden
Population	France, Ireland, Latvia, Luxembourg, Slovakia, Slovenia, United Kingdom
Reform	Ireland
Social Exclusion	France
Special Affairs	Germany
Without Portfolio	United Kingdom, Poland
Women	Austria, Germany, Luxembourg, New Zealand

1. In some cases the minister may not be a full member of cabinet, or may be a junior minister.

for coordination has been particularly evident in the budgetary process, with en-
velope budgeting in Canada and Sweden as the prime examples (see Bouckaert,
Peters, and Verhoest 2010). This approach also has its disadvantages. In particular,
the boundaries between policy areas, and therefore between cabinet committees,
are not always clear. The boundaries between policy areas may be becoming even
less clear; for example, social policies, labor market policies, and even education
policies have become intertwined through competitiveness concerns to a degree
not previously experienced. Therefore, there may be a proliferation of coordinating
committees, and the consequent need to coordinate the coordinators.

Ministers without Portfolio, or with
Additional Coordinative Portfolio

One means of generating improved coordination within a cabinet system is to
utilize ministers without portfolio tasked to coordinate programs within a broad
policy area. Another related method would be to assign departmental ministers
additional coordinating portfolios. For example, in the Netherlands one minister
has been assigned the additional responsibility for coordinating all programs being delivered to immigrants, as well as programs designed to regulate their entry
and their participation in the labor market. Ministries for families and children
have now become rather common in democratic political systems. In other cases
ministers have been assigned the responsibility for integrating the services provided to women, or in one exceptional case to coordinate the range of services
for the middle class.

While the system of coordinating ministers has the advantage of designat-
ing an individual to be responsible for coordination of a policy area, it also has
several important drawbacks. The most obvious is that it can overload an already
busy minister, if the coordination role is added to a functional portfolio.[6] Further,
although the minister is responsible for coordinating a range of other programs,
this responsibility is unlikely to receive the same priority as running the programs
within his or her own department. The programs in the ministry have more visible
clients and the success or failure of the minister in serving those clients will be more
visible than the results of performing a more diffuse coordination role.

In the case of a minister without portfolio assigned primary responsibility for
coordinating programs, such an individual may have more time to spend on this
activity but may not have other necessary resources. In some cases (Canada) these
ministers may be considered to be mere patronage appointments rather than real
members of government. In particular, a cabinet minister without a departmental
power base may not have sufficient political clout within the cabinet to bring his
or her colleagues along if there is a need to coordinate their policies. This apparent

weakness, however, may be counteracted by assigning these roles to politicians with strong political links to the prime minister. That can be successful with a strong prime minister committed to programs, but may not be possible in many countries with weak prime ministers holding together unstable coalitions.

Junior Ministers

Rather than have a minister accept additional responsibilities and add to an already extensive range of duties, some governments have instead developed a cadre of junior ministers that can help coordinate the ministries and perhaps accept responsibility for services to designated groups of clients, or perform other special functions that cut across conventional departmental lines of responsibility. Table 4.3 gives lists of junior ministers in several governments to provide some sense of the range of activities that can be addressed by these political executives.

To some degree junior ministers will have some of the same problems encountered by ministers without portfolio. Being designated "junior," these officials almost certainly have less power in government than will ministers or probably even senior

Table 4.3 Examples of Junior Ministers in Two Governments

Canada (2013)

Atlantic Canada Opportunities Agency
Western Economic Diversification
Quebec Economic Development
Northern Ontario Economic Development
Southern Ontario
Status of Women
Seniors
Democratic Reform
Sport
Small Business
Chief Government Whip

United Kingdom (2013)

Policing, Criminal Justice and Victims
Civil Society
Universities and Science
Status of Women and Equalities
Children and Families
Disabled People
Welfare Reform
Health Quality
Immigration

civil servants. If these aspiring political leaders are asked to coordinate a range of services and manage cross-cutting issues controlled by powerful ministers they may have only limited success. Further, they may be placed in confrontational positions with the senior ministers and may perceive the job as a political detriment rather than a step up the political career ladder.

The junior minister may, however, be able to transform weakness into strength through less confrontational means of addressing coordination issues. Given that a ministerial structure with junior ministers for coordination will likely have other junior ministers at roughly the same stage of career serving as the putative coordinators, networks and collaborative arrangements, rather than political confrontation, may be a more appropriate means of addressing the demands of the position. To some extent that style would conform to the general layering of interactions within governments, with various lower-level groups—civil servants and perhaps political advisors—meeting to prepare decisions for ministers and finally for cabinet.[7]

Ministerial Organizations Themselves

We have been discussing the need to coordinate across cabinet portfolios or their equivalents, but cabinet departments can themselves develop mechanisms for policy coordination. One that has been tried in a number of countries is the creation of "superministries" that incorporate within their own structures a wide range of programs that otherwise would have to be made compatible across departmental structures. At one extreme the Swiss government is limited to seven government departments, so that if their portfolios are relatively homogenous they should be able to produce substantial internal congruence of policy. The current configuration of programs contained in these ministries does not appear to represent the most coherent plan for policy coordination, e.g., a Department of Defense, Civil Protection, and Sports.

At less of an extreme, in Australia the Hawke government in 1983 reorganized government to create a smaller number of large ministries and created an inner cabinet that had some capacity to coordinate policies across the entire range of government services. Canada created the immense Human Resources and Skills Development Canada to cover virtually all human services for which the federal government was responsible.[8] The British government had tried a similar strategy much earlier, and the Nixon administration in the United States had proposed creating four "super-departments" in the federal government (Nathan 1975). More recently the government of China adopted several superministries, with the most visible being the environment, given the immense pollution problems there (Qiu and Li 2008).

While it may appear logical to locate as many similar programs as possible within a single ministry, the coordination gains from that structural decision may be more apparent than real. First, there will have to be a significant subministerial structure, which may engender its own difficulties in coordination, vertically as well as horizontally. Likewise, if a minister has a too large a ministry with too many internal divisions (especially if each has a junior minister) he or she may encounter the same problems in producing coordination as might a prime minister with an equal number of ministries to coordinate. Finally, the location of all the apparently related programs within the single department may lead to complacency and the assumption that the problems have been solved while the problems actually persist.

Several American cases will illustrate these problems. The US Department of Defense was created in 1947 to attempt to create a more integrated national security apparatus. The assumption was that within this single department the rivalries that had characterized relationships among the services would be reduced, or even eliminated. After over sixty years those rivalries appear as alive as ever, and manifest themselves in differences in strategic priorities, procurement, and a host of other ways (Flynn 2005). The internal difficulties within the Department of Homeland Security will be discussed in Chapter 5.

The superministries represent the extreme version of a general practice in reorganization to merge organizations to attempt to improve efficiency and coordination (Hult 1987). The target of mergers is more likely redundancies in service than the attempt to create synergies among complementary programs, but even for this seemingly easier goal reorganizations are often less than successful (Thomas 1993). That said, the probabilities of achieving policy change through reorganization appear greater than the usual target of improving efficiency and reducing expenditures.

Placing a number of programs together within a single ministry also may have other effects on policy and management. By placing the principal coordinative responsibility within a department, the decisions tend to be made more by career officials than by political officials; if departments remained more fragmented, politicians would have to debate those issues at the cabinet level in order to produce better policy coordination. Developing larger departments, in turn, may free up the cabinet to make more fundamental decisions about policy priorities. At the same time, however, ministers will always have priorities even within their own departments, so creating the large departments may assist some interests and leave many others without advocates in cabinet.

Lead Agencies

Rather than moving organizations into a superministry, another option for achieving greater coordination is to use lead agencies to provide direction to other

organizations. Some policy areas may be better managed if a number of organizations cooperate but there is one organization that is central to the policy area and
should take the lead. For example, economic policy is increasingly complex and in a
globalized environment is styled as "competitiveness policy." Economic policy now
involves (among others) foreign ministries, ministries of education and labor, and
numerous regulatory organizations as well as the ministry of finance. Even with
that, however, the ministry of finance or its analog is central to this policy area and
usually will be the principal source of policy and control over other organizations.
The Finnish government's (see Chapter 5) attempts to coordinate through a device
built largely on procedure has some elements of the lead agency concept as well, as
each of the programs is housed in a ministry that has the principal responsibility
for the program.

While the lead agency principle is commonly used, like all other mechanisms
for coordination it has its strengths and weaknesses. The primary strength is that
this method of coordination is flexible and can be adapted easily to changing circumstances. If there are shifts in the relative importance of the different ministries
in the group concerned with a policy, then it can be easy to shift responsibility for
leadership among the participants in the process. On the other hand, however,
the organization meant to provide the leadership in coordination is an interested
party and may therefore not function as an honest broker among the (potentially)
competing interests involved in the policy area.

A special case of the lead agency is the lead individual. One approach champi-
oned, if briefly, by the Major government in the United Kingdom was to treat the
senior civil service as a corporate resource and to have the most knowledgeable
individual, regardless of rank, be responsible for taking the lead on a policy area.
While this approach to governing did emphasize the need to coordinate the role of
expertise in coordination, it also went against many of the folkways of Whitehall and
therefore was not acceptable to many participants in the process. The mechanism
of czars, mentioned above, to some extent replicates this pattern.

Advisory Committees

One way to approach the problem of coordination of programs is to have a means of
mutually representing the interests of relevant programs. This can be done through
the creation of broad advisory committees for departments or bureaus containing
representatives of other organizations. For example, in the Scandinavian countries
(Norway in particular) each ministry will have an advisory committee composed
of representatives of interest groups as well as other ministerial departments. Any
significant policy initiative by the ministry must be referred to this advisory committee. This system works well in these countries, with their traditions of consensual

decision making and well-developed interest group universes. Even without that tradition this method can at least inform interested departments of actions and perhaps allow them to be settled (in cabinet or by other means) earlier than they might otherwise be. Further, like most other existing mechanisms for coordination, the agenda for these committees is set by existing organizations using conventional conceptualizations of policy.

One variant of the advisory committee mechanism is the use of management boards. With the increasing use of disaggregated government organizations in a number of countries (e.g., agencies in the United Kingdom) there may be a need to use the same governance system as was developed for organizations of this type in Scandinavia. In the Scandinavian countries from which this model of organization was derived, the use of boards composed of government and lay personnel is a means for providing a broad perspective on the functions and role of the organization and hence a broader perception of the policies being developed. To the extent that other government organizations are represented on these boards they can help produce enhanced coordination. For example, the boards used for policy direction and oversight in Sweden contain a variety of government officials who can advance the ideas and interests of their own organizations and hence produce a certain amount of coordination without formalized interventions.

Agencies with Portfolios Relevant to Coordination

Ministries or agencies can be developed that have direct responsibility for coordinating services for a specific target population or geographical area. At a minimum these organizations can act as advocates within government for the interests of those segments of the population. Examples of organizations of this type serving particular demographic groups are the Administration on Aging in the United States, the Ministry for Family and Seniors and the Ministry for Women and Youth in Germany, and the former Ministry for the Middle Class in France. Examples of these organizations serving geographical areas are the "regional ministries" in Canada, e.g., the Atlantic Canada Opportunities Agency, the Ministry for Macedonia and Thrace in Greece, and the Ministry for the Mezzogiorno in Italy.

The development of organizations of this type does bring attention to the needs of particular client groups, or regional groups, but it is far from a guarantee that those interests will be served in the way in which they need to be. These ministries and agencies often are not perceived to be central players in government, so that even though they may sit at the cabinet table they may not have much influence over major players such as the principal large social and economic ministries. In many instances the client-based organizations may be seen as being too close to the clients by other actors in government, but also as being too close to government by the groups whom they are meant to serve. They are, as Jonathan Malloy (2003) argues, organizations that exist "between colliding worlds."

In addition, these ministries may provide some services for the target groups but still must ensure that services being received from other ministries are compatible and beneficial for their clients. In other words, these ministries may be just another version of the division of services among departments, albeit at a somewhat higher level. Further, as cross-cutting issues become more significant, the more traditional definitions and limitations characteristic of existing programs and ministries may not push consideration of the issues ahead quickly enough. Having a ministry for women, for example, may let political leaders assume, and argue, that these issues are "solved."

Interministerial Organizations

Another obvious means for coordinating the activities of existing programs, and to explore the needs for new structures to cope with cross-cutting issues, is to develop organizations within the interstices of existing organizations. All governments have some forms of interministerial governance, although governments differ in the extent to which those structures are articulated and the power they can exercise over policies. For example, interministerial committees are utilized in almost all governments but in some their decisions are central to policy outcomes, while in others the decisions are at best advisory to cabinet and the prime minister. What follows here is a brief enumeration of some of those mechanisms.

Task Forces, Working Groups, and So On

When government is going to enter a policy area for the first time, or when there is a great deal of confusion about the best way to conceptualize a cross-cutting policy issue, a standard response is to create a temporary "task force" or "working group." These are sometimes given executive authority, e.g., some *projets de mission* in France or *Projektgruppen* in Germany, but generally these organizations are oriented toward problem identification and clarification—a central need for cross-cutting policy issues (Timsit 1988). A major example has been the establishment of major agency, program, and expenditure reviews in Canada (including one in social policy on pensions). These appear to be very much recognitions of the need to think more broadly about the issues facing an aging population and the governments that provide them services. In addition, the financial crisis in many if not most countries since 2008 has prompted the creation of numerous interministerial organizations intended to coordinate responses to the crisis and establish priorities for addressing the issues (see Peters, Pierre, and Randma-Liiv 2010).

If the cross-cutting issues can be "resolved" in a limited period of time, or if a clear définition of the issues can be developed in the limited time span allowed for most of these special organizations, then this approach is perhaps the most desirable manner to address the coordination problem. They can provide a clear focus and perhaps clear answers to a limited problem. If that success is not possible—and that is usually the case—then these organizations either go out of business with little being accomplished or become simply another set of players in the complex network that will surround the difficult, cross-cutting policy issues.

Another way to think about interministerial organizations is as "virtual organizations"—organizations that may have no permanent structure and/or membership. This style of organization has been advocated by some Canadian civil servants interviewed in this project as a mechanism for generating coordination without creating yet another permanent structure. The argument is in part that creating another permanent organization with the goal of enhancing coordination will itself soon require additional coordination as issues change and new patterns of interaction among organization become the dominant concerns. Still, reaching agreements about when and under what circumstances an organization will cease to exist is not the most pleasant thing for most public officials—for them it is thinking about death.

Interministerial Committees

Another flexible means for attempting to deal with cross-cutting issues is to employ committees of the organizations affected. Almost all government use some form or another of these committees. This practice is perhaps best developed in France, with committees existing at the level of officials, ministers (or their cabinets), and finally to coordinate between the prime minister and the president (Fournier 1987). Co-ordinative committees of this sort have also been well developed in the Antipodean systems. Like all committees formed to link existing organizations, committees of this type will have a difficult time in advancing the definitions of policy far beyond those that already exist. If, as argued, there is a need in many policy areas for some potentially sweeping redefinition of the issues to be considered then these committees are unlikely to change policies significantly (Schön and Rein 1994). Granted broader powers than is usually the case, committees of this type might be able to advance more innovative ideas about policy, but would tend to be only as effective as their most committed member.

Specialized Coordinating Organizations

Another approach to policy coordination is to develop special organizations with the task of ensuring coordination for clients. One example of this was the Model

Cities program in the United States. This program was one component of the War on Poverty in the 1960s and early 1970s, which sought to identify all the services available to residents of poor inner-city neighborhoods and to coordinate those services in order to provide the full range of services to clients (Gilbert and Specht 1977). The time during which Model Cities was in operation was in many ways very much like the present, in terms of the perceived need to rethink an area of policy and to attack social policy questions differently.[9] For a variety of reasons (financial, bureaucratic, and others) Model Cities enjoyed only limited success, but it was one means of incorporating some rethinking of the problems with service delivery. In particular, this program forced a number of organizations delivering services to think about how they could cooperate more effectively with organizations having similar objectives, and how they could better serve their disadvantaged populations. It had the additional consequence of centralizing a good deal of power in city halls and increasing the responsibility of mayors for social programs.

Under Prime Minister Blair the British government has also undertaken several initiatives to address social and economic problems that cut across several ministries, most notably the problem of "social exclusion" (Ling 2002). The European Union as a whole has also undertaken programs in social exclusion as a part of its increased initiative in social policy. These programs are managed out of the Policy and Innovation Unit in the prime minister's office or through smaller organizations in the deputy prime minister's office, but they have substantial influence across government and are a means of integrating a wide range of social and economic services in government. While these organizations to some extent depend upon the authority of the prime minister they also represent a more specialized approach to these problems that operates to integrate policies and to overcome many of the problems of departmentalism within the public sector.

COORDINATION THROUGH MARKETS

Markets are, as already noted, by their very nature mechanisms for coordination. The nature of the market in economic theory is that markets are institutions that coordinate almost automatically. The market brings together buyers and sellers through the price mechanism. Relatively few contemporary economists would expound such a simplistic, automatic view of the market, generally pointing out that there are important costs of organization and the existence of friction—transaction costs—within markets. In the most extreme cases those transaction costs may best be overcome by substituting formal organization for the presumed freedoms of the market (Williamson 1995), but other, less extreme mechanisms may be available to reduce transaction costs.

Likewise, few economists would argue that markets function as perfectly as the neo-classical model would assume, so means must be found to overcome those failures (Wolf 1993). At a minimum, however, markets can be institutions for using more or less voluntary action to coordinate the activities of otherwise autonomous individuals and organizations. In developing coordination capacity the process of contracting in essence becomes one of "relational contracting," in which rather than having specific functions and services identified in the contract, the intention is to create more enduring relationships among the participants. Instruments such as partnerships (Pierre 1998) and more formalized versions of networks may approximate the idea of relational contracting by institutionalizing a more continual process of interaction among the participants.

Therefore, markets or market-like mechanisms must be created if there is a desire to use this means of coordination. Political leaders may indeed be committed to using the market, either for ideological reasons or because they believe that coordination can be achieved with less investment of scarce political capital than might be necessary if more direct, hierarchical means of bringing programs together were to be used. Further, creating markets may enable the participants in the political process to coordinate their activities without having to have direct intervention of political or administrative superiors, and hence each new situation requiring coordination may be "resolved" without separate decisions. To the extent that this automaticity can be institutionalized, administrative remedies can be substituted for more difficult political choices.

Perhaps the simplest market mechanism that can be used to produce enhanced coordination is to make money available to would-be coordinators. Coordination involves using scarce resources, and public organizations may not be willing to invest the effort required unless they are given additional funds to sweeten the deal for them. Using financial rewards as an instrument for inducing coordination may be enhanced by linking funding to performance management, assuming that the performance system can be designed to include indicators of cross-program performance. While those indicators are notoriously difficult to develop, if they could be linked effectively to resource allocation then some of the resistance to coordination might be overcome.

The use of quasi-markets within government itself has become one of the more common approaches to bringing actors together and producing enhanced cooperation. One of the better examples of this type of coordination can be seen in the reforms in the National Health Service in the United Kingdom and analogous changes implemented in Sweden and several other countries (Jerome-Forget, White, and Wiener 1995). These internal markets attempt to separate the purchaser roles and provider roles that are fused in a hierarchical provision of services and to utilize market mechanisms to make arrangements between those purchasers and providers. Bargaining among the actors, and the resultant contracts, are employed as the means to specify the levels of service purchased at a particular price, and the competition inherent in the contracting is assumed both to reduce costs and to improve quality (Walsh 1995).

The internal markets used in health care, education, and social services, among other policy areas, may be a special case of using contracting as a means of bringing together interested parties using a market device. As noted in Chapter 2, the contract is a generic tool for bringing together individuals in either the public or the private sector, or for bridging the divide between the two. In the best of all worlds, or a world based more on collaboration (see below), these formalized arrangements might not be necessary, and indeed in many cases they merely formalize a reality that has arisen through less formal and more cooperative means. Still, the specification of obligations under a contract is a means of ensuring that the policy intentions in the policy area will be met to the extent that it is possible to do so.

In summary, market approaches to public administration and policy offer perhaps better means of understanding coordination problems than of resolving them. The general concept of collection action problems, so central to reasoning in political economy, helps to define the issues but does relatively little to resolve the problems.

COORDINATION THROUGH NETWORKS

Some of the examples of coordination through hierarchy developed above also contain some elements of networking, and the market conceptions about coordination may have even more network elements in their dynamics. Any form of coordination to some extent implies working cooperatively with other people and organizations, and that behavior can easily be described as networking (see Bakvis and Juillet 2004). Dahl and Lindblom (1953, 238) describe this as "coordination through reciprocity and spontaneous control." Despite the generality of the mechanism, there are some aspects of governing that do involve more or less pure examples of employing network concepts, with coordination coming through the personal or institutional connections of individual actors (see Marin and Mayntz 1991; Carlsson 2000). The examples to be given here involve those actors more or less voluntarily attempting to work together to solve common problems, and particularly to solve problems for the clients of their programs. These organizations and their leadership may always be cooperating "in the shadow of hierarchy," as Fritz Scharpf has argued (1997), but still they do choose to cooperate.

The networks utilized to coordinate in the public sector may be entirely within the public sector itself or may include actors from both the public and the private sectors. At the extreme the relevant networks could be composed of private sector actors only, using pressures from clients or stakeholder groups that are involved in different programs as the means of having those programs cooperate. Indeed, much of the theoretical literature on networks concerning policymaking in the public sector focuses on private sector actors, assuming that the public sector is perhaps incapable of reacting flexibly and rapidly when coping with pressures from the outside (Kooiman 2003). In this view the private networks have a substantial superiority to government and are able to get their way in making and implementing policy.

Although "networking" is often discussed as autonomous action on the part of public and especially private sector actors, to be effective in actually coordinating public services the networks may require some direction and some structuring by government. The leadership in the public sector must play a central role in that leadership. At a minimum, effective coordination in networks will require some level of connection between that leadership level and the organizations that are involved in the policy area. The political leadership, if it adopts a real interest in networks, must at once maintain some hierarchical control in governing as well as be a component of a more egalitarian structure. Playing this dual role is easier if the leaders involved have been active in the policy areas in which they are involved as ministers, but it is still a difficult process.

Despite the rather dismissive attitude of much of the network literature toward government itself (at the extreme see Rhodes 1997), one of the most important of the networks for coordinating the activities of the public sector has long existed within government itself. This network has been composed of the established connections among civil servants, especially civil servants at the top of government hierarchies. These civil servants often have worked together for years, and therefore would know each other and could often solve problems of coordination with a simple phone call, or a quiet chat.[10] Further, these officials generally were longer-serving than their nominal political masters and therefore could maintain the necessary connections among organizations and programs over time. Coordination is usually considered to have horizontal and vertical dimensions across organizations, but there is also an intertemporal dimension that may be important for individuals and organizations as well, with coordination across time being important for individuals involved in the process as well as the policies themselves.

The networks of civil servants vary significantly across countries, based in part upon the nature of the civil service system. Perhaps the model of such a system is the "village" that existed in the upper levels of the British civil service, with long-serving career officials who have worked together for decades often capable of working out interorganizational problems informally (see Peters 1987). Further, these civil servants generally have worked in a variety of ministries during their career and hence are more capable of empathizing with the problems of other organizations and programs that would be civil servants who have worked only in a single policy area. The capacity to coordinate is further enhanced by the similar social and educational backgrounds of many members of the political class with those of the senior public service, so that the inhabitants of the village at the top of government would be very similar.

The French model of the administrative *corps* provides another model for co-ordination through a civil service network (see Tanguy 2013). The basic concept of the *corps* in the French bureaucracy is that the elite of the public service will be employed through one of several cadres of civil servants that pervade the public sector. The members of these "fraternities," and now also "sororities," are in essence members for life and have some sense of connection with the other members. That connection with other *corps* members can be used to coordinate more readily their actions with other members of the *corps*. Further, as many members of the *corps* go into the private sector, these structures also constitute a means of coordinating between the public and private sector, especially in making and implementing economic policy.

The personnel at the apex of the American federal government might not be expected to provide much help in coordinating public policy. The "in and outers" who generally change with every change of political party in the White House, if not change of individual presidents even if from the same party, do not provide the continuity in office that would be found in the two administrative systems described above. There is, however, greater continuity than might be assumed. Increasingly, there is an "issue network" (Heclo 1978) surrounding each policy area and the in-dividuals in those networks remain involved in the policy even when they are not in government. That having been said, however, there may be less movement across policy areas than in the above administrative systems, and therefore the participants may be expert but their expertise may be rather narrow, making them less effective participants in a process for coordination.

Much of the above discussion of the civil service has been written in past tenses of various sorts. Although the civil service has been a model of the capacity to coordinate within government through a network, many of the reforms of the public sector during the past several decades have tended to denigrate the civil service as an institution and therefore to make coordination less likely through that structure. In particular, the idea that there should be a career civil service that is to a substantial extent distinct from the private sector has been under attack from the ideas of NPM (see Maor 1999). For the advocates of NPM, employment in the public sector should be open to competition, just as are positions in the private sector. Creating this open competition is assumed to enhance the performance of individual civil servants, as well as government as a whole, and to have governments produce better-quality services at lower costs.

While the evidence about the effects of competition among civil servants on performance is somewhat mixed (on pay for performance see Ingraham 1993; Halligan and Bouckaert 2007), what is clear is that effective mechanisms for policy coordination also have been devalued in the process. Different countries have adopted the NPM ideology to varying degrees, so that France, for example, has been able to maintain most of its civil service networks in and around government (see Rouban 2003; Bezes 2012), while in the Westminster systems (Halligan 2004) the civil service career is no longer exclusive, a feature that had helped to create and maintain those networks within the public sector.

As well as the decline of the career civil service as a separate career, with insulation from competition, the decline of the civil service as a collective resource for governments also appears to have resulted from the spread of NPM. The emphasis in many civil service systems has been to develop the individual managerial capacity of each top-level manager rather than to think of the cadre of executives in the public sector that can produce a higher level of collective results (Randma-Liiv 2014).

In summary, networks can provide support for attempts to improve coordination in the public sector, but their influence in many cases is remote from the formation of policy. That having been said, networks of public and private actors in a policy area often are situated at the center of the implementation process and therefore can be important for building coordination from the ground up and building coordination around clients who are receiving services through multiple networks and therefore can attempt to influence the overall distributions of goods and services to their group through their cross-cutting memberships in networks. Thus, in this case, the selection of the particular type of coordination would be associated with the selection of a bottom-up versus top-down style of coordinating, and the networks would have only an indirect capacity to exert influence on the policies being adopted by government.

COLLABORATION

The final mode of approaching the challenge of coordination is collaboration, or attempting to alter the manner in which the participants in the policy process think about the possibilities of cooperation with other organizations, and hence the way in which they think about the possibilities for delivering more "joined-up" services (see also 6 2004). The fundamental idea involved in collaboration is to alter conventional thought patterns, from perceiving coordination as a threat, or at best an impediment to efficient administration, to seeing it as an opportunity for the organizations involved. That opportunity is even more apparent for the clients who should receive better, integrated services with less difficulty for themselves. There may be few structural or procedural changes associated with a strategy of building collaboration, but rather the central element is changing patterns of thought among the participants in the policy process.

Given the emphasis on ideas, collaboration is more relevant for conceptions of coordination that utilize integration of policy ideas, rather than organizational methods for control and the imposition of that coordination. This view of coordination tends to emphasize the formulation stage of the policy process, assuming that if the actors involved can get the policy ideas correct then the remainder of the process will produce coordination policy results. The emphasis on policy integration has been especially pronounced in environmental politics, perhaps given the numerous competing ideas and the need to infuse environmental ideas across the entire gamut of public sector activity (Lenschow 2003; Briassoulis 2005).

Although altering patterns of thinking by negotiating among organizations and their programs can be important for coordination, an even more basic point is that ideas themselves can be important for coordination. At the most extreme, ideologies can coordinate across the full range of programs when the party or leader in charge of government is able to convince the participants in government as well as the general public of the correctness of the approach. At a less extreme level ideas about policy goals or policy designs can be used to provide a common perspective for the participants and to reduce conflict over organizational goals, even in rather diffuse policymaking situations. For example, in economic policy, ideas such as Keynesianism and monetarism have helped to integrate decisions across a range of actors (Hall 1989). At an even less extensive level of the use of ideas, a policy idea may pull together disparate parts of policies that might not otherwise be compatible (see May et al. 2005; Dery 1998).

Given that this approach to creating improved coordination depends largely on changing values it is clear that the necessary instruments are training, bargaining with potential allies in other organizations, and leadership. In particular, Eugene Bardach and his collaborators (see also Agranoff and McGuire 2003) discuss the mechanisms for building collaboration in terms of instruments such as motivating employees and changing the attitudes of lower-echelon employees in public organizations. These scholars have discussed building the capacity of these officials in terms of "craftsmanship," which involves factors such as flexibility, high involvement, empowerment, and training (Bardach 1998, 307). Thus, they see collaboration arising in the construction of "post-bureaucratic" organizations in the public sector.

This approach to enhancing collaboration is one aspect of more general movements in the management of public organizations that stress participation and empowerment rather than either bureaucracy or market mechanisms (see Peters 2003). The central position assigned to the "street-level bureaucrats" in this model of collaboration is central because these are often the principal actors in the coordination drama, especially when viewed as an administrative rather than policy process (see Warin 2002). These public employees must interact with each other on a regular basis and must find the means of producing more integrated outcomes for clients as a result of their interactions. The assumption (supported by substantial research) is that these lower-level workers will be more likely to be effective in generating coordination if they perceive that they have more control over their own jobs and their organizations.

This approach to coordination has some clear connections with the instruments associated with networking models of coordination, given that the emphasis is on how people at the bottom of organizations connect with one another to solve the problems created by formal structure. Bardach (1998) discusses that networking primarily in terms of the interactions of members of different public sector organizations, but the same logic could be applied to networking with members of private sector organizations, with the employees serving the boundary-spanning roles discussed by Malloy (2003). That is, these individuals may play roles in different types of organizations and therefore induce greater trust and cooperation among potential partners than they could even if they were collaborative members of a single organization or institution.

Given the similarity, noted in Chapter 2, of the concept of collaboration to several concepts associated with the normative institutionalism, some of the instruments involved in institutionalization in that approach would also appear to be applicable to building better coordination among organizations. In particular, public managers need to create a "logic of appropriateness" that supports efforts at cooperation. Cooperation, rather than competition or conflict, must become a central value for the organizations involved in collaboration, as discussed by Bardach (1998), if that cooperation is to be successful. Thus, even if there are formal structures established to facilitate coordination among actors in the public sector, those structures must be "infused with value" (Selznick 1957) so that the participants will naturally respond to situations with answers that build public value that extends across more of government than the single organization.

Further, the managers in organizations attempting to institutionalize a pattern of collaboration will need to create routines, standard operating procedures, and perhaps "rationalized myths" that support the shift in operational values within the organizations. It may not be sufficient for the actors involved in coordination to have the appropriate values, but the achievement of the goal of coordination can be facilitated if those actors have created routine responses to situations that lead them to think first of how to cooperate rather than first about what they can do for themselves. Bardach's (1998) discussion of the success of building collaboration among state and local government organizations in the United States demonstrates the extent to which the routinization of action can be crucial for that success. For example, he shows how developmental patterns among cooperating organizations made their cooperation a matter of course, rather than something about which there had to be any significant discussion among the participants in the policy area.

One interesting contrast between the logic of collaboration and the logic of normative institutionalism is between a top-down and a bottom-up approach. The normative institutionalism places a great deal of emphasis on the role of the manager in creating the internal logic for the organization (see Brunsson and Olsen 1993), while the collaboration approach places somewhat greater emphasis on the autonomous action on the part of the lower-echelon employees. Such action by the lower echelons may come within a context and an organizational culture created by managers, but the locus of the initiatives is clearly lodged with the employees in the collaborative approach.

The most obvious source of the differences among those theoretical approaches is in the purpose of their analyses. The normative institutionalists are concerned with how to create and change institutions, while Bardach is more concerned with getting an array of organizations to work together effectively. Collaboration also means that the analysis is somewhat concerned with the process through which those organizations *deinstitutionalize* themselves (Oliver 1992). That is, to collaborate effectively an individual organization may have to suppress some of its own internal operational code in order to work effectively with other organizations in the pursuit of common goals. Strongly institutionalized organizations may create such strong belief patterns in their members that compromise or collaboration becomes almost treason to the organization (see Peters 2005).

In summary, collaboration as an approach to coordination depends primarily on building routines and patterns of thought that will institutionalize coordination among organizations in the public sector. The collaboration approach has both bottom-up and top-down elements. On the one hand, the approach appears to depend upon the lower echelons of public workers in the field who have real clients and need to bring together packages of services for those clients. Those workers have the opportunity to interact with one another and to frame the manner in which those services are delivered collectively. On the other hand, leadership will be important for creating a climate of action, and further organizational factors such as the capacity to mobilize resources must be considered. Still, all those elements will be insufficient if individuals at the bottom of the organizations are not interested in producing cooperation.

HYBRIDS

When I discussed the various theoretical approaches to coordination in Chapter 3, I concluded by noting that many ideas about coordination are in reality hybrids of the four more or less "pure" models. Almost any major program of social or political action tends to involve some level of hierarchy to be able to enforce the decisions, but that hierarchy may be mixed with any or all of the other sources of coordination. Likewise, to some extent any mechanism for coordination involves some element of networking given that multiple organizations are being linked to create some pattern of interaction.

JOINED-UP GOVERNMENT

As noted, perhaps the most significant efforts by governments to address coordination do not fit neatly into the four categories advanced here. The concept of "joined-up government" and other attempts to create "whole of government" solutions to public problems have strong roots in hierarchy, but also contain some elements of networking and some elements of collaboration (Bogdanor 2005; Pollitt 2003). At the extreme, the British government talked about creating "holistic government" (6 et al. 2002), implying that not only would there be formal coordination through hierarchy but there would also be an attempt to create greater policy integration through more collaborative means.

The notion of "joined-up government" was advanced first in the Blair government as an attempt to address the seeming extreme disaggregation of governing produced in the Thatcher and Major governments, largely through the creation of so many executive agencies. The diagnosis was that the creation of agencies and the emphasis on managerial autonomy had made government even less integrated than in the past. In addition, it was argued that there were an increasing number of "wicked problems" that did not fall conveniently into the department and agency structure of government and therefore required more holistic involvement of actors across the public sector (Kavanagh and Richards 2001).

This conception of holism in governing emphasizes the hybrid nature of joined-up government. If there is the perceived need to cope with "wicked problems" then utilizing merely hierarchical methods to attempt to address those problems will be inadequate and some elements of networking and collaboration will necessarily be involved. Students of policy integration have argued (Weber and Khademian 2008) that their perspective is crucial for coping with wicked problems, but that emphasis on ideas may not be effective unless there are also hierarchical mechanisms for enforcing the cross-cutting ideas.

Although originally a British invention, the notion of joining up government spread to other settings, albeit in a number of different rubrics. Further, the different versions of the same fundamental idea had goals for differing levels of integration of policy and administration. For example, governments in the Antipodes were very clear about the need to restore policy control in the center of government (Chapman and Duncan 2007; Christensen and Laegreid 2007), and to make government function as a single entity. This approach emphasized more political than administrative factors, despite the role that administrative change played in creating the need for the recentralization of the system.

In other countries, operating in other administrative traditions, the need to restore the center of government and create greater coordination was perhaps not so pronounced, but it was still evident. Two examples—Finland and the Netherlands—make this point most clearly. Both of these administrative systems adopted a good deal of the NPM agenda and moved a good deal of policy control out of the center of government. The Finnish government sought to overcome this decentering of the public sector by developing a series of cross-cutting programs that sought to impose the priorities of the government on the administrative system (Kekkonen and Raunio 2010). The Dutch adopted a strategy more like superministries but with clear attention to the concept of joining up government (Karre, Van der Steen, and Van Twist 2013).

The attempt to make government holistic and to cover the "whole of government" was perhaps excessively optimistic. As I have been arguing throughout this volume there are a number of well-established barriers to coordination, much less the creation of a holistic vision of government. And many of these barriers are functional and can facilitate making good policy, if only policy defined in rather narrow, sectoral perspectives. While all policies tend to have some relevance for all other policies—even if only for their budgets—assuming that they can best be made and managed in the round appears somewhat misguided. And if the idea of "holism" is taken to an extreme it is difficult to determine just how government could be organized.

The attempt to build a "joined-up government" is admirable but in many ways is old wine in new bottles. We began this volume by noting that the pursuit of better coordination has been a part of government since the beginning of government. The slogan from the Blair government actually added little of substance to that pursuit, other than emphasizing the enduring nature of the issue. The problem of segmented government was exacerbated by the ideas of NPM but that problem was there before NPM and will almost certainly be there after the slogan has been forgotten by everyone other than administrative historians. Further, other than highlighting the importance of coordination this initiative contained little new substance.

SUMMARY

There is no shortage of mechanisms available to government in their attempts to improve coordination. The examples of instruments in this chapter represent many of the more commonly used, and more successful, mechanisms, but governments continue to search for that philosopher's stone that will solve all their coordination problems. When in doubt most governments will revert to the hierarchical, structural remedies that comprise the largest number of examples discussed above, but changing patterns of management in the public sector are tending to alter this pattern. For example, accepting varieties of the NPM would push governments in the direction of either using market solutions or attempting to build more participatory, collaborative arrangements.

We have attempted to demonstrate that there is no magic bullet for producing coordination among public organizations and programs, and that even if one group of programs does become well coordinated, it may well be that the need for improved linkages between those programs and still other programs may become more evident. Further, governments may incur substantial costs when they pursue coordination, and achieving that desired end may in fact reduce the effectiveness of the individual programs within the group. The costs of coordination may differ for different instruments, and in different settings, so therefore understanding in some particular cases is important for building the more nuanced comprehension of coordination that appears necessary for administrative theories in the public sector.

Governments must make difficult decisions about how they will attempt to coordinate their policies and their administrative actions. These are important political decisions, and most governments have tried a range of these options with varying degrees of success. To some extent the options adopted represent some aspects of the political system; for example, the role of presidential organizations within presidential systems. In other cases, however, there are ideas such as "joined-up government" that become "ideas in good currency" and guide public action. And both reforms within government such as the NPM and crises such as the financial problems beginning in 2008 may add pressures for coordination.

The next chapter will present four more detailed studies of coordination. These cases have hardly been selected at random, but they were chosen to show the potential of a number of possible instruments for coordination. The cases also cover a range of political systems, ranging from the large, presidential United States to the small, semi-presidential Finland to the parliamentary system in the United Kingdom to the rather diffuse political system within the European Union. These are all wealthy and mostly democratic systems (with the possible exception of the European Union), but many of the same issues would have arisen had we chosen less affluent systems. I will attempt to make some comparative sense out of these disparate cases, but there are too many variables and an insufficient number of cases to be able to make any firm statements. The results from these cases will still provide substantial insight into the processes of coordination, and some of the conditions for successful coordination.

5. Case Studies in Coordination

The preceding four chapters have discussed numerous dimensions of the coordination question in public policy and public administration. This analytic and theoretical discussion has pointed to the wide variety of approaches to and interpretations of coordination, and indeed a variety of different concepts that can be employed to express the perceived need to make government organizations work together more effectively. Likewise, I have identified a number of instruments utilized by governments as they attempt to achieve this elusive goal of a "joined-up government."

It is now time to attempt to put some meat on these theoretical bones and present several cases of attempts to coordinate and to produce more effective governance. Attempting to cover all the various dimensions of coordination and coherence touched on above would require a very large number of cases. I have instead chosen four that represent some of the important dimensions, and point to both success and failure in attempting to produce that sought-after coordination. Also, the cases cover several different governments, as I hope to demonstrate that these issues are not at all confined to single countries or types of systems but rather tend to be universal. Also, these are rather obviously "mini-cases," designed to be more illustrative than definitive.[1]

The first case will focus on the creation and maintenance of the Department of Homeland Security (DHS) in the United States. This is a clear example of the strategy of creating superministries to internalize the coordination problems that had existed across organizations. And like many other attempts to employ this strategy, the outcomes were mixed. Just because organizations—especially organizations as diverse as those brought into the DHS—are put under the same umbrella, we should not assume that they will in fact be cooperative and coordinated. They will maintain their own organizational cultures and values and attempt to continue along their well-worn paths.

The second case will address attempts to coordinate around clients. In particular, I will be concerned with attempts to protect children from abuse and exploitation. The problem here is that perhaps *because* children are vulnerable and because they require multiple services from the public sector, a large number of organizations are involved. And those multiple organizations each have a partial image of the needs of the child, and a capacity to address only a small portion of those needs, and therefore tend not to produce a more comprehensive output for their clients.

The third case will be the development, and then the death, of the policy programs in Finland. These programs represented attempts to integrate policies and management in major areas of public sector activity that were priorities of the governing coalitions. This was an interesting experiment that was largely successful during the course of two coalition governments but that then was terminated during the third, even broader coalition. This case demonstrates the importance of the link between politics and administration in producing policy coordination, as well as the potential perils involved in these efforts.

The final case will be concerned with the Open Method of Coordination in the European Union. This means of addressing coordination comes close to the logic of collaboration discussed above (pages 65–68). This mechanism was devised in response to demands to create a more competitive economy within the EU, and the need to integrate a wide range of policy areas to achieve this task. In this case, hierarchy was unavailable as the mechanism for several reasons, and therefore the EU had to devise mechanisms to coordinate both across countries and across policy areas in a more collaborative manner.

These four cases will be only rather brief discussions of these inherently complex political and administrative events. Even those relatively brief discussions, however, will illuminate the dynamics of coordination, as well as some barriers to achieving the goal of greater coherence. None of these cases can be considered a complete success story, but none are total disasters, either. They therefore present a rather realistic conception of the struggles involved in attempting to make the public sector, along with its counterparts in the private sector, function more effectively and cooperatively.

CASE I: THE DEPARTMENT OF HOMELAND SECURITY

In Chapter 4 I identified the use of superministries as one of the various hierarchical and structural strategies for improving coordination in government. The basic logic of this approach is to include within a single structure all the agencies and programs that must cooperate in order to produce a desired outcome. The United States had done this in 1947 when it created the Department of Defense (Ries 1964), and after the attacks on New York and Washington utilized the same strategy in creating the DHS. President Bush saw this approach as a means of overcoming the fragmentation that had played at least some part in allowing the terrorist attacks to succeed.

In many ways blaming the failures of security that led up to 9/11, and made the successes of those attacks possible, on coordination problems appears to be justified by the available evidence. The record that has emerged from the National Commission on Terrorist Attacks on the United States (9/11 Commission) appointed to investigate the happenings of that day has indicated that the extremely decentralized structure of governing in the United States did have a great deal to do with the relative ease with which the hijackers evaded detection and were able to execute their plan (National Commission 2004).

Likewise, Donald Kettl, a distinguished student of American bureaucracy, has examined the facts and concluded (2007, 22) that "the problem lay in connecting the dots. Investigators did not find any smoking guns—clear incontrovertible evidence—that showed that senior officials knew enough about the plans for the September 11 attacks in advance to be able to prevent them. But the investigators did find a large number of tantalizing clues that, if connected, would have provided evidence for the need to take decisive action."

The first response of President George W. Bush to the terrorist attack on September 11 was to create (Executive Order, October 8, 2001) what was in essence a homeland security "czar" in the Office of Homeland Security. This rather small office was located within the White House Office, with direct access to the president (Carter 2006). Tom Ridge, then governor of Pennsylvania, resigned his state position in order to become the leader of the new anti-terrorist program at the federal level. At the beginning of the "war on terror" Governor Ridge was given very limited resources, other than moral suasion and the backing of the president, to attempt to pull together the numerous organizations and programs involved in homeland security. In particular, he had no authority with which to counteract the legal mandates that organizations could use to justify their continuation of the status quo (Allen and Miller 2002). As former senator Gary Hart argued, "Without budgetary or statutory authority, Ridge is doomed not to succeed. If he only has the power of exhortation, the disparate agencies will do what he asks only when it is approved by their own superiors" (cited in Daalder and Destler 2002a).

On March 1, 2003, the DHS was formed out of twenty-two pre-existing agencies. These agencies (see Table 5.1) ranged from relatively large police-type organizations (US Customs Service, now Customs and Border Protection) to small research organizations (Plum Island Animal Disease Center). These organizations were drawn from eight cabinet departments and one independent executive agency. The structure created was very large, with approximately 175,000 public employees (approximately 12 percent of the total federal civilian workforce)—only the Department of Defense and the Department of Veterans Affairs had larger workforces. The size of this workforce has continued to grow, and by 2013 there were over 200,000 employees in the DHS.

The assumptions behind selecting the organizations involved in the DHS were clear, but the decisions to leave certain other organizations out of this new super-department were less clear. The most obvious question that was raised at the time was the exclusion of the intelligence community from the DHS (see Gellman and Miller 2012). Given that many of the issues surrounding the success of terrorism were

Table 5.1 Organizations Included in the Department
of Homeland Security at the Time of Formation

US Customs Service (Treasury)
Immigration and Naturalization Service (Justice)
Federal Protective Service (Treasury)
Transportation Security Administration (Transportation)
Federal Law Enforcement Training Center (Treasury)
Animal and Plant Health Inspection Service (in part, from Agriculture)
Office of Domestic Preparedness (Justice)
Federal Emergency Management Agency (Independent)
Strategic National Stockpile and National Disaster Medical System (Health and Human
    Services)
National Incident Response Team (Energy)
Domestic Emergency Support Teams (Justice)
CBRN Countermeasures Teams (Justice)
Environmental Measures Laboratory (Energy)
National Defense Analysis Center (Defense)
National Domestic Preparedness Office (Justice)
Plum Island Animal Disease Center (Agriculture)
Federal Computer Incident Response Center (General Services Administration)
National Communications System (Defense)
National Infrastructure Protection Center (Justice)
Energy Security and Assurance Program (Energy)
US Coast Guard (Transportation)
US Secret Service (Treasury)

addressed to failures of the intelligence community excluding these organizations from the DHS makes little apparent sense. If the security-oriented organizations such as Customs and Border Protection within Homeland Security were to be effective, they needed to have ready access to the intelligence community.

Although logically it would appear sensible to include intelligence in this department, the power of the intelligence apparatus in the Department of Defense, and the CIA as an independent agency, prevented that integration from occurring. While the failure of intelligence organizations to coordinate among themselves and with the remainder of the public sector was central to the success of the 9/11 attacks, they were capable of maintaining their autonomy from the DHS through skillful bureaucratic politics, as well as some more reasonable arguments about the need for these organizations to function with fewer impediments than might others (*National Journal* 2001).[2]

The decision not to include the intelligence community in the DHS was perhaps not as misguided as it might appear. First, although these organizations will focus a good deal of their efforts on terrorist threats, they also have numerous other responsibilities. For example, the Federal Bureau of Investigation is responsible for investigating numerous federal crimes such as bank robbery and kidnapping, and has a strong internal culture that emphasizes gathering evidence for prosecuting criminals rather than developing intelligence that might prevent the crimes. Also, the fundamental nature of the intelligence organizations, and particularly their handling of highly sensitive materials, was at odds with the more mundane tasks of many of the other organizations included in the new department. The intelligence organizations feared that their missions would be compromised by direct involvement with those other organizations.

Even without including the intelligence community, the internal, and external, coordination issues in the DHS are significant. First, externally, overall homeland security policy is coordinated in the White House by the Homeland Security Council, an analog of the National Security Council that attempts to coordinate the activities of the Departments of Defense and State. The Homeland Security Council is chaired by the president and contains secretaries from five cabinet departments in addition to several officials from the DHS. While that council may provide presidential clout for coordination, the practical problems of getting all these officials to cooperate across departmental lines is daunting.

The above discussion of inclusion and exclusion of organizations has focused on the principal goal of the DHS in preventing terrorism, but the other tasks of the department also require coordination. For example, in dealing with its responsibilities in managing natural disasters the DHS must coordinate with organizations such as the Department of the Interior, the US Department of Agriculture, the Small Business Administration, and the Department of Housing and Urban Development. Some of the functions in these agencies might have been included in the DHS, e.g., the capacity to fight forest fires, but have not been. This selection of competencies in turn means that the coordination issues have not been eliminated but only moved around.

The existence and scale of this organization emphasizes not only the importance of homeland security in contemporary American government but also the difficulty in designing a structure that can internalize all the issues and actors in a policy area. Even with a huge department, there is the continuing need to work with other organizations within the federal government, and this does not begin to cover the issues of coordination with other levels of government. For example, every US state has its own structures for dealing with threats—both terrorism and natural disasters—and the DHS must work with them whenever there are perceived threats. These attempts to create cooperation involve many if not all of the same cultural and organizational differences encountered when attempting to coordinate within the department itself (Cohen, Cuellar, and Weingast 2006).

Management Challenges

The internal coordination issues in Homeland Security are even more daunting. As the new department was created, the managers faced an immense challenge if they were to be successful in using this massive department as a means of effectively coping with threats to the United States. In terms of the underlying management theory that has guided the development of the DHS, the classic notion of "organization by purpose" has been central (Sayre 1958; Yi 2003). This is true for the department as a whole and is also true for the second level of structuring within the department, e.g., Emergency Preparedness and Response. The assumption is that organizations will be most effective if they have a common purpose that can be used to guide their action, rather than being motivated by service to a particular set of clients or a common process.

The inclusion of so many different organizations with so many different organizational purposes, albeit all to some extent related in one way or another to homeland security, makes organization by purpose more difficult to manage (USGAO 2004b; 2004c). As already noted, the inclusion of so many organizations creates a great deal of internal inconsistency, and hence there is a need to manage a massive volume of activity, as well as a good deal of complexity (Krauss 2003). The purpose of part of the department is to prevent potentially dangerous foreign nationals from coming into the country, while another part of the organization is preparing to cope with the consequences of any attack that may occur but also having to prepare for more mundane (if more likely) disasters such as floods and tornados. Still other parts of the organization are responsible for protecting the lives of the president and vice president.

One aspect of coordination and its associated task of strategic management is to create coherence and the compatibility of multiple policy programs. That task, which is difficult at the best of times, is made all the more difficult by the vast range of activities included within this one sprawling organization. The common, and extremely important, primary purpose of the organization may mitigate that difficulty to some extent, but still there could be cultural difficulties. Thus, the dominant purpose of the organization that may unite these components and their employees may be mitigated by the various interpretations that different organizations within the department may assign to that purpose. For example, organizations that are concerned primarily with law enforcement are likely to interpret the meaning of homeland security very differently from the research organizations or those agencies interested in processing intelligence or in responding to disasters once they have already occurred.

Although the focus on the overarching purpose of this department could create some integration within the organization, the internal structuring created to manage the DHS may both contribute to coordination and detract from it. The design that was created for the new department had four main lines of action, in addition to the top management surrounding Secretary Ridge. These lines, organized as "directorates" within the department, are:

1. Border and Transportation Security
2. Emergency Preparedness and Response
3. Science and Technology
4. Information Analysis and Infrastructure Protection

On the one hand each of these directorates tends to integrate some of the agencies within the DHS, but at the same time they have divided the department into those various strands that might be thought to have little to do with one another. As perhaps is true for any attempt to create huge departments such as this in government, the level of integration that can be achieved is indeed more limited than intended.

The structuring of the department into those several directorates is an attempt to manage internal diversity and complexity, but even then there are substantial variations in the purposes of the components contained within a single directorate. For example, the Border and Transportation Security directorate contains what was the Federal Protective Service, in essence a police force; several research activities from the Department of Agriculture; and the Federal Law Enforcement Training Center, having come from the Department of the Treasury. Again, all these programs have some connection to protecting the borders of the United States, but they certainly go about it in different ways and with very different policy styles.

One managerial strategy for coping with these different organizational backgrounds has been to essentially subsume them within the directorates and attempt to minimize their organizational identities. Therefore, if one examines the official organizational chart for the DHS one sees that with the exception of the Coast Guard and the Secret Service the pre-existing organizations do not appear as separate entities. On the one hand this strategy might expedite the integration of the constituent organizations, given that their identities will be subsumed into the larger structure. On the other hand, however, these directorates are themselves rather amorphous, as is the DHS as a whole, so that creating any organizational identity and commitment may be difficult. The old cultures may persist, but just not be as evident to the managers as they would be if the organizations were more clearly defined.

While internal organizational cultures may present some coordination problems, they also provide some benefits for the organization as a whole. Organizations that have common purposes tend to function together more effectively and can use their organizational ideology to motivate their employees. Thus, for Homeland Security and for other organizations there is a need to balance the demands for commitment and the need for coordination within and without the organization. The creation of the directorates within the DHS is an attempt to create a halfway house between maintenance of the individual cultures and the creation of a common internal culture.

Coping with the Vertical Dimension of Coordination

The bulk of this discussion has been on horizontal coordination among federal organizations included, or not included, in the DHS, but an additional dimension of vertical coordination should also be discussed, if only briefly. Indeed, the need to involve state and local governments and their "first responders" in any plan to cope with terrorism is worthy of a book on its own, given the challenges it poses and the central importance of these players in producing effective policy in the area (see Pluvoise-Fenton and Pionke 2004).

The DHS has made some initial movements toward that vertical coordination. For example, in 2004 the DHS created a National Incident Management System to provide some coordination in identifying and managing major fire events (Lester and Krejci 2007). While fire fighting had never been a major federal priority, the need to coordinate responses to major incidents was in part a role of the Federal Emergency Management Agency (FEMA) that was absorbed into Homeland Security. Further, FEMA now is responsible for a wider array of incidents at the state and local levels and is meant to coordinate responses to those crises across levels of government.

The vertical coordination problems encountered here are not dissimilar to those encountered in other vertical coordination situations, but the difficulties are to some extent exaggerated by the perceived urgency and by a substantial lack of trust among the actors. The source of the sense of urgency is rather obvious, but it appears to be perceived rather differently by the several actors involved. The DHS has stressed the need for crisis preparations by the numerous fire and police departments—almost 15,800 general-purpose law enforcement agencies and approximately the same number of fire departments (many volunteer) across the United States. Most fire and police departments, however, are having their own capacities stretched by their normal responsibilities in protecting their communities and do not have the resources to respond to all of the wishes of the DHS. The DHS, on the other hand, sees their mandate as perhaps the central concern for government and therefore is not particularly interested in the other demands on local organizations.

The lack of trust among the actors appears to flow in both directions. The DHS and other federal agencies have been reluctant to share substantial information with local governments, fearing that there would be leaks and misuse of what is considered sensitive information. There have been numerous complaints from police and fire

departments and other emergency services being given little substantive information despite changes in the threat levels facing the United States.[3] As already noted,
secrecy can be a major barrier to effective coordination, even when coordination
is crucial for achieving the central goals of the organizations.

In addition to believing they are kept "out of the loop" concerning intelligence
but also because of broken promises about funding and support (O'Beirne 2003;
USGAO 2007), many local government officials appear to feel that their services are
being relied upon—sor even assumed by the federal government—and are having
requirements imposed upon them, but that the federal government has helped little
in supporting their preparations. This complaint is one more variant of the familiar
arguments about "unfunded mandates" imposed upon subnational governments
by the federal government, but one that has perhaps even more resonance with
local citizens (Posner 2007).

Although these problems and misunderstandings about the use of resources
and the use of privileged information certainly exist, the two sets of actors in this
coordination problem need each other to be effective. The federal government
cannot re-create the network of local responders in the face of any crisis. The
subnational governments, on the other hand, need federal intelligence support
and also federal financial support to be effective in their tasks. The political task,
a variant of other coordination tasks, is to get these actors to collaborate. In this
case the structural solutions do not appear available, so that other, softer versions
of coordination must be pursued. For those solutions to be successful there must
be mutual trust among the actors but history has tended to eliminate or at least
to reduce that trust.

Into the Future

Much of the discussion above focuses on the first years of development of the DHS.
Although the department has been in business for over a decade at this writing,
the coordination issues internally and externally continue to emerge, and older
ones are not necessarily resolved. As already noted concerning the Department of
Defense, creating internal unity in a large, sprawling organization is not easy and
some of the problems may be expected to persist, but the development of new
coordination issues illustrates some of the inherent difficulties in coordination in
the public sector.

As noted in the theoretical chapters, the use of words like *security* or *competitiveness* to describe policy areas implies the integration of several strands of
policy around a major goal. The title of the DHS implies that integration, and the
development of additional policy issues has emphasized the need for integration.
For example, as food security has come to be a national and international issue,

the DHS has become more directly involved with the Department of Agriculture and USAID in thinking about national and international risks to the food supply (USGAO 2013b). Similar issues have been raised about the security of supply chains for American producers in international trade.

Summary

To date it is difficult to argue that the DHS has failed in its primary task of preventing domestic terrorism in the United States. Its performance in other tasks such as border protection against illegal immigration and effective response to natural disasters has been more mixed, and more controversial politically. To some extent there have been no direct challenges in the primary area of the department, whereas some of the failings have been widely publicized. And there are still numerous coordination issues in areas such as intelligence and emergency response that may limit the ability of the organization to function effectively.

While many of the most basic coordination problems facing Homeland Security, notably the coordination with the intelligence community, have not really been solved in any meaningful way, security tends to become an encompassing policy goal. Any politician who wishes to sell his or her pet project can do so more readily by linking it to security. While this may be good for the department from the perspective of bureaucratic politics and its ability to influence government as a whole, it does exacerbate the difficulty of maintaining a clear mission and focusing on central policy concerns. Thus (see below) coordination may not be a panacea but one of several virtues that require balancing.

CASE 2: THE PROTECTION OF CHILDREN

As well as organizing around purposes, governments can also coordinate around people, especially the segments of society that require a range of services from the public sector. Children and the elderly are the two social groups generally serving as the targets of integrated public sector action. Both require a range of services such as health, transportation, and social services and both are deemed more entitled to services from the public sector, even in neo-liberal societies, because of their not being in the labor force. Children have a particular symbolic strength for the public sector, so that targeting services to children is perhaps less of a political issue than it would be for other groups.

Because children are a powerful political symbol, useful for justifying what an organization or policy entrepreneur wants to achieve anyway, services targeted to children may be proposed and managed across a range of programs and departments

Table 5.2 Examples of Children's Programs
in the US Federal Government

Agriculture: Women, Infants and Children Nutrition Program
Defense: Department of Defense Educational Activity Office
Education: Multiple education programs
Health and Human Services: Administration for Children and Families
Interior: Native American education
Labor: Child labor law enforcement
Transportation: Regulation of child safety seats, etc.
Veterans Affairs: Medical and pension benefits for children

in government. This is an obvious source of coordination problems, but it is also the source of many real-life problems for children and their advocates. Most cabinet departments at the federal level in the United States have programs that deal with the needs of children (see Table 5.2) and the average local government has any number of actors involved. Further, outside the executive departments the courts are major players for the needs of children, deciding issues of custody, protection, and guardianship that can have a profound influence on the life chances of individuals.[4]

Despite their symbolic power, children often have been poorly served by the public sector, and some of those failures have been a result of the poor coordination of public services (Pecora 2000). The innocence and vulnerability of children is a foundation of their symbolic power in public policy but also is a reality that contributes to the policy and administrative failures when dealing with children. The simple fact that they may not be capable of voicing their problems, or perhaps being believed if they do voice them, makes children highly dependent upon parents or upon public sector officials acting *in loco parentis*. And because so many actors share part of that responsibility, the problems of coordination may be intense.

Although there may be a number of other circumstances in which the public sector fails children, abuse by parents and other caregivers is certainly the most egregious example and demonstrates clearly the problems of coordinating around clients. Although the general findings in these cases of abuse have been that children who are being abused may be seen by a variety of public sector officials—teachers, nurses, doctors, social workers, and policemen—each of these public employees sees only a part of the picture but fails to discuss the case with others who have seen the same child. Further, the abusers tend to make the detection problem more difficult by purposefully taking the child to different hospitals, or moving across jurisdictional lines.

Cases of child abuse arise in all cultures (see, for example, UNICEF 2012), but several high-profile cases in the United Kingdom have made the problem more apparent there and have also demonstrated how difficult it can be to produce adequate coordination of protective services for children. The first of these was the death of Victoria Climbié in 2000 and the second the death of "Baby P" (Peter Connelly) in 2007. Both deaths occurred in North London and involved some of the same child-care authorities. The obvious question raised in Parliamentary debates (White 2008) and elsewhere is why there was apparently no improvement in protections offered to children.

When she died in a London hospital, Victoria Climbié was only eight years old. She had been the victim of systematic abuse by caretakers for most of her life, having been brought to the United Kingdom from the Ivory Coast (via France) when she was seven years old. The available evidence suggests that police, social workers, and staff of the National Health Service missed at least twelve opportunities during the last months of her life to remove her from the abusive home (Laming 2009). Some of that failure by the potential protectors of the child may be attributed to general unwillingness to address an awkward situation that may result in accusing a parent or other caregiver falsely. Some of the failures also may be attributed to poor individual work by social workers and others and inadequate funding for each of the public organizations involved. But no small portion of the blame for the failures can be attributed to inadequate coordination among those three services, as well as little connection with the education authorities, all of whom had suspicions about the poor treatment of this one child.

Peter Connelly died at an even earlier age—seventeen months. Although the abuse of this child lasted much less time, some of the same coordination issues were involved. Peter Connelly had been seen by a social worker who suspected abuse but the evidence was not deemed sufficient to take the child into protective care. Likewise, the child was seen by several doctors who did not detect or who chose to ignore serious injuries. Only at the stage of the autopsy was the extent and duration of the abuse suffered by the child apparent to the authorities—some of whom had been involved in the Victoria Climbié case.

The Climbié and Baby P cases present perhaps the most difficult coordination problem of all the four cases discussed here. On the one hand it involves coordination across several different policy areas—health, social services, education, and the police. Representatives of all of these programs interacted with the clients in question, but did not talk to each other adequately in order to provide the range of services, or even the basic protections, that these clients needed. At the same time several different facilities or decentralized organizations within each of these various policy areas had something to do with the client, and there was little coordination even within the single policy areas. This was especially true for the social services that should have been the principal source of protection for the child, but seemed to have had no institutionalized means of tracking the clients across the multiple providers. Thus, this case illustrates problems of coordination that links horizontal and vertical problems of coordination.

The horizontal dimension of coordination is perhaps the clearer of the two issues for child protection. In the case of the deaths of both children a number of organizations in the public sector had had contact with the children and apparently had suspicions about the mistreatment they were receiving from their (so-called) caregivers. There was, however, no effective mechanism for the officials—police, teachers, social workers, nurses, etc.—to communicate easily with one another, or even to know that the other organization was involved with the child. Without that mechanism in place, any opportunity to coordinate action to protect the children fell to overworked social workers, who simply did not pursue the issues (Laming 2009).

The vertical dimension of coordination to some extent mirrors the horizontal. Not only were different types of services involved but they had different geographical boundaries so that they might not naturally understand their joint jurisdictions over the children. This inherent problem in coordination was exacerbated by the caretakers for the children purposefully going across jurisdictional boundaries in order to evade detection of the abuse. The negative impact of boundaries was evident even in a centralized unitary regime such as the United Kingdom, and these impacts can only be expected to be greater in more decentralized regimes.

The media exposure of the Victoria Climbié affair produced a good deal of reaction and several proposals for reform. In addition to improving the training of medical and police personnel to recognize and report on abuse, the British government responded in several ways. One response was to empower a Minister of Children (created in 2003) to integrate a range of services for children available from different government departments and local authorities. Later, a Green Paper (consultative document) entitled *Every Child Matters* (2003) provided an insight into the government's thinking about possible extensions of the role of the public sector in protecting children. The structural implications of these policy changes are perhaps profound and will involve a good deal of collaboration and cooperation (Miller 2003). Further, the Office of Standards in Education (OfSTED) has begun to establish criteria for managing and implementing these policies, thereby to some extent putting education into the role of the lead agency in this field.

The political mobilization for child protection initiated after the death of Victoria Climbié resulted in the passage of the Children Act of 2004. Among several provisions in the act was the creation of the statutory position of Director of Children's Services in local authorities and the creation of Children's Commissioners in England and Wales. Separate legislation provides for analogous officers in Scotland and Northern Ireland, with those officials having somewhat greater powers than those in England and Wales. All these officials have taken as their principal responsibility the implementation of the United Nations Convention on the Rights of Children, as well as national legislation for the protection of children (see Thomas 2011).

As has been true in any number of cases the structural solution for coordination may not really be the solution. In the case of the Director of Children's Services the rapid turnover in these officials has meant that they cannot provide the coherence required (Wiggins 2013). Local governments have also developed numerous interagency committees and similar organizations designed to bring together all the relevant actors in the policy area and to assist the involved agencies in cooperating in protecting and serving children. Further, a series of pieces of legislation have been adopted in the UK Parliament, as well as in the assemblies in Scotland and Wales, that have created new powers for the protection of children. But none of these structural solutions appeared sufficient to prevent continuing problems of child abuse.

Despite the emphasis placed in this book, as I will be arguing in the final chapter, coordination—and especially a formal mechanism for coordination—is not always the answer to the problems of governance. Certainly better coordination among agencies and across territorial jurisdictions could have increased the probabilities of these children surviving and perhaps have reduced significantly the length of their abuse, but there is no guarantee that they would have been saved. Building systems of coordination is important for public services, but they may not be effective unless the individual public servants involved are committed to achieving the goals of their programs and prepared to invest time and energy in the programs (see Marinetto 2011).

The potential importance of individual actors involved in coordination around abused children is analogous to Kettl's concept of contingent coordination (2003; see above, page 43). Kettl observes that, at least in the case of natural disasters, the coordination process was more informal than hierarchical and relied on the personal initiative and networks of individuals rather than on structure or rules. Protecting these abused children might have been more probable with individuals working across organizations personally, rather than relying on formal structures to make the connections. While this reliance on individuals makes a great deal of sense in terms of avoiding formal structures, it also may put individual public servants in very difficult situations, having to decide how far to move beyond their safe, bureaucratic routines (see Boin and Nieuwenburg 2013).

For the programs directed at children the ordinary day-to-day pursuit of improved service may be more affected by coordination than are the extreme cases such as those motivating this small case study. On a daily basis children, and other groups of clients such as the elderly and the disabled, require a range of services from multiple organizations in the public and private sectors. Those services will be less expensive and almost certainly more effective if they are well coordinated. Organizations such as UNICEF (Innocenti Research Centre 2003) working for the protection of children and the expansion of services for those children, have pointed numerous times to the need for policy integration, but the folkways of governments, among many other things, tend to keep the services divided and piecemeal.

This case study focused on the protection of children in the United Kingdom, but the same story could have been told for many other places in the world. There is a very strong desire to protect children from abuse but the many actors involved in that process may make achieving that goal difficult. Further, rules designed to protect privacy in health and education institutions may also prevent even the most dedicated actors from putting together information on abuse. The British government has attempted to address these issues with a variety of hierarchical and network instruments but the problem remains one difficult to address effectively.

Although this case has been in practice the most difficult, in theory it should have been the easiest. Coordination around clients should be relatively easy since there is an individual who is present and who needs a variety of services—or in this case the single service of protection. Further, in this case the clients in question are children, who tend to be given special status in public policy as well as in society in general. But this case also illustrates that children, or any other vulnerable group, are at the mercy of their caregivers as well as the public sector organizations responsible for their protection.

CASE 3: POLICY PROGRAMS IN FINLAND

At the very end of the twentieth century the Finnish government, like many others, became aware of the high levels of fragmentation in their public sector. This was more a function of the traditional "silo" structure within that system than of the numerous reforms driven by New Public Management (NPM), which had been adopted in that government. Unlike their neighbor Sweden, for example, the cabinet is virtually nonexistent as a collective decision-making institution in Finland and ministers enjoy substantial autonomy. In addition, the rather extreme version of multiparty coalitions in this government further divided policies.[5]

One response to the problem of fragmentation was the idea of "health in all policies," meaning that all organizations in government would be required to consider the health implications of their policies and attempt to enhance health outcomes whether that was their primary policy area or not (Melkas 2013). This cross-cutting program emphasized the need to consider the health impacts of government actions in all areas, not just in important social policy areas such as health and education. This approach therefore provided the foundation for integrative policymaking, using primarily ideas rather than coercion.

A more comprehensive response to this fragmentation was adopted in the government of Prime Minister Paavo Lipponen in 2000 (Kekkonen and Raunio

2010). In this attempt to increase coordination and policy integration, "policy programs" became components of the coalition agreement formed after each election. Thus, in addition to the general statement of government policies for the period of the electoral mandate, the coalition would select several cross-cutting programs that would not only reflect the policy commitments of the coalition but would also be strategic attempts to intervene in the economy and society more efficiently than might be possible with programs being managed within an individual ministry.

For example, in the first array of policy programs the Liponnen government selected creating higher levels of employment as one of the policy programs. The Finnish economy was reasonably strong but maintaining employment was still a policy priority. The Ministry of Labor was, of course, central to this program, but it also affected the Ministry of Trade and Industry, the Ministry of Agriculture and Forestry, the Ministry of Education, and the Ministry of Foreign Trade (see Table 5.3). Although Labour would take the lead on this program, other ministries would contribute to achieving the goals, and some strategy for coordinating these contributions would be essential to achieving the policy goals.

In the last government to use this methodology (2007–2011) for coordination there were three programs (Prime Minister's Office 2011). One program was to some extent a continuation of the employment program from the first exercise. A second program focused on health promotion, extending the concern for health well beyond the boundaries of clinical medicine, and the third was concerned with a broad array of issues affecting women, children, and families. The analysis of these programs and previous ones by the National Audit in Finland was, however, less than supportive and emphasized (among other things) the need to maintain accountability in ministers and also the ability to use more conventional mechanisms such as interministerial committees to address the same coordination needs.

Although this mode of strategic intervention and coordination was important for the Lipponen and two subsequent governments, the capacity to coordinate given to the program leadership was minimal. In addition to a lead minister there was a senior public servant designated to guide these programs. But relatively few resources were attached to the programs, so that all these program leaders had was, as one of them put it, the "power to beg" (personal interview, May 2004). These leaders at the outset of the initiative had no resources to induce the cooperation of the existing ministries. To some degree, like the Open Method of Coordination in the European Union (see below), this method of coordination depended upon collaborative methods, rather than on the use of hierarchical controls.

In addition to the absence of financial incentives that were available to the program managers in this arrangement, there was almost no capacity to change personnel allocations. Further, the independence of ministers in the Finnish

Table 5.3 Composition of Ministerial Groups
for Policy Programs in Finland

Employment Policy
    Lead Minister   Minister of Labor
    Members   Minister of Foreign Affairs
                     Minister of Health and Social Services
                     Minister of Trade and Industry
                     Minister of the Environment

Entrepreneurship Policy
    Lead Minister   Minister of Trade and Industry
    Members   Minister of Defense
                     Minister of Social Affairs
                     Minister of Justice
                     Minister of the Environment

Information Society
    Lead Minister   Prime Minister
    Members   Minister of Defense
                     Minister of Transportation and Communication
                     Minister of Education
                     Coordinate Minister of Finance

Civic Participation
    Lead Minister   Minister of Justice
    Members   Minister of Education
                     Minister of Regional and Municipal Affairs
                     Minister of Culture
                     Coordinate Minister of Finance

government (Tilli 2007) makes it difficult for other actors in government—even a prime minister—to affect their behaviors significantly. This tendency was perhaps exacerbated by the general tendency of NPM to emphasize the independence of actors in government and the desirability of pursuing their individual organizational goals (Pollitt and Dan 2011).

Despite some weaknesses in the design of this method for achieving more strategic coordination, the program approach did produce some real and significant governance benefits. At one level this approach encouraged a greater appreciation for strategic thinking within government. The enhanced understanding of the linkages among policies and the need to consider those linkages in a longer term was an important contribution to policy management in this system. This sense appears to have persisted even after the programs themselves have been terminated (personal interview, September 2013).

Although there were some successes coming out of the program approach in Finnish government, the termination of this governance innovation demonstrated some of the continuing problems of this and analogous attempts to coordinate. The most obvious is that any attempt to impose broader priorities on existing organizations in the public sector, especially when those organizations are headed by political leaders, is likely to encounter opposition. Governments tend not to be very effective in developing comprehensive strategies but rather continue functioning in their comfortable silos unless there are good reasons to alter that behavior. In the case of Finnish programs the resistance was subdued, and covert, but still this or any change in working routines is likely to encounter some resistance.

Unfortunately, at least in its earlier manifestations, the programs in Finnish government were not capable of providing the ministries, nor the ministers, good reasons to alter their behavior. Having few if any resources to induce the ministries to participate in the cross-cutting programs, the program managers had to depend upon the cooperation and good will of the participants in the process. This capacity to induce cooperation was further weakened because of the relatively weak governmental structure and the related capacity of ministers to manage their ministries and pursue policies relatively autonomously.

In the case of policy programs in Finland, politics (see Chapter 2) was a major source of the downfall of the attempt at coordination. Finland has had coalition governments since World War II, and these coalitions often have contained a number of parties and parties from across the political spectrum—so called "rainbow coalitions." The election of 2011, however, produced an even broader six-party coalition (Nurmi and Nurmi 2012) that made maintaining the program management approach all the more difficult. Reaching agreements on priorities and creating adequate cooperation among such a wide range of parties produced the downfall of an admirable experiment in managing coordination and indeed in managing multiparty government considered more generally.

In addition to the impacts of the party system on the program management system, there are also challenges based on efficiency and accountability. The auditor general argued that there were better ways of achieving the same ends of policy coordination and strategic management that did not require maintaining this new system. In particular, the parallel system of cabinet committees, as well as the reintroduction of regular meetings of the senior civil servants from each ministry, were argued to achieve many of the same purposes of enhanced coordination without the expense of the additional system (personal interview, September 2013).

In summary, this was an innovative attempt to create greater coordination and strategic thinking in the Finnish government. In some ways it was a success, given that it did produce working programs that appeared to be successful in at least some policy areas. On the other hand, however, it did not survive more than two changes in government, so if the intention was to generate more long-term thinking and policymaking then it was a qualified success at best. But if the goal was to instill a pattern of thinking then it can be considered successful—even if Finland was already one of the more future-oriented governing systems in the world.[6]

CASE 4: THE OPEN METHOD OF COORDINATION IN THE EUROPEAN UNION

The European Union summit held in Lisbon in 2000 stated as a principal goal for the EU to be the most competitive economic area in the world by 2010 (Rodrigues 2009). This ambitious goal was to be achieved through utilizing a wide range of instruments working across the full gamut of policy areas that have an impact on the competitiveness of economies. While conventional conceptions of economic policy involve primarily organizations clearly linked to the economy, e.g., ministries of finance, ministries of industry, and regulatory agencies, this goal would also include programs such as education, labor market programs, and social welfare issues. These policies have indirect impacts on the competitive strength of an economy, especially a contemporary knowledge-based economy.

For the EU this broad approach to economic policy presented a distinct governance challenge. Although the treaties that function as the foundation for EU policy action clearly provide it substantial authority in economic affairs, the union's authority in areas such as social policy and education that have been considered increasingly significant for competitiveness remained largely in the hands of the national governments. Therefore, some creative mechanism was required to be able to produce the policy integration required in the Lisbon Strategy, and that mechanism was to be the Open Method of Coordination (Borrás and Jacobsson 2004).

The Open Method of Coordination (OMC) actually involves several types of coordination. The first and most obvious was the integration of a range of policies that had relevance for competitiveness within each of the member nations. This involved then coordinating policies that were heavily impacted by and to some extent controlled in Brussels with other policies that had remained national and at times might have actors involved who would be suspicious of the role of the EU. This coordination was compounded by the control, or at least strong impact, of subnational governments in some of these policy areas such as education. That issue was, of course, particularly relevant in federal regimes.

The other dimension of coordination was that between the various member nations of the EU. Even if the individual countries were to retain control over their national policies, the drive to enhance competitiveness within the union as a whole would be strengthened if all the participants were to adopt roughly the same policies and try to implement those policies in a more coordinated manner. Although analogous to coordination of states or provinces in federal systems (Waugh and Streib 2006), this mode of coordination was different in that the analog of the central government in this case had little or no formal authority in the policy areas being coordinated.

The OMC works though regular meetings of officials from the member countries. Although officially described in a more elegant manner the style of these meetings is very much "show and tell." That is, at the meetings the representatives of each country report to the others what they have been able to accomplish during the intervening months to contribute to the goal of enhanced competitiveness. Given that no one wishes to have to report negatively to colleagues and appear to be laggards in the project, this need to demonstrate progress places pressures on the country representatives, and indirectly on governments as a whole, to produce changes.

A second part of the meetings of the OMC is determining new goals and how to advance the cause of competitiveness even further. From some interviews this process appears to be analogous to the process that Scharpf (1988) describes for European integration more generally, with rather slow movement because of the need to reach something at least approaching unanimity. Given the significantly different levels of competitiveness in the member economies the process has difficulties in going faster than the slowest economy or the government least willing to change its internal policies and practices in several important policy areas. And given that there are also rather profound differences in policy perspectives among the countries, the politics of competitiveness may also not contribute to success in this endeavor.

There are several factors that appear to influence the effectiveness of the individual countries within the EU in being successful in reaching the goals agreed upon by the meetings of the OMC participants. As already noted, there are marked differences in the nature of the economies, even among the largely developed economies within the EU. These differences mean that it may simply not be possible for new members such as Slovakia or Lithuania to make the required adjustments in labor market and social policies, and even some older members such as Greece and Portugal have also encountered difficulties.

Second, some governments are not as committed to achieving these competitiveness goals for the EU as have been others. Countries such the United Kingdom, and at times the Scandinavian countries, are less willing to make these changes in domestic policies just because it will assist in some European project emanating from Brussels. And the willingness to adapt national policies to goals of economic competitiveness also appeared to depend on the political control of the government, with parties of the Left appearing somewhat more reluctant to make changes in labor market protections or social policies that might in other lights be considered impediments to international competitiveness.

The OMC involves some mixture of networking and collaboration to produce its effects. On the one hand the regular meetings of the officials from the member countries, and their continuing interactions between those meetings, represent the institutionalization of a network concerned with achieving the stated goal of competitiveness, even if all the participants are from within the public sector (Borrás and Peters 2011). That said, the method through which this network can create its desired effects is largely collaborative, with the actors using various forms of argument to persuade and cajole one another to move the project forward.

Although it began as a mechanism for helping to achieve the competitiveness goals of the EU, other forms of this method have since been initiated to attempt to solve other policy problems (Morth 2004). The policy domains included under the several treaties functioning as the foundation of the union exclude a number of policy areas that a national government would control, in large part because those national governments wanted to maintain control. For example, the EU has had increased powers in criminal justice but still does not have nearly the range of powers of a national government (Guild, Carrera, and Atger 2009).

The Bologna Process in higher education is another example of the informal process of policy coordination among countries in the EU (Heinze and Knill 2008). Again, the EU lacks the formal authority to regulate higher education, or education taken more generally, so it developed a negotiation process among the higher education authorities to ensure greater uniformity among the national systems and greater ease in moving across systems. Again, this coordination has been achieved through "soft law" and negotiation rather than through hierarchy.

The OMC and associated informal coordination processes appear to have enjoyed some success, perhaps because the discussions are being conducted within reasonably well-defined policy domains. This restriction is clearest in the case of the Bologna Process, in which all the participants are involved in higher education, speak the same professional language, and have relatively common goals. Even in the case of the original OMC the participants tended to come from a relatively narrow range of policy areas and hence could cooperate more effectively. This similarity made the networking easier and also helped to focus their interactions on a clearly defined range of issues.

The OMC demonstrates the role of networking, along with collaboration, in producing coordination in public policy. There is no real hierarchical authority[7] that can shape these interactions in the OMC, but the participants appear to have developed effective patterns of interaction among the relevant actors. Further, they appeared to have some capacity to frame and reframe issues in ways that advanced the policy goals that were being sought. That said, the overall competitiveness goals for the European Union appear not to have been attained.

SUMMARY

None of these four cases can be argued to "prove" anything theoretically about policy coordination or about the manner in which public sector organizations cooperate, or not, in the provision of public services. These cases do, however, illustrate the types of issues that arise when attempting to coordinate and in particular they illustrate the barriers that exist to effective coordination. If indeed coordination is so crucial to effective governance then actually finding this philosopher's stone appears to be a long and torturous process. The good news, however, is that politicians and administrators continue to pursue this goal despite the numerous barriers.

Two of the cases presented here represent complete, or at the very least partial, coordination failures. The clearest failure to produce coordination is in the case of the two abused children (and thousands like them whose cases have not become as prominent in the media) in the United Kingdom. This failure is somewhat surprising, given that the case deals with clients who have significant symbolic power and that the problems are severe and in many ways obvious to both responsible officials and the public. Those factors should have been sufficient to motivate action. However, the absence of mechanisms to facilitate coordination, and the lack of adequate time and "slack" within the organizations involved can prevent effective coordination.

The DHS also represents a failure of sorts. As already noted, there have been no domestic terror attacks in the United States since the formation of the department. But in other aspects of coordinated performance the success has been less demonstrable. Although apparently performance in this area has improved, the reaction to Hurricane Katrina was disastrous and demonstrated weaknesses in the ability of the complex organizational structure to produce effective action (Morris, Morris, and Jones 2007). Further, if one of the goals of this reorganization was to create a common internal culture within the organization it is not at all clear that this level of internal coordination has been achieved.

The Finnish case of program management represents a partial success in strategic coordination. During the first three governments in which it was used this methodology for producing greater coordination produced some significant impacts, with some apparent improvements on the strategic capacity of governments. These governments were able to create programs that cut across the conventional lines of existing ministries and agencies and provided more integrated services for citizens. But in this case politics became a major part of the downfall of the effort at coordination as the addition of more parties to the coalition government made maintaining the cooperation more difficult.

Finally, the OMC may be considered as close to a success in coordination as any of the cases. That success may be in part because the goals were somewhat ambiguous and it was therefore unclear just what would constitute success. As the name implies, the OMC is more of a method and a process than it is a targeted outcome for a particular level of policy integration. As primarily a means to an end, rather than the coordination goal itself, the process becomes as significant as the outcomes. The continuing discussions among the national actors involved provided for opportunities to address, if not necessarily solve, policy issues related to competitiveness.

In all these cases the structural elements of coordination appear to be the chosen means of intervention more than does agency. That is, in all these cases there was an emphasis on building structural and procedural solutions to the problems of governing. These structures are all reasonable solutions to the problems of coordination but apparently do not perform as well as they might. That appears to be at least in part because they depend upon the actions of the individuals within them. This failure is perhaps most evident in the case of child abuse, where individuals have not been able to use the structures created after the Climbié affair, and another similar tragedy occurred. In all the cases, however, the structures do not appear to be as important as the roles played by individual public officials.

Following from the above conclusion, it also appears that coordination is better conceived as a lower-level administrative activity than as a grand policy initiative. Even when there is a coherent policy initiative, i.e., the OMC, the success of the program appears to come through the interactions of individuals rather than because of the ambitious policy. While the treaty limitations of the European Union limited the ability to attempt imposition, the interaction among national representatives may still be more productive than attempting to impose a standard solution.

Another of the related observations coming out of these cases is that coordinating administration may be more productive than attempting to create policy integration or coordination. As noted above (Chapter 2), attempting to build agreement on policies and policymakers may generate more political conflict than working to produce cooperation among administrative organizations. Those organizations confront real clients who have real needs for coordinated policies. Further, the networking across organizations may be more evident among administrators working in decentralized settings that facilitate coordination than it is among actors at the top of the silos.

In summary, these cases demonstrate the difficulties involved in coordination but also demonstrate that the task is not insurmountable. Even in the more extreme cases of failure in coordination there were some improvements in the capacity of the governments involved to provide coordinated services to the public. At a very minimum the question of coordination and integrated services had become more recognized as a central concern for policymakers. In some cases massive failures were instructive, while in others the modest success in enhancing coherence in governing helped to concentrate thinking about increasing effectiveness even further.

These cases also illustrate that the various theoretical approaches to coordination presented earlier do indeed appear in practice. Although the cases demonstrate that the theoretical models do appear, the real-world interventions described here also tend to be hybrids of those basic approaches to coordination. For example, the OMC in the EU is, in essence, a network approach and it also involves collaboration among the actors around the idea of competitiveness. And the representatives of the individual countries may have been capable of relying on authority within their own governments in order to implement the agreements reached through negotiation.

To this point I have been stressing the importance of coordination for effective policy and administration. In the final chapter I will step back somewhat from that advocacy and examine some of the limits of coordination.

6. Is Coordination Always the Answer, and Can It Be?

Throughout this book I have been searching for the philosopher's stone of greater coordination and coherence in the public sector. I hope that I have made two points clearly: coordination is important, and the goal of greater policy coherence is difficult to achieve. The complexities and pressures of contemporary government make achieving coordination an exceedingly difficult task. Each of the four mini-cases discussed in Chapter 5 demonstrated that some aspects of performance in the public sector could almost certainly be improved by increasing the degree of coordination among the programs involved in delivering the service. These studies, and numerous other examples throughout the book, demonstrate that would-be coordinators have encountered substantial barriers in achieving their goals.

The emphasis on coordination in this volume, however, should not be taken to indicate that coordination is a panacea for any and all problems confronting politicians and civil servants as they attempt to govern. It is not. Indeed, in some cases enhanced coordination may actually harm performance of public tasks and make citizens less well-off than they might otherwise have been. Further, even if it does create some benefits, effective coordination of organizations and programs may have significant negative side effects that require balancing different values before significant investment of time and resources is made for improving coordination. Like most values in public management, emphasizing coordination is likely to imply de-emphasizing other values (Simon 1947), and therefore political and administrative leaders must decide what and when to coordinate.

The second major question that emerges from the examination of coordination and the efforts that have been made by so many governments at so many points in time is *how* to go about improving the policy process. To some extent that question is related to the first about whether investment in coordination is worthwhile, given that the application of sufficient hierarchical authority may be able to produce greater coordination, but at a significant cost in terms of the expenditure of real resources, political capital, and perhaps effectiveness of the individual programs. On the other hand, if governments are willing to adopt somewhat less directive mechanisms, and softer instruments, for coordination then the likelihood of their desired outcomes might be less, but so would the investments of resources and also the political exposure in the case of failure.

Coordination is certainly an important attribute for public administration and public policy, but it may be only a start, albeit an important start, toward making the public sector more strategic and coherent. Simply putting programs together is one thing, but attempting to move toward selecting broad goals and relating the conventional program structure of ministries and agencies to those goals will perhaps be the next wave of development of the public sector (Stewart 2004). That strategic sense will imply coordination not only in the delivery of current services but also will involve linking programs around more comprehensive and longer-term goals.

This shift in the style of governing to some extent reflects a "recentering" of government after several decades of decentralization (Peters 2004b; Dahlström, Peters, and Pierre 2010). Both New Public Management (NPM) reforms and more participative "governance" style reforms have emphasized the need to permit greater latitude for action for both managers and the lower echelons of public organizations. Those reforms so weakened the central governing apparatus in many countries that presidents and prime ministers did not believe themselves capable of providing the strategic direction that would be needed to make governments truly effective actors. Building coordination devices is one step in that direction, but it is far from the end point in the developments needed.

The final general question that emerges from this examination of coordination is how we know that coordination has been achieved. The study of public administration has not invested as much in developing quantitative measures of the attributes (Peters 1988) we study as have other areas of political science, and although we certainly know coordination when we see it,[1] measuring that coordination in other than a qualitative sense is at present difficult if not impossible. The research presented here is certainly consistent with that qualitative tradition, but from the evidence gathered here we may be able to begin thinking about how to address the difficult, but not impossible, problem of measuring success in coordination.

These four issues will frame the conclusion to this study of coordination in the public sector. The principal focus of the concluding chapter will be on what we have learned and the possible limits to the benefits to coordination. All four of the questions, however, will be used to attempt to provide a more complete picture from a set of case studies that in some ways may appear quite disparate and to some extent incommensurable.[2] For example, two of the cases developed here represent almost pure examples of attempts at coordination, while one (the Finnish case) is an attempt to create a more strategic sense for government, while the Open Method of Coordination (OMC) in the European Union may decentralize decision making even further. Each of the four provides some insights and together they can provide the basis for understanding what happens when governments attempt to get organizations to cooperate.

Coordination is important, but it is not always the solution, or even a help, in solving difficult management problems. But when is it possibly even a barrier to achieving desired ends through public policy? The case studies have presented some answers to those questions, or perhaps only inklings of answers, but there are also some more fundamental points from the literature on public management that must be considered when thinking about the limits to coordination.

The Rationality of Redundancy

One reason that we may not want to coordinate programs in the public sector is that there often is, as Martin Landau (1969) has argued so persuasively, substantial rationality in redundancy for some of the functions performed in government. Many of the examples that can illustrate this point come from national security, and by extension now are relevant for Homeland Security. Indeed, the multiple intelligence sources that have been derided so much in the examination of the events leading up to 9/11 might have been an advantage if the organizations had been more cooperative. The multiple actors using multiple methods in different arenas should have provided the greatest probability of detecting the threat and thus being able to counteract it than a single coordinated effort relying on a more limited number of sources.

The argument for redundancy is based primarily on the collection and processing of information, especially when that management of information is done within organizations. There is more than a little literature pointing out that organizations are not particularly good at using information (Wilensky 1967; Stinchcombe 1990). There are typically distortions—both purposive and random—in information as it flows through hierarchies, and the capacity to link to the environment effectively is often compromised. Therefore, having multiple channels, and perhaps multiple types of distortion, will improve the quality of decisions.

Further, the specialization inherent in most organizational settings means that each organization is likely to be gathering information on a limited number of subjects and with a limited number of detection methods (Rosacker and Olson 2008). Having a single organization responsible for detection of threats, for example, may mean that not only could that source of information fail at any one time (radars going down, for example) but even when working as well as possible, it might still not be able to detect all the relevant threats, or collect all the relevant information. Thus, the coordination solution of a single organization and a single methodology for detection may not be the most effective.

Although much of the logic of redundancy in the public sector applies to detection of threats and is most relevant to the defense sector, the same logic applies to other programs in the public sector. The analogy for governments coping with crime is rather obvious, especially when government must confront organized crime such as drug cartels. Likewise, multiple channels of detection and service provision in social policy may be able to locate and serve a wider variety of the socially excluded than can more linear, integrated models of service provision.[3] Even the case mentioned in Chapter 2 (page 37) of alternative approaches to antitrust policy may enable government to address a wider variety of anticompetitive behaviors than would any one definition of the problem, and a single organization involved in the policy area.

Although policy analysts, critics of the public sector, and many actors within government itself (especially performance-based auditing agencies such as USGAO[4]) frequently emphasize the inefficiencies of redundancy in the public sector, participants in these processes may not find them such a problem. For example, a study of local law enforcement officers (Delone 2009) found that many of these officers actually liked the duplication of services across local governments and with the state police. This redundancy provided them extra security and capacity to respond more effectively to problems in their communities.

Jonathan Bendor (1985) moves the argument on behalf of redundancy from the detection of problems to the production of services. His arguments are in essence the same as those of the market economists arguing against monopoly. That strand of thinking had been applied by Niskanen (1971) to argue for creating greater competition in government, and Bendor proceeds to extend the argument to the more general proposition that competition and some redundant provision will enhance the quality of services in a variety of public settings. While the analyst coming from the public administration tradition may question some of the economic and market assumptions underlying this approach, the evidence that Bendor presents from local governments in the United States does make a strong case on behalf of competition and the reduction of monopoly.

Thus, redundancy, duplication, and apparent waste may not really be wasteful, but paradoxically may actually enhance efficiency. Governments therefore have to make decisions about which of their functions are sufficiently important to be worth the creation of redundancy and therefore have an enhanced probability of not failing totally. The National Aeronautics and Space Administration (NASA) has been famous for the levels of redundancy that it builds into its systems, but several disasters have made it evident that even double and triple protections do not always ensure success. The more extreme argument would be that *most* public services would be better provided were there some redundancy, with agencies having to compete for clients and budgets rather than enjoying the benefits of monopoly.[5] Even if one does not accept market arguments as the most appropriate way to address public problems, creating alternative conceptions of how best to address problems may provide better ways of solving the problem.

Specialization and Autonomy

Designing public administration reflects a tension between two important drives, much as Herbert Simon discussed the tendency of organizational analysis to focus on one end or the other of fundamental dichotomies. One of the more important of these dichotomies is specialization and coordination. The fundamental premise of this book, and of a good deal of contemporary activity in the public sector over recent years, has been that most governments have gone too far toward the specialization end of that dimension, and there is a need to accentuate the coordination end of the dimension more. That said, there is a good deal to be said for the virtues of specialization and permitting public organizations to become expert in a limited range of policy issues.

Our earlier book on specialization and coordination (Bouckaert, Peters, and Verhoest 2010) demonstrated the continuing struggles of governments to find some balance between the virtues of coordination and the virtues of specialization. In this sample of advanced democracies, all the governments were engaged in continuing reforms attempting to find the correct mixture of these two important aspects of governing. None of the seven countries was able to achieve an enduring equilibrium as both politics and external circumstances dictated additional movements along this dimension of organization.

The value of specialization should be evident to anyone who has worked within an organization, public or private. Whether that specialization is in the form of ministries concentrating attention on particular policy issues or is in the form of organizations focusing on accounting, procurement, or other technical processes, organizing around specializations is logical and remains the foundation for structuring the public sector. Similarly, specialization remains important in recruiting individuals to the civil service in many countries, with the dichotomy of specialists versus generalists continuing to be important in understanding how public personnel systems function (Scott 1988).

As well as being structured around the specifics of policy, some public sector organizations appear to be more effective if they are granted a good deal of autonomy. Autonomy has been one of the tenets of the NPM, but even before those ideas became popular some organizations had been granted autonomy, especially organizations responsible for economic regulation (Bernstein 1955; Thatcher 2002). But although the autonomy of regulators is also in many ways a virtue, it can generate the same overlap, duplication, and inconsistency identified in other cases of limited coordination (Aubin and Verhoest 2014). Again, there is a need to balance competing virtues in public administration, with independence of regulators being traded off against policy integration in economic and consumer protection policies.

Uncertainty

The above discussion of the possible utility of redundant channels of communication also implies the importance of uncertainty as a premise for the design of public policies. Although the political process often demands that there be a sense of certainty about the causes of public problems and the efficacy of the proposed solutions, in reality much of what government does is done without very sure understanding of the root causes of problems or the probable consequences of choosing one solution or another. Therefore, although politicians and civil servants are unlikely to admit this, a good deal of policymaking is experimentation, using interventions in the economy and society without any certainty that those interventions will be effective (see Dunn 1998).[6]

Citizens certainly do not want to hear that government is experimenting upon them, so the experimental nature of public programs is not often discussed as explicitly as it might be, even among the policymakers. Richard Nelson (1967) provided one of the most important discussions of the inadequate knowledge base of many programs and the trial-and-error decision making that may be involved in public policy. Nelson contrasted NASA putting a man on the moon with the difficulties associated with "solving" the problems of poverty and social exclusion in the American ghetto. While the moon landing was dramatic, and required extremely good engineering, the scientists and technicians involved were for the most part working with well-established theories and technologies. In contrast, designing programs for ameliorating or alleviating social problems, and especially the problems of the underclass in American society, required an understanding of social dynamics that did not then exist.

That necessary information base for addressing social problems does not as yet exist (see O'Connor 2001).[7] Therefore, to design good social programs continues to require a good deal of experimentation, with trial-and-error learning. In such a setting excessive coordination might imply that there was a clear direction for policy that had been agreed upon and should be followed, a choice of policy styles that would be clearly false. Rather, the existing regime following adoption of the "workfare" laws during the Clinton administration allows the states substantial latitude to experiment with alternatives, albeit within the general framework of the law (Soss 2000). The states have again become policy laboratories and if the mechanisms in place for learning and sharing are effective then there is a better opportunity for developing workable programs than if there were premature closure of the options for policy being considered.

Uncertain Futures

If we frame this discussion of uncertainty in terms of the ideas in Chapter 1, the movement toward a single agreed-on set of goals and programs might be seen as "holistic governance" (6 et al. 2002). This style of governing has been presented as a desirable end point for systems of governing but in reality may institutionalize poor, or at least suboptimal, programs. That is, negotiating toward some agreement on goals may well get individual governments into the same "joint decision trap" that Fritz Scharpf (1988) has described for intergovernmental relations. The desire, or necessity, to negotiate toward common, agreed-on goals among a set of organizations may produce government by the lowest common denominator, and hence may miss opportunities to provide higher-quality programs that less collaborative solutions might produce.

The experiences of the Federal Emergency Management Agency (FEMA) in the aftermath of Hurricane Katrina helps to make this point. This agency had made good progress in developing a capacity to cope with disasters, whether natural or made by humans. After 9/11, FEMA lost its independent status and was made a part of the Department of Homeland Security (see Chapter 5). The evidence from the aftermath of the Katrina disaster is that the organization had lost a good deal of its focus on the more probable events, such as hurricanes, in reaction to the national concerns over terrorism. The evidence emerging after this hurricane was that although every police officer in Wyoming has a protective suit against chemical attacks, the capacity to cope with natural disasters has been assigned lesser importance. This coordination from above and attempts to create a common approach to policy has diminished organizational flexibility.

The desirability of adopting the highly coordinated, holistic approach to governing is diminished given the uncertainty that all governments face about the future states of the world with which they necessarily have to cope. The issues that are emerging for government now—wicked problems such as climate change, water, food, etc.—involve complex interactions among physical variables and political forces (Duit and Galaz 2008). In contrast to more linear policies such as pensions or transportation, the uncertain futures in these areas of wicked problems require greater flexibility and also may require avoiding premature closure in some highly integrated policy framework.

MANAGING INNOVATION AND CREATIVITY

One of the first limitations on coordination arises when governments manage innovative activities and attempt to marshal creative people to achieve public purposes. The increasing importance of science and technology in modern society has made these scientific activities (including the social sciences) more important for the success of government (Bijker, Bal, and Hendriks 2009). The problem may be that the usual hierarchical models for managing these organizations do not work as well as for scientific activity as they may for other types of organizations and other types of employees. In particular, scientific and professional workers are less likely to accept controls over their behaviors, even those that are intended to make their activities more in line with the policy priorities of government. Among the scientific community the fear of an official science or official arts would be likened to controls over science in Stalinist Russia (Sofer 1994).

In addition to the general problems of management, attempts to coordinate the activities in which these types of workers are engaged may not be the best strategy for achieving the goals of improved research productivity. This simple truth about managing research was perhaps best illustrated by the "War on Cancer" during the Nixon administration in the United States (Rettig 2005). The president was for various reasons determined to find a cure for cancer during his administration and attempted to launch an all-out effort to find that cure. He was in the end dissuaded by biomedical professionals from pursuing that course, given that basic science could not be rushed or coordinated and that the best thing that could be done would be to continue to fund slow, patient research.

The pressure for the "War" did lead to increased funding for cancer research but not the linear, coordinated effort that some nonscientists wanted (see Johnson 2003). This does not mean, however, that this approach to scientific management will necessarily fail. The obvious counterexample is the Manhattan Project, which created the atomic bomb during World War II (Hughes 2002). The analogy with the Manhattan Project may not, however, work for policy problems that are not as clearly structured as was understanding and then utilizing atomic energy (Yang and Oppenheimer 2007).[8]

More recently, a conflict has arisen between the Department of Homeland Security (DHS) and the Department of Energy (DOE) over the management of research in the DOE national laboratories (USGAO 2004b). The DHS has immediate, practicality-oriented demands for research from the DOE's labs, while the latter wants to maintain its longstanding emphasis on basic research. Despite contracting arrangements, this fundamental difference in conceptions of the role of these laboratories continues, with the DOE continuing to argue about the difficulties, and the undesirability, of managing and coordinating some of these best scientists in the world.

Professionals and scientists who are working in public organizations are in roles that may span conventional boundaries. On the one hand, these individuals must retain their strong commitment to their scientific careers and practices, must retain that manner of working that involves independence and open exchange of ideas. On the other hand they are members of organizations that have public duties and public accountability (see Remington 1988). The competing pressures on the behavior of these employees makes it difficult for the public sector to manage them effectively and also may make them more difficult to coordinate. Many coordination programs attempt to impose those public responsibilities on the employees, and to involve them in public service in a way that may undermine their ability to conform to usual standards of professional conduct.

The question of managing creativity is not just a question of managing the individuals but is also a more general question about how to promote greater creativity in organizations such as laboratories and universities that are inherently involved with creative enterprises. Almost by definition creativity is difficult to manage and to coordinate, and the notion of coordinating creativity is oxymoronic. A number of studies of science have indicated that while "normal science" is coordinated and follows well-trodden paths, more important innovations tend to come about through less programmed and less predictable processes. Further, even when dealing with normal science, it is generally difficult to predict and to coordinate the most fruitful avenues for continuing research.

THE NEED FOR DIVERSITY

The typical rational approach to policy is that uniformity is a virtue, so that vertical coordination of programs across all areas of a political system is often considered a virtue in making policy. This logic is especially manifest in unitary political systems, but even in federal regimes, or quasi-governmental systems such as the European Union, there may be tendencies to advocate uniform solutions to policy problems and stress coordination solutions to the perceived problem of divergences. Even with the rather "soft" form of coordination implied in the OMC (see Chapter 5) there is the presumption that uniformity is desirable.

That presumption concerning the virtues of uniformity may not be justifiable in the reality of many cases. For example, part of the logic of federalism is to permit the subnational units to make some of their own decisions about policy and to have alternative solutions to policy problems (see Tillin 2007). Justice Louis Brandeis once famously described the states as the "laboratories of democracy" (*New State Ice Co. v. Liebmann*; see also Greve 2001), meaning that the opportunities for adopting different policies in the various states permits governments to try out alternative means of solving policy problems without having to commit to a single solution in advance. This logic, of course, mirrors that of coping with uncertainty through experimentation discussed above.

The uses of diversity may, however, extend beyond being a means for coping with problems of uncertainty. In any political or administrative system of any size there may be real differences among the units that make a single solution less viable or less desirable. For example, adopting the single European currency means that a common, coordinated monetary policy is being applied by all members of that aspect of the European Union's overall economic package.[9] There are, however, significant economic differences among the members of the Euro Zone—at this writing Spain, Greece, and Italy have high levels of unemployment (12 percent or over) while others such as Germany and Finland have strong economies. In this case what is appropriate monetary policy for one may not be appropriate for the others. The European Central Bank appears to have a bias toward controlling inflation, rather than stimulating growth, so that the less buoyant economies may not be well served by this version of coordination in economic policy.

Individual organizations are themselves diverse, and many government organizations perform multiple tasks. An emphasis on performing a single task, driven by the need for coordination with other organizations, may divert any agency in government from fulfilling its range of obligations. For example, the emphasis on terrorism has the potential of diverting the Federal Bureau of Investigation from its other, and perhaps dominant, function of domestic law enforcement. The evidence from the first few years of its working with the Department of Homeland Security is not conclusive, although some enforcement activities of the FBI do appear to have been weakened (USGAO 2004d). Likewise, to the extent that an agricultural organization becomes heavily concerned with food safety because of some crisis, it may divert its attention from other important aspects of farm policy that support agriculture rather than regulate it (Smith 2004).

PRIVACY AND CIVIL LIBERTIES

At least one of the cases here illustrates the need to think about the potential that successful policy coordination has for the abuse of individual rights within a liberal democratic state. In particular, the Victoria Climbié case points out that attempts to coordinate information about clients may produce data banks that would invade the privacy of the children in question and perhaps even more that of their parents. Almost all citizens would want to protect these potential victims from abuse, but many citizens would also ask what the price might be for that protection. Likewise, the follow-up to the coordination failures surrounding the events of 9/11 in the United States indicates that governments may attempt to impinge on civil liberties and coordinate information collection in the name of coordination (and anti-terrorism)[10] and again that these efforts may be well meaning but may have important negative side effects—they may be, in Sieber's (1980; see also Hood and Peters 2004) terms, "fatal remedies."

Contemporary governments face a set of conflicting demands when considering how to collect and collate information. On the one hand governments require large quantities of information in order to govern effectively. The public policy cases we have presented here all depend to some extent on the capacity of governments to collect, process, and coordinate information from multiple sources. Further, if governments can, for example, put together information about tax payments, income, and expenditures of citizens, they may have a better chance of identifying and correcting tax evasion that costs them millions of dollars each year. Likewise, if governments can effectively put together information concerning social payments, income, and taxation they may be able to reduce levels of fraud in social welfare.

In some countries there are specific legal or even constitutional restrictions against collecting and collating information about citizens. In Germany, for example, there are strong protections against putting together information about individual citizens from multiple sources and that prevent government organizations from sharing information (Bamberger and Mulligan 2013). These protections have been in place in the United States also, but, as noted, have been eroded to some extent as a result of fears about terrorism; the Patriot Act, for example, permits collecting and collating information that previously had been private or had been kept separate. The fear of many civil liberties groups is that if governments can assemble information and coordinate their actions then individual liberties will be severely undermined. As in so many other areas of public policy there is a definite trade-off between coordinating information gathering and protecting individual civil liberties.

The issue of sharing information for coordination becomes even more difficult when the private sector becomes involved. For example, in order to provide a more coordinated and efficient system for identifying potential terrorists attempting to get on airplanes in the United States, the Transportation Security Administration had proposed supplementing its information on travelers with private databases such as employment records, credit reports, and the like. This plan was opposed vigorously by civil liberties organizations, which considered it to concentrate entirely too much personal information in the hands of one government agency and to be the source of potential abuse by government.

CONTROL AND INTERNAL REGULATION

Attempting to coordinate and centralize in the public sector may produce some efficiencies in service provision by eliminating duplication, but it also eliminates the possibilities for using several important forms of control over public organizations. We usually think of the internal regulation of the public sector being made primarily through hierarchy, with each level of an organization exercising control over the next subordinate level, working up and down the hierarchy. Competition and mutualism are, however, significant alternatives to hierarchy (Hood et al. 2004) and can be a more efficient and effective means for ensuring that members of public organizations perform as expected by the remainder of the public sector. These controls are perhaps most effective with individual organizations and individual civil servants, but they may also have some more general applicability.

Competition and mutualism depend upon there being multiple organizations either providing the same services or complementary services and upon individuals having some means of assessing the work of their peers in government. For example, the increased use of "naming and shaming" to place pressure on failing organizations in government, and using organizational report cards (Weimer and Gormley 1999), are means of pitting organizations against each other and using that competition to spur them on to improved performance. That technique is hardly new, however, and Franklin Roosevelt developed multiple organizations to deliver his New Deal programs, allowing them to compete and then choosing the best-performing organization to continue.[11] Likewise, the higher civil service often functions as an important network of professionals who observe each other's behaviors and assess how well the individual civil servants are performing (see Hood et al. 2004).

The ideas guiding the NPM, now implemented in most public sectors around the world, have produced another justification for competition and lower levels of coordination than governments have typically considered desirable (Maor 1999). The market logic behind much NPM thinking has stressed the use of competition as a mechanism for enhancing efficiency and forcing organizations in the public sector to reveal more about the true costs of production of their services. In the NPM critique of traditional bureaucracy the monopoly held by public sector organizations enabled them to mask costs and to extract excessive funds from their sponsors—the legislature (Niskanen 1971). Therefore, creating redundancy, and thereby perhaps reducing levels of coordination, may in fact *enhance* the efficiency of public organizations when compared to the presumed target of coordinators as a single organization providing a single service. This logic is, of course, similar to those made by advocates of redundant solutions to public problems (see also Landau 1969; Bendor 1985).[12]

The breakdown of discipline and internal controls in the Abu Ghraib prison during the Iraq War may be taken as one example of the possible uses of competition in controlling behavior, even in such extreme circumstances. One of the reasons cited for the development, and persistence, of the abuse of prisoners within the prison was that control over the prison was changed in the course of war, and had become unified in one organization—an Army Reserve Military Police Battalion. Previously that one organization had had to share responsibility with other army units and the Central Intelligence Agency, and the multiple organizations had to some extent served as checks on one another. Even if not in direct competition for the control of the prison, having more than one organization watching each other may have constituted a check on their behavior.[13]

POLITICS

To this point I have been discussing coordination largely from the perspective of policy and administration, but any activity that is so central to the actions of government is fundamentally political, and if that political dimension is neglected then significant misjudgments are possible. In principle coordination decisions should be Pareto-optimal, with the outcomes making all the participants better off, or at least no worse off. In reality few decisions in the public sector meet that rather rigorous requirement, and most instead do involve making decisions among competing uses of resources, or alternative conceptualizations of policy priorities. As Harold Seidman (1998, 227) wrote, "Coordination is rarely neutral ... inevitably it advances some interests at the expense of others."

Although coordination may always be an administrative good, and a positive outcome for policy analysis, in political terms it is often not so positive. Political leaders, especially in coalition governments, may find that coordination requires to some extent weakening a commitment to their own programs and their own clients and therefore may be a poor political choice for those leaders. As we have already noted, good policy coordination may not be as visible to the public as more direct benefits, so efforts to coordinate that tamper with existing programs may be suboptimal choices for a minister or a prime minister. Citizens do recognize poor coordination when they have to go from one office to another in order to deal with a seemingly simple personal issue, but their recognition of the benefits of effective coordination may not be as strong.[14]

If indeed political leaders want to achieve greater policy coordination then, paradoxically, the best way of reaching that goal may be not to politicize the issue, or at least not to do so more than it inevitably must be politicized. Above (Chapter 3), we spent a great deal of space discussing the role of hierarchical leadership from political leaders in the process of coordination, and indeed most of the methods for coordinating policy emphasized the need for political leadership. Those methods are important, but may arise once the issues have already become stated and the process has become politicized. If, as in the collaborative and to some extent the network approach, coordination can be made more of a natural outcome of the interaction of individuals than a political stratagem, then it is more likely to be successful.

To produce political action for coordination, some form of political mobilization will be required. The fundamental political task is to build coalitions that are capable of surpassing the identifiable political interests of the individual organizations and create a majority that will emphasize coordination over the virtues of maintaining the individual programs. The socially excluded are one group requiring this type of political mobilization, but the potential beneficiaries of enhanced coordination of social programs often have limited political "clout," and hence political leaders may not be interested in investing political capital to address this problem. That problem can be overcome in part by appealing more to middle-class values of efficiency and cost reduction in order to justify the investment in coordinated service provision.

A political perspective on coordination emphasizes the role of political entrepreneurs in working across organizations and policy areas. The role of these entrepreneurs will make coordination more effective but it may also increase the bias in the direction of the coordinated policy. Those policy entrepreneurs will be performing a public service in coordinating policies, but they also will be promoting their own conceptions of good policy in the domains that they are attempting to coordinate. And the most successful of these entrepreneurs may be using the coordination process as a means of developing new, or at least revised, versions of policy.[15]

ACCOUNTABILITY

Perhaps the most important reason for questioning the efficacy of coordination is accountability. Accountability is one of the most commonly discussed terms in the study of public administration, but the frequency with which it is used should not be taken to mean that this concern is trite or insignificant (Gregory 2012). Indeed, much of the reason for the amount of ink spilled on the issue of accountability of public administration is that it is such a crucial concern in a democratic political system. This is true for the continuing concerns of academic analysts (see Thomas 2012) with accountability, but it is also true for practitioners in government, given that they are responsible for what happens to citizens and their money. Those political officials must therefore find mechanisms for identifying responsibility and tracking the use of resources.

Accountability is often difficult to enforce, even in simple public programs. To be able to enforce accountability requires that the institutions or individuals overseeing the actions of other individuals or organizations within the public sector be able to track activities and the use of public funds. As government becomes more complex, whether because of the increased use of contractors and not-for-profit organizations to provide public services, or because of the use of more complex instruments, those difficulties in tracking responsibility become all the more acute (Considine 2002;

Skelcher 2004). Public programs may be delivered by several tiers of organizations, linked together through contracts, negotiated agreements of other types, or simply through long relationships and trust. Whether things are going well or poorly in such a policy area, it will be difficult to understand the reasons for the outcomes.

The complexity associated with many schemes for coordination may make it even more difficult to assign responsibility. As already noted, attempts in the United Kingdom and other countries to move resources into comprehensive programs in urban areas have met difficulties or been terminated because of the virtual impossibility of central agencies being able to follow lines of financial or personal responsibility. Similarly, when multiple lines of authority are merged or intended to work in close collaboration sharing facilities and funds, then the central controllers are likely to become uncomfortable. When coordination strategies involve extensive devolution to individual actors, e.g., permitting "street-level bureaucrats" to make decisions about assembling packages of benefits for clients, those central agencies may become even more nervous (Smith 2012).

In fairness, three of the four cases presented in this book have developed methods of coordination that may to some extent enhance accountability for the outcomes of programs. The American case of homeland security places a great deal of the accountability for domestic security in that department and its secretary.[16] If things go badly, there is little doubt that the secretary of Homeland Security will be among the first individuals at whom the fingers will be pointed. In the case of Hurricane Katrina the director of the Federal Emergency Management Agency, Michael Brown, was fired after the terrible performance of the agency.

Also, in the British case, the creation of the various "czars" for children within the constituent countries of the United Kingdom places much of the responsibility for the safety of children on the shoulders of those officials and their staff. That having been said, however, the relative obscurity of these officials compared with cabinet ministers (even those of the devolved governments) and the long history of parliamentary accountability of ministers in Britain may make accountability difficult to enforce with respect to these officials. The Finnish case is somewhat more ambiguous, with the four ministers and the four civil servants immediately responsible for these programs sharing direct accountability for the outcomes but all the ministers of the organizations involved maintaining some crucial aspects of accountability.[17] Further, the programs themselves were relatively amorphous, so that identifying program failures may have been difficult.

The fourth case demonstrates a rather extreme case of the diffusion of responsibility for outcomes in a policy area. The OMC is rather indeterminate and has no real center at which blame or praise can be directed. While the commission may in the end be responsible for policy in the EU, the method chosen as a central feature of an important policy area such as employment and economic growth diffuses a good deal of responsibility to the members. This strategy may, however, be a conscious plan for handing the poisoned chalice to the member countries. Given the difficulties in many countries—France and Germany as the clearest examples—it may be a good organizational strategy to avoid direct responsibility for this policy area.

WHAT HAVE WE LEARNED?

The four case studies included here are, of course, only a very small sample of the cases of coordination that governments encounter every day. Further, they were selected on a purposive basis to illustrate something about various approaches to coordination, or the impact of different types of policy issues, on the capacity of governments to coordinate. Even this small and selective sample does, however, lead to some conclusions about the capacity to coordinate. These conclusions are, of course, extremely tentative, but they do appear to be borne out in other writings on coordination in the public sector.

Leadership Is Important

The first observation from these stories about coordination is that leadership is important. While the naive observer of government might expect all public officials to have an interest in providing citizens with more coherent public services, the reality may not be so benign. For one or all of the reasons already discussed (see Chapter 1), political and administrative actors may resist coordination rather than be willing participants in creating more coherent services. Thus, the well-meaning official seeking to produce better coordination may need some help in thinking through how to produce that improved service.

One of the most important elements of creating coordination appears to be effective leadership, whether that comes from the political or the administrative officials in the public sector. Whether a leader depends upon hierarchy or upon more normative arguments (collaboration, networking) to produce the changes in behavior, it does seem that leaders are required. For example, in the Finnish case, the respondents noticed differences among the four policy programs based at least in part on the capacity of the individuals in charge (both the ministers and the civil servants) to influence the behavior of the other participants. Likewise, some critics of Homeland Security in the United States (Wechsler 2002) have argued that there has not been sufficient leadership in the organization to overcome the inherent administrative difficulties of bringing together so many organizations with such a range of missions and internal administrative cultures.

The prior question in the study of creating coordination, however, may be how leaders can become motivated to make the needed coherence central to their definition of their office tasks. As already noted, an increasing number of presidents and prime ministers may see the need for greater coordination and strategic management from the center, but they cannot do everything (see Peters 2004a). To be successful the individuals at the top of government will have to motivate the second or third or even lower tiers of government to provide that necessary direction to the system of governing. The leaders for coordination may be located far down in the hierarchy and indeed may be at the very bottom of the organizations where collaboration and networking are the dominant models employed to produce the needed coordination.

Structure May Be Necessary but Not Sufficient

The usual reaction to problems of coordination and coherence in the public sector is to create new structures charged with imposing some form of control over other organizations and individuals responsible for delivering public services. All the cases I have presented here have some structural or organizational element in the response of the public sector to the problem of coordination. This attempt at a solution was clearest in the case of the Department of Homeland Security in the United States, but even the more process-based format found in Finland and in the OMC have some structural elements. While other, less tangible means of producing cooperation among actors may be fruitful, in most instances actors in the public sector will attempt to institutionalize the cooperation through some form of structure.

Although structure is a common remedy for the problems of coordination, the evidence amassed here demonstrates that it is only part of the solution. The Department of Homeland Security is a case in which structure was assumed to be the answer for the need to provide enhanced security to the American public. This solution was based in part on the perception that a good deal of the failure to provide effective security prior to the attacks on New York and Washington was poor coordination and that poor coordination had been in large part structural in its origins. That structural solution, as already noted, may have exacerbated the difficulties in providing services rather than improving those services.

Ideas Are Important

I have already argued that leadership is important in coordination and that structure also plays a significant role, but there is a third element that is important for coordination, and that is the role of ideas. Attempting to govern through the use of authority, and structural manifestations of authority, may be possible, but it may also be expensive, involving a good deal of time and effort in order to gain compliance. On the other hand, gaining compliance on a normative basis is less expensive once the participants in the political process are convinced that one set of ideas is the most appropriate means of addressing particular policy problems. Convincing other actors that one's own ideas are correct is difficult, given that the existing ideas of that individual and/or organization are often deeply entrenched and may have been successful in the past. In government those ideas are also supported by an organization and perhaps also by professional training and "epistemic communities." Still, ideas do have a major role in policy change (Hall 1986; Béland and Cox 2011) and if they are developed appropriately they can be used to create common policy approaches and to motivate cooperation among actors.

The four cases I have developed above show varying levels of impacts of ideas, but all have some element of one actor attempting to convince others about the best conceptualization of a policy problem and of solutions. The clearest case is the OMC in the EU, in which the diffusion of ideas among countries and the use of "best practice" are the means to create coherence in social and employment policy among the members of the EU. While the European Commission emphasizes the autonomy of the actors involved in the process of diffusion, there is, however, some role of authority as well as spontaneous learning. The creation of the Department of Homeland Security represents another use of an idea, although in this case it is the rather simplistic use of the idea of promoting security in the face of a perceived terrorist threat. Similarly, the idea of protecting children is hardly controversial or an innovation, but still it can be used to motivate the participants in the process of providing services for those children.

From a more theoretical perspective, promoting coordination through the use of ideas reflects much of the thinking of historical institutionalism. The persistence of patterns of making and implementing policy that new ideas about coordination and coherence must overcome is very much in the pattern of "path dependency" (see Thelen 2004). Further, these earlier ideas often have been successful, and the positive feedback from those successes has reinforced them (Pierson 2000). The difficulty for the would-be coordinator is to find a new idea sufficiently powerful (like homeland security in the context of the post-9/11 world) to move individuals and organizations off the well-trodden path and to create a "punctuation" in the equilibrium characterizing the policy.

Although ideas may have some importance and some capacity in their own right to produce policy change, and perhaps improved policy coordination, those ideas may need policy entrepreneurs (Kingdon 2003) to make them operational. Indeed, political actors may have to create the ideas needed to make coordination effective. This process of "framing" (Payan 2006) is usually discussed in reference to initial policy formulation, but is equally relevant for coordination. Again, to explain behavior, and success and failure, in the area of policy coordination we need to have some sense of agency. Who is to take responsibility for coordination, and for putting ideas into operation? The first variable I discussed in this catalog was leadership, and that variable comes into play here, with good ideas needing leadership, just as leaders without good ideas may have little reason (or capacity) to lead. That need for ideas is at least as true for collections of organizations that are being coordinated as it is for any individual organization (Huxham and Vangen 2003).

Coordination Is Not Always Politically Important

Another of the lessons that can be extracted from the cases is that coordination is not always politically important. This lesson may be the "flip side" of the lesson above about leadership; if the important political leaders of the society are not willing to invest in creating coordination and coherence then it is not likely to happen. There should be ample evidence by this point that coordination does not come naturally to most organizations in the public sector, so political commitment is required.

This statement about political indifference to coordination may appear somewhat paradoxical, however. The cases here all involve some political investment, and in at least one of the cases (Finland) a great deal of involvement of the very top of the political pyramid. That commitment, however, is not forthcoming, and political leaders may want to avoid responsibility for coordination, and perhaps especially for coordination failures. For example, although the Blair government has made a good deal out of its commitment to "joined-up government," in practice some of the strategies discussed in Chapter 5 indicate that government has been distancing itself from the coordination process.

In many settings coordination will not only not be a political priority, it may be a political liability. If there are strong ministries linked to powerful interest groups and supported by a public bureaucracy that is itself recruited around those departments, then coordination is not likely to be a high political priority. Attempting to produce coordination will step on so many toes that unless a prime minister, or a central agency, is willing to use political capital to engage in a political battle with those interests the other ministers will not be willing to spend much time or energy in coordination. In that setting coordination may have to occur at the bottom of government rather than at the top if it is to occur at all.

Coordination May Be Only the Beginning

Coordination, especially the negative coordination that is the most common outcome of political processes, is only the beginning of the needs to make governments perform in a more coherent manner. Government programs may be designed or managed in a manner that prevents them from conflicting with one another, but that does not prevent the extra value added that may be attainable through more "holistic" or coherent means (6 et al. 2002). Therefore, the usual means of creating coordination, especially the commonly used hierarchical methods, may only be a beginning in searching for the mechanisms needed for a more coherent and effective governance. The collaborative approach that depends upon changing ideas and creating a common understanding of the policy issues may, however, be able to create more strategic governance.

Numerous governments have begun to address this need for a more coherent style of governing. The example from Finland (Chapter 5) represents some movement toward such a coordinated and coherent approach. Other governments are beginning to make efforts toward more strategic approaches to governing. More than a decade ago the New Zealand government began to think in terms of strategic planning for government and finding ways of integrating the goals of individual ministries into those more comprehensive goals. The "Whole of Government" program adopted in Australia (Australian Public Service Commission 2005; Halligan 2006) is somewhat less clear on grand strategies for government but does develop some ideas on how the public sector should bring together the range of programs that it administers into a more comprehensive whole.

Several of the cases developed above are now moving toward more strategic and integrated approaches to policy. For example, although there has been a good deal of effort already in developing cooperative arrangements, policies for supporting children in the United Kingdom may be moving toward even higher levels of coordination. For example, in Wales the Welsh Assembly, the Department for Education and Skills, and the Children's Commissioner are involved in creating an "integrated children's system" to monitor the welfare of the children (DfES 2005b). Also, in the United States, the Department of Homeland Security has been attempting to develop a more comprehensive strategy for national security that can address the overall needs of the country for internal and external security (Department of Homeland Security 2007). That strategic plan has been augmented by the National Security Strategy adopted in 2010 with a "whole of government" approach (Garamone 2010). The policy integration produced through Human Resources and Skills Development Canada is now being expanded through a "Social Union." The complexity of that task is making developing that strategy difficult, but the need for such a comprehensive approach has been identified clearly.

Coordination as a Contingent Phenomenon

As might be expected in public administration or any other field in the social sciences, there is no single, dominant explanation for coordination and hence no strong theory on which to base practical advice for people charged with governing. The best we may be able to do is to develop a set of contingent statements about how to coordinate and even about whether to coordinate. There are in fact two nested questions that need to be addressed. The first is how much political and organizational capital to invest in coordination, and the second is how to invest those scarce resources. Although discussed separately, these questions are related, given that the availability of a method for coordination with a reasonable probability of success may influence the decision about whether to coordinate at all.

How Much to Invest in Coordination?

The first decision for an official, whether political or administrative, charged with managing a set of programs, or even an individual program, is how much to care about achieving better coordination. Most available evidence is that most decision makers answer this question rather easily with an answer such as "very little, thank you." These officials then proceed either to permit the organizations for which they are responsible to carry on with business as usual, or make a few rather tepid statements that may enhance levels of coordination and coherence and in fact do very little. From time to time political leaders (or at least their staffs) will invest heavily in coordination, e.g., Tony Blair in the United Kingdom and Lyndon Johnson with the Model Cities Program in the United States, but most political and administrative leaders find it more productive to invest in direct service delivery issues, and in specific programs, rather than in coordination.

The decision to make this investment in coordination is in essence a cost-benefit analysis, expressed to some degree in service outcomes for clients, and to some extent in political outcomes for the major decision makers. That is, what real benefits are created for the recipients of programs if a greater effort is made to coordinate programs and their delivery? In addition, some benefits may also be lost if there is greater coordination of programs, because the individual programs are not delivered as fully or effectively. Likewise, do politicians gain any significant approval from voters if they are successful in achieving greater policy coordination, or can administrative leaders gain any benefits in their budgetary and policy battles if they can demonstrate a real commitment to coordinating with other programs that might be providing similar or complementary benefits?

The issues raised in Chapter 1 to some extent help to provide the means for assessing the probable real benefits of coordination for the clients of programs. For example, coordinating complementary programs may produce more real benefits for clients than will coordinating programs that are essentially the same and thereby eliminate redundancy. Taxpayers may appreciate the tax savings created by the reduction of redundancy among programs, if they are able to identify them, but clients are more likely to notice and to appreciate more comprehensive services. On the other hand, eliminating redundant regulatory programs may provide substantial real benefits for businesses but be less visible to average taxpayers (and voters).

For the majority of coordination devices the political benefits will be relatively slight for the leaders who advocate the administrative changes required. Coordination often can reduce the costs of government and may improve the quality of services if the correct connections among organizations are made or the right sets of information are channeled to the administrators of programs. But for most citizens the focus of political attention tends to be on the particular program or programs that benefit them directly, and they are less likely to be concerned with the larger and more complex picture of government as a whole. Coordination is a public good that, by benefitting everyone to some extent, really benefits no one in particular and hence is of little political value.[18]

A second and related question for political leaders is how far to extend the attempts at coordination. The example of the Department of Homeland Security (Chapter 5) pointed out that although a massive government department was created, it still could not internalize all the coordination problems. Therefore, as well as the continuing internal problems of coordination, that department still has continuing interactions with a wide range of organizations, notably over twenty intelligence organizations. Likewise, in the case of the Finnish attempts to institutionalize a series of coordinating programs and procedures, there are still overlaps among those programs, and, in the words of one of the participants in the process, a need to coordinate the coordinators. Finding unambiguous criteria for whether to include a program in a single large organization or to force other forms of coordination appears impossible with contemporary levels of theoretical development, so that would-be coordinators must continue to rely on judgment, simple rules of thumb, and trial and error.

And in all these cases it is important to remember that coordination is expensive, and the benefits may accrue in the future, when the political official may be out of office. Therefore, the politician may have to make more difficult calculations about how much to invest in coordination than does the administrator. Administrative officials may have a longer time perspective and therefore be more willing to expend scarce resources on improving coordination. That coordination may also be more effective, as attempting to get organizations and individuals to work together around individual clients may be more achievable than attempting to overcome policy differences at the political level.

Choosing a Method of Coordination

Part of the purpose of examining the four cases developed above, and collecting less detailed information about a number of other cases of coordination, is to be able to develop some generalizations about this important aspect of policymaking. The four cases are themselves far from sufficient to test any budding theory of coordination, but they do serve one of the purposes that Harry Eckstein (1975) identified for case studies—they are important heuristics for beginning to build the generalizations we would need for such a generalized theory. That is, each of these cases can be used to illustrate a particular aspect of coordination, and the strengths and weaknesses of this style of bringing together divergent public programs into a more coherent whole. The success or failure of the approach is, of course, dependent upon the particular circumstances of the case—leaders, resources, political pressures, etc.—but each case can still be instructive and provide inklings about the generalities that underlie this area of inquiry.[19]

If I now return to the arguments presented at the beginning of this book, I was concerned with the relative abilities of different theoretical and analytic approaches to coordination to explain the outcomes observed in these four cases, as well as the numerous other cases of attempted coordination in the literature. However, we should not expect any one approach, or any one set of instruments for coordination, to be the solution for all the manifest problems that have been identified; those problems are too varied and too numerous for such a simple outcome. Rather, the selection of the instrument for coordination should be seen as a contingent phenomenon, with part of the logic of looking at multiple cases of government coordination programs being to attempt to identify what may work, and what may not.

Two forms of contingency are involved in examining alternative approaches to coordination in the public sector. One contingency is a political question of the most acceptable forms of intervention, given the constellation of political forces in the policy area, and perhaps more broadly in the political system as a whole. This is analogous to the arguments that some scholars have made about the use of policy instruments, with more coercive instruments being acceptable more readily in some cultures (see Woodside 1986 on Canada). Further, seemingly in all systems these command and control instruments have become less acceptable over time (Salamon, 2000; Heritier and Lehmkuhl 2008).

The other contingency is more administrative, and reflects the difficult analytic problem of matching types of policy solutions with the needs of the case in which they are being applied. How well can we characterize the problems confronting government and match those with solutions? Both of these contingencies are important for determining the ultimate success of a strategy of coordination, but unfortunately they may not covary. Solutions that are politically feasible may not be those that will produce the most desirable outcomes once they are implemented, and optimal strategies for achieving administrative ends may not be accepted by politicians or by social partners in the governing process.

The political contingencies involved in selecting a particular style of coordination are dependent upon a number of factors. For example, the selection of a network strategy depends upon the availability of network actors who can perform the tasks. It may not be sufficient to have networks in a few policy areas, but rather if the bottom-up logic for coordination implied by this approach is to be effective the networks must be present across the public sector.

As noted earlier (see Chapter 3), for the network logic to coordinate across policy areas, the members of the networks must be involved in cross-cutting structures that enables them to place political pressures on government from several different directions. Indeed, if network memberships are more narrowly defined, then they may simply reinforce the ministerial stovepipes in government, rather than providing a means of overcoming them.

The logic of the use of markets as a means of coordination depends perhaps more on cultural elements than it does on the existence of particular groups in the society. Certainly the ability to utilize contracting and other market instruments depends upon the availability of the institutional supports for such mechanisms, such as functioning market institutions, and a sense of the efficacy of internal contracting in the public sector (Cooper 2003). Markets are more acceptable forms of resource allocation in some societies than they are in others, so attempts to utilize the quasi-market devices described earlier may not work in those less market-friendly systems. That having been said, however, these market-based reforms have been adopted, seemingly with some success, in Scandinavian countries (Hansen 2011) that might have been expected to be less than receptive to such formats for making policy.

Given that hierarchy is inherent in almost all governing systems, if not all, this approach to achieving coordination should in general be acceptable in almost all political systems. For the hierarchical approach to be viable, however, we will have to be interested in the alternative hierarchical remedies that have been proposed and the relative utility of each in different settings. Two of the cases presented above use clearly hierarchical remedies to enhance coordination, while the Finnish remedy also has strong hierarchical elements. Why were these particular variants of hierarchy chosen, and what are the consequences of selecting them as opposed to others? These cases are all the more interesting given that the United States originally adopted a czar plan for Homeland Security but then adopted the more structural solution of combining numerous organizations into the single huge department.

Based on theories of organizations and institutions, and evidence from numerous attempts on the parts of governments to implement mechanisms for coordination, I can present some rudimentary hypotheses about the choice of one or another of these options. For example, the central hypothesis would be that the extent to which governments are functionally segmented may influence the extremity of the mechanisms that may be needed to overcome the institutional barriers in the administrative system (Egeberg 2012). For example, the functional segmentation in the US federal government is relatively high,[20] so there may need to be more extreme interventions to overcome the division among organizations. Thus, the full-scale reorganization appears to have made substantial sense in the case of building the Department of Homeland Security. Likewise, the Finnish government is described by all the participants as being very strongly divided internally, and hence the relatively weaker program for coordination, using largely procedural remedies, may not in the end be sufficient to overcome those barriers.[21]

In addition to the above argument, the nature of the internal structuring of government may also influence the type of response that is politically viable, and necessary, when confronting the need to coordinate. Again, the highly differentiated structure within the American federal bureaucracy, with the individual agencies having a legal status and direct political contacts with Congress, means that controlling those organizations will require employing stronger methods than might be needed in systems in which ministerial departments are more significant coordinating structures (Seidman 1998). In contrast, the relatively low level of internal structuring in many policy areas in the United Kingdom, even after the implementation of the Next Steps agencies in many of those policy areas, may allow a less powerful organizational principle, such as the czar, to be reasonably effective in improving coordination.[22]

The political milieu of government is also important for explaining the approaches to coordination. The single-party control of most Westminster systems is very different from the coalition government of Finland and the essentially "no-party" governance arrangements within the European Union (Hanley 2007). The absence of a single dominant party in government removes one potentially important source of policy coordination. A single party is capable of integrating many policy differences in cabinet by working within the party itself, although we should not assume too much. Many political parties are themselves coalitions of factions and individual aspirations so that the party may simply be a holding company for all of those alternative conceptions of policy. Just as creating the Department of Homeland Security moved the coordination problems into that one organization, so, too, does relying on the "catch-all parties" typical of Westminster systems place the coordination problems within the party.

Further, it may be fallacious to assume that the dominant party style of governing may indeed produce the most effective policy coordination. There may be political barriers with different ministries being headed by members of different political parties. That said, many multiparty systems also have a consensus style in governing that may create stability and even coordination across programs (Lijphart 2008). The coordination in consensus politics may be explained less by formal hierarchy within cabinet than by the continuing need to cooperate across many cycles of election and government formation.

Measuring Coordination

Finally, we should consider how we could enhance the scientific understanding of coordination and find means of providing usable measures of coordination. The four cases developed in the preceding chapter tended to use primarily qualitative evidence, yet we could make statements about the success and failure of governments across policy areas. I have already mentioned some indicators of coordination in the introductory chapters. For example, we can ask how many ministries or departments have something to do with a particular policy function, e.g., education. In most governments, the answer will be that more than one does, and often many play a role in this and other policy areas.[23] Likewise, we can identify the number of budget categories that address similar problems, but in different organizations, and to what extent those categories are directed toward the same clients (Dewar 2002).

This simple enumeration of the actors involved in policy areas, or of the budget lines, will almost certainly be insufficient to assess the real impact of poor coordination—as already noted in several places, redundancy actually can be beneficial for performing public tasks rather than a detriment. Therefore, we will need to identify some more robust mechanisms to assess the impact of coordination, and especially coordination failures, on clients. For example, what does a client have to do in order to receive the full range of benefits to which he or she is entitled?[24] Are these services "joined up," or are they still delivered through different organizations? And are the services in question merely administered together, or are their fundamental assumptions and objectives also integrated so that the services delivered really do create some coherence?

Also, to some extent, coordination may be the "dog that doesn't bark." Can we assume that coordination is proceeding adequately if there are no obvious policy failures, or if the public is not complaining about the problems created by inadequate coordination? For example, Americans appeared to assume that many of the problems in emergency responses made so evident by September 11, 2001, had been solved. They believed that, at least until the inadequate responses to Hurricane Katrina made it clear that the coordination problems in at least some dimensions of security still existed and almost appeared worse than they had been previously. Or are citizens so accustomed to inadequate coordination in public programs—the all-too-common trek from one office to another and then to another to obtain needed services—that they do not even bother to comment, much less complain? In short, many coordination problems are hidden until the issues become apparent when the systems in question are tested.

Another approach to measurement is to determine to what extent governments have used instruments designed to enhance coordination. Jennings and Ewalt (1998), in studying coordination of job training programs in the American states, identified several dozen instruments that were being used by at least one state to coordinate programs in this complex policy area. They simply enumerated the number of such instruments that each state used, and assumed that greater coordination occurred when there were more instruments in use. That assumption has some apparent validity, but still does very little to assess the extent to which those instruments were effective in altering behavior of the organizations involved in the policy area, nor does it assess the informal mechanisms for coordination that may be at least as important for success.

The study of telecommunications in several European countries (Aubin and Verhoest 2014) utilizes measures of coordination that are not dissimilar to the measurements used by Jennings and Ewalt, but it has added more dimensions of measurement. In addition to procedural measures this telecommunications research has examined media records to understand the conflicts that have occurred. Further, this study sought to measure the horizontal and vertical dimensions of coordination simultaneously, thus capturing the complexities of coordination with the European Union.

The above discussion of measuring coordination makes it abundantly clear that measurement, and the quantitative analysis that has been central to the contemporary social sciences, have a very long way to go in assessing this area of public life. Most of the measures that are now available are either indirect and/or involve an extensive amount of information about case-by-case outcomes. Neither of these answers to the measurement problem is entirely satisfactory if we are to move this important aspect of political and administrative behavior more in the mainstream of political analysis. We would like to be able to provide more quantitative and direct measures of this phenomenon, but those have been elusive. The search for those measures does need to be extended, however.

The Future for Coordination

This discussion has pointed to any number of barriers and difficulties in producing coordination. This discussion has also pointed out that coordination is an ageless problem in the public sector. All that is true, but perhaps policymakers need to begin to think even more seriously about developing capacities for coordination and coherence as the nature of policy problems continues to evolve. The major issues that will be confronting governments will be issues such as climate change, food, population, poverty, and the like. All these issues do not fit neatly into conventional policy domains and the associated organizations, and therefore almost inherently require coordination (see May, Jochim, and Pump 2010).

The planners Rittel and Webber (1973; see also Levin et al. 2010) argued that issues such as these, which they characterized as "wicked problems," are not amenable to the usual mechanisms for policymaking, given that not only was causation undetermined and complex but also the boundaries of these policies were undefined and therefore indefinite. In other words, coordination across the usual policy areas is almost inherent in addressing these policy issues.

Food policy represents an important example of problems of this type (Peters and Pierre 2014). Contemporary food policy is not just about the Ministry of Agriculture. As well as production, food policy also involves issues of consumption and attempts to control obesity even in middle-income countries such as Mexico (Malkin 2013). It also involves regulation, so that the food distributed and consumed is pure. Food policy will increasingly involve linkages with climate policy, both in terms of the likely effects of demands for biofuels make on food production, and the likely effects of climate change on the viability of certain crops in different geographical locations.

Not only does the nature of the issues likely to confront government appear to push governments toward greater concern with coordination, but the nature of politics also may be pushing in that same direction. After the decentralizing and deconcentrating trends associated with NPM, the increasing "presidentialization" of politics and increased attempts to govern from the center (Dahlström, Peters, and Pierre 2010) appear to be the dominant style for governing. And this type of more centralized decision making may be linked to the nature of the problems being faced, given that the wicked problems described above may require more strategic interventions.

CONCLUSION

This book is definitely not the last word in policy coordination. Although I believe that the discussions of theory and the case studies have added to our collective understanding of coordination, the problem will persist, and perhaps even intensify, in the real world of governing. Governments now have a greater understanding of the problems they confront when they attempt to coordinate, and they also have a larger array of instruments available to help them in that task. Likewise, academic students of policy and administration have also invested a good deal of time and energy attempting to understand how coordination occurs and what approaches can best explain the outcomes of attempts to coordinate. Despite those advances, the problem persists and is unlikely ever to go away.

The cases presented here, and many others that could have been presented, all illustrate the importance of increasing coordination both horizontally and vertically.

The governance problems being addressed by these reforms were very real, and none of the interventions has truly remedied the underlying problems, although it is fair to say that all have had some salutary consequences. These cases illustrate the variety of interventions available to would-be coordinators, and some of the pitfalls of each possibility. And they also help illustrate the complexity within the public sector that makes coordination at once necessary and difficult to achieve.

The cases discussed here also make clear the types of difficulties involved in coordinating public programs. Not only do would-be coordinators have to overcome the resistance of entrenched organizational interests, they also must confront political barriers to cooperation among organizations. Sometimes these political challenges may result from an incomplete commitment to coordination on the part of the political leaders. Those political problems may also result from an inadequate conception of what a more coordinated and effective policy solution might look like. Ministers may be selected on the basis of their interest in a particular policy area, or their commitment to a particular clientele, or they may become captured by their own ministry that has such specialized interests (Bäck, Debus, and Dumont 2011). Those politicians may therefore be incapable of seeing a broader picture of what the policy needs of the society are. The political problem may be, however, to find ways to mobilize around coordination and around more comprehensive solutions to policy problems. Prime ministers and presidents have some interests in this type of political mobilization, but the service and efficiency gains from coherence may not be as apparent to citizens as the quality of individual services.

A better scientific comprehension of coordination, as well as a better political understanding of the behaviors involved, will help both scholars and practitioners. But they should not be expected to solve the fundamental problem of division within the public sector. The factors that produce coordination problems are not likely to go away, and as already indicated, they may actually be increasing. Almost every government from the beginning of government has attempted to improve its internal coherence, but most have made little progress. The few who have made significant improvements in their internal coordination have been faced with major crises, or have strong internal cultures of coherence, or have simply been fortunate.

But coordination and coherence are not the only values that require consideration when designing public organizations, and the public sector more broadly. Specialization, organizational autonomy, and meeting political demands are also important factors within the public sector, and those values need to be balanced with the needs for coordination. Indeed, finding an appropriate balance between coordination and specialization may be an even greater challenge in managing within the public sector than simply creating higher levels of coordination.

Notes

CHAPTER I. INTRODUCTION

1. See Hood (1986) for an interesting, if discouraging, catalog of coordination problems in the public sector.

2. Even at this stage of development of the state this ability to coordinate from the center appears to involve some heroic assumptions. See for example, S. E. Finer's descriptions in his *History of Government* (1997).

3. Offices such as the *intendants* in the ancien régime in France were responsible for ensuring something approaching uniformity. These officials evolved into the contemporary office of the *préfet*.

4. For example, if individual programs have a very high error rate, e.g., in ascertaining eligibility for social services, then coordinating the programs may only compound the errors.

5. The "coercion" here implies the use of hierarchical authority, whether between ministers and their officials or between superiors and subordinates within an organization. As such the major resource being used is authority rather than norms.

6. In particular, the Conservative government created large numbers of executive agencies, disaggregating ministerial departments into quasi-autonomous organizations. This model has been adopted in a number of other countries (Pollitt, Talbot, Caulfield, and Smullen 2004).

7. For example, community-based mental health programs at times find it difficult to coordinate effectively with more institutional-based programs, and as a result clients may fall through the cracks *within* the broader policy area, rather than the cracks between types of policy.

8. See the discussion of measurement in coordination later in this chapter for some assessment of the amount of coordination generated.

9. This is especially true given the absence in the European Union of some horizontal coordination devices that might be present in a national government. For example, despite the increasing role of the President of the European Commission, the absence of instruments such as political parties and strong central agencies makes coordination more difficult in the EU than in most national governments.

10. Central agencies (Campbell and Szablowski 1979) are organizations such as Ministries of Finance that provide few if any services directly to citizens but rather are concerned primarily with providing services, and particularly with regulating, within the public sector. See also Peters, Rhodes, and Wright (2000).

11. While desirable from a coordination perspective, this type of integration may encounter problems with privacy laws that prevent sharing of data across government departments. Those governments in the European Union present particular difficulties for this style of coordination because of strong statutes protecting individual privacy.

12. What was perhaps most remarkable about the poverty trap was that its existence was widely known, with statistics about it being published in official documents such as *Social Trends* in the United Kingdom, but little was done about it.

13. That phrase has come to encapsulate coordination problems in intelligence and security in the United States. As we will point out in a subsequent chapter, the responses to these problems have not necessarily made it easier to connect those dots.

CHAPTER 2. BARRIERS TO COORDINATION

1. These information asymmetries are central to many of the rational-choice arguments about the inefficiencies of public bureaucracies and the difficulties that their sponsors (meaning legislatures) encounter when attempting to control those formal organizations. See Niskanen (1971) and Page (2003).

2. Often the undercover agents will appear to be the most committed of the participants in the illicit organizations in order to provoke the other members, and therefore agents from other law enforcement organizations will spend their time pursuing their own counterparts—hardly the desired outcome.

3. For example, in New Zealand, the government in 1994 introduced a system of Strategic Results Areas (SRAs) that reflected the goals of the system as a whole. Those SRAs then cascaded downward to Key Results Areas in the individual departments (Boston 1992).

4. This risk would exist in the private sector as well, although the possible rewards for taking the risk are likely to be greater. If individuals in the public sector are unlikely to recoup any of the rewards of risk or innovation personally then they have little reason to engage in those risks.

5. Within the Advocacy-Coalition Framework (Sabatier and Jenkins-Smith 1993), there is a similar understanding of the politics of policy change.

6. As we will point out in Chapter 5, however, having the organizations in the same cabinet department is no guarantee that they will in fact coordinate more effectively.

7. For example, "purple coalitions" in the Netherlands and "rainbow coalitions" in Finland and several Eastern European countries have extended across the political spectrum from Left to Right. That having been said, Chapter 6 will point out that the Finnish government has made significant advances in managing policy issues and in creating coherence even in the face of these "rainbows." In this case the issue of coordination appeared able to transcend partisan differences, in part because of a strong and effective civil service.

8. The notion that poverty is largely a function of the political and economic cultures of the poor has become very politically incorrect but has been expressed by some notable scholars (Banfield 1970).

9. As noted, this redundancy may be desirable given that it provides greater probabilities of identifying and correcting antitrust problems in the economy.

10. The danger, of course, is that these professional values may make it more difficult for them to cooperate and coordinate with other elements of their department. For example, the health professionals within the Department of the Interior may find it difficult to cooperate with the rest of an organization concerned primarily with natural resources, parks, and wildlife.

11. For example, the major outbreak of hepatitis in the Pittsburgh area appears to have resulted from green onions used in a Mexican-style restaurant. These onions had been imported from Mexico and had not had adequate screening and inspection before being served, despite the existence of numerous health inspection programs at all levels of government.

12. For example, the Office of Management and Budget has developed a set of government-wide goals and performance indicators (Office of Management and Budget 2003) usually referred to as PART. Also, as a part of their large-scale performance program the government of New Zealand has developed an extensive set of indicators that cut across departmental and program lines.

13. In comparative politics these issues in research design are usually discussed as "sampling on the dependent variable" (see Geddes 2003). While it is appealing to select cases that characterize a particular outcome, e.g., successful democratization or successful coordination, the absence of contrary cases makes it impossible to assess the sources of those successes.

CHAPTER 3. APPROACHES TO UNDERSTANDING COORDINATION

1. This is, of course, the familiar structure-agency problem that pervades a good deal of social science theory (Hay 1995).

2. Gulick's work is an example of classic organizational theory that, although it has been criticized from any number of directions (see Simon 1947), still constitutes one of the basic roots of thinking about organization and management in the public sector.

3. That purpose for government organizations is often enshrined in law, and public managers tend to be very concerned with the need to pursue their legal mandates.

4. Of course, there may well be important coordination issues within the single cabinet department. Agriculture is perhaps more unified than many departments, but even then there may be conflicts between elements that are more regulatory and those that are more supportive of agricultural interests.

5. Rural merchants and rural bankers do receive a good deal of indirect support from the Department of Agriculture. As well as simply maintaining viable farms with families who buy things from the merchants, programs like crop loans are generally managed by local business and financial interests.

6. Coalition governments do, of course, vary markedly in the ways in which the leadership can exert control over the members of the cabinet. Although the rubric in most systems is that the prime minister is *primus inter pares,* the tendency has been for prime ministers to gain increased powers over other ministers and others in the civil service (for the extreme, see Savoie 2008).

7. This is the economic language used by Niskanen (1971) in his analysis of the public bureaucracy and its relationship to Congress.

8. The experience leading up to the events of September 11, 2001, indicated the extent to which those connections among organizations were important, as well as the extent to which they were deficient. See Chapter 5.

9. In this case I was rather too slow to fulfill my side of the bargain, but did so in the end.

10. Thus, this pattern of decision making is analogous to satisficing or bounded rationality rather than optimizing behavior.

11. This is especially true if the excluded groups are those who have been generally less accepted as social partners—minorities, immigrants, women, etc. Exclusions of this sort are more common in part because of lower levels of organization among these groups, but that simple fact will not limit the political damage.

12. Buchanan and Tullock (1966) argued that when designing institutional structures there were two sets of costs that needed to be considered and those costs were inversely related. Exclusion costs were the costs imposed on individuals as a result of the exclusion of their ideas from the final decision, while decision-making costs were those resulting from difficulties in making their choices.

13. The long development of models of interest intermediation between state and society beginning with the corporatists and coming through to ideas of policy concentration has emphasized the connections between groups and particular bureaucracies.

14. Some communities, such as the medical professions, might easily claim to operate in the public interest, or at least in the interest of their patients, but the evidence is also that they will use their positions and their dominance over expertise to pursue their own interests as well.

15. On the other hand, there may be some element of "learning by doing" so that if mechanisms can be found to encourage network behaviors then some change in attitudes may result.

16. On the concept of "public value" see Moore (1996).

17. The energy policy emerging from the Bush administration, for example, was created by

avoiding the underlying conflict in the policy area and permitting only a limited and carefully selected number of participants to be involved. In essence this approach to the policy avoided the need to think about collaborative approaches.

CHAPTER 4. THE INSTRUMENTS OF COORDINATION

1. Presidents and prime ministers have always been political, but with increasing media attention and virtually continuous campaigning few chief executives find that they devote much time to the details of policy (see Clarke, Stewart, and Whiteley 1998).

2. Much of the work of the CEA is more technical, being tasked with providing the president economic forecasts and other data necessary to make macroeconomic policy. Despite that, the organization cannot escape political realities and so may have to develop forecasts that please the president as well as reflect reality.

3. Although the American government has created a very large number of czars, other governments such as the United Kingdom (Fawcett and Rhodes 2007) and Germany have similar officers to facilitate coordination.

4. That having been said, the staff of the National Security Council tends to be very jealous of its prerogatives and its direct accesds to the president, as compared to the more distant roles for analysts in the Departments of State and Defense (see Newmann 2003).

5. Denmark is the clearest example of such a weak cabinet system in which the ministers are essentially individual entrepreneurs.

6. As an example, see the Finnish case discussed in Chapter 5.

7. In the Finnish case, for example, the political advisors network around each of the government programs was important for preparing decisions and enhancing cooperation among the ministries (see Chapter 5).

8. For a critique of the structure, and especially of its consequences for management, see Good (2003).

9. At present workfare is being substituted for traditional welfare programs in many countries, and the demographic pressures on public pensions are forcing some rethinking of that mainstay of the welfare state.

10. Various studies of the civil services have documented those close connections, especially the studies such as Granastein's 1982 *The Ottawa Men* (they were almost all men then) and Heclo and Wildavsky's (1974), which were conducted during the golden age of governing in the several decades after World War II. Some administrative systems have been able to maintain their privileged position, and their capacity to coordinate, even after the advent of NPM.

CHAPTER 5. CASE STUDIES IN COORDINATION

1. In terms of the classification presented by Eckstein (1975) these cases would be heuristic rather than theory testing. They are means of exploring the interactions among variables instead of testing any hypotheses derived from theory.

2. There were subsequent attempts to rein in some of the autonomy of the individual organizations through the creation of the Director of National Intelligence (the "intelligence czar") in 2004. This office was designed to coordinate the sixteen federal organizations, including agencies

from six cabinet departments as well as the independent CIA, with significant responsibilities for intelligence collection. Although seemingly a powerful office, the evidence is largely that the autonomy of the intelligence organizations has been maintained.

3. The now famous (or infamous) color-coded threat levels have gone up and down numerous times since being created. For a critique, see Bobbitt (2004).

4. Similar issues and needs for coordination have arisen in the care of the elderly. See USGAO, 2004.

5. At the time the policy programs were adopted there were a mere five parties in government, while in 2013 there were six.

6. For example, the parliament has the distinctive feature of a "Committee for the Future." See Arter (2007).

7. Leaving aside the moral authority of the European project to many of the participants in the process, there is no formal authority at the European level undergirding most of the actions taken through the OMC. To the extent that there is any authority it remains within the member states.

CHAPTER 6. IS COORDINATION ALWAYS THE ANSWER, AND CAN IT BE?

1. This statement of course echoes the famous statement by Justice Potter Stewart that although he could not define pornography, he knew it when he saw it.

2. On the concept of commensurability in comparative politics, see Blatter and Haverland (2012). These cases were not used per se for comparison but rather served to illustrate alternative approaches to coordination and some of the strengths and weaknesses of each. Hence, any conclusion drawn here will be more illustrative of some patterns as they will be capable of confirming relationships among variables.

3. This attribute may become more important as the concept of "social exclusion" begins to replace other, less expansive terms to define the targets of social programs. Social exclusion is itself a "joined-up" term that implies bringing together a range of social and economic services.

4. The USGAO now publishes an annual report on redundancy and duplication. The most recent is *Actions Needed to Reduce Fragmentation, Overlap and Duplication* (USGAO-13–279SP).

5. Critics of NASA from the private sector now argue that its monopoly control of space travel has in fact impeded development of space travel because of its excessively cautious and bureaucratic approach to this "industry."

6. It may not be so much the unwillingness on the part of analysts to admit to the inadequate scientific and technical basis on which policies are made, but rather that politicians do not understand that weakness.

7. If anything, the increasingly ideological nature of American politics has reduced the level of objective social scientific research on these issues and replaced that with rather proverbial wisdom coming from both the Right and the Left.

8. It may be that the Manhattan Project only looks neat and linear in retrospect, while for those involved at the time it had many of the same problems that a war on cancer would have for contemporary observers.

9. Denmark, Sweden, and the United Kingdom among the "old" members of the EU have chosen not to join the Euro Zone. Several of the thirteen new EU members are already Euro Zone members, although most if not all aspire to membership and have begun to align their financial policies with those of the European Central Bank.

10. In particular, the Patriot Act (Bradley 2002) allows the federal government to collect a variety of individual level data that once would not have been acceptable and to put that data together with other data sources in order to attempt to identify possible terrorists living within the United States.

11. For example, the Public Works Administration (PWA) and the Works Progress Administration (WPA) were created at approximately the same time in order to get people back to work. The WPA was more successful and persisted, while the PWA was terminated.

12. Landau is much more clearly in favor of redundancy than is Bendor, arguing that constructing redundant systems is often a remedy for the inherent weaknesses of most organizational mechanisms for processing information.

13. Elsewhere, we have conceptualized this form of control as "mutualism," emphasizing that one organization or individual can serve as a watchdog on another—policemen working in pairs, for example (see Hood et al. 2004).

14. When told of the virtues of the "one-stop shop" for public services, one cynical citizen said "Great—now I will not have to go to six or eight offices in order to be told no."

15. As already noted, policy tends to be made through implementation as well as through the usual methods in legislatures. Therefore, as coordination is being developed even at the implementation stage there can be significant transformations of policy.

16. The first secretary of Homeland Security, Tom Ridge, was not reluctant to accept that responsibility, having been quoted as saying that he was responsible for outcomes in this area of public security.

17. Remember that the programs per se have no appreciable funds and even less direct authority to implement the programs and must rely upon the line ministries that do have the necessary resources.

18. That is, if a program or political action benefits everyone it may have little special appeal and hence may be not be an effective foundation for political mobilization.

19. This book has focused on coordination as a particular administrative and political problem, but the findings and basic analysis would also be applicable to many other aspects of policy and administration.

20. All governments are segmented, but several factors tend to strengthen that segmentation in the United States. For example, civil servants tend to be recruited and remain within a single department for their entire careers, thus having a limited perspective on the full range of government activities. Further, most major agencies have their own enabling legislation and their own legal mandates that can be used as a means of warding off coordination efforts.

21. As noted (page 118), some of the participants in the process who were interviewed thought that more drastic action was needed to produce the desired level of integration of programs across the government.

22. The degree of autonomy actually exercised by agencies in the United Kingdom is actually less than some of the literature coming from the United Kingdom might have one believe. This perception of autonomy for those organizations may be a function of the tight controls usually exercised over organizations in British government. See Polidano (1999).

23. For example, in the US federal government, at least six cabinet departments in addition to the Department of Education are engaged in some activities that could be labeled education.

24. The World Bank, for example, assesses the amount of red tape and the number of actors involved in issuing business licenses as one measure of the quality of governance.

References

6, P. 2004. "Joined-Up Government in the Western World in Comparative Perspective: A Preliminary Literature Review and Exploration." *Journal of Public Administration Research and Theory* 14: 103–39.

6, P., D. Leat, K. Seltzer, and G. Stoker. 2002. *Towards Holistic Governance: The New Reform Agenda.* Basingstoke, UK: Palgrave.

Agranoff, R. 1991. "Human Service Integration: Past and Present Challenges in Public Administration." *Public Administration Review* 51: 533–42.

Agranoff, R., and M. McGuire. 2003. *Collaborative Public Management.* Washington, DC: Georgetown University Press.

Albert, S., B. E. Ashforth, and J. Dutton. 2000. "Special Topic Forum on Organizational Identity and Identification." *Academy of Management Review* 25: n.p.

Alexander, E. R. 1995. *How Organizations Act Together: Interorganizational Coordination in Theory and Practice.* Luxembourg: Gordon and Breach.

Allen, G. 2003. *The Last Prime Minister: Being Honest about the UK Presidency.* Charlottesville, VA: Imprint Academic.

Allen, M., and B. Miller. 2002. "Bush Seeks Security Department." *Washington Post,* June 7.

Allison, G. T. 1971. *Essence of Decision.* Boston: Little, Brown.

Althaus, R. R., and D. L. Yarwood. 1993. "Organizational Domain Overlap with Cooperative Outcomes: The Departments of Agriculture and State and International Agriculture Policy in the Carter Administration." *Public Administration Review* 53: 357–67.

Amorim Neto, O. 2006. "The Presidential Calculus: Executive Policy Making and Cabinet Formation in the Americas." *Comparative Political Studies* 39: 415–40.

Anderson, G. 1996. "The New Focus on the Policy Capacity of the Federal Government." *Canadian Journal of Public Administration* 39: 469–88.

Andeweg, R. 2000. "Ministers as Double Agents? The Delegation Process between Cabinets and Ministers." *European Journal of Political Research* 37: 377–95.

———. 2003. "Studying Government." In *Governing Europe,* edited by J. E. S. Hayward and A. Menon, 33–60. Oxford: Oxford University Press.

Arter, D. 2007. "The End of Social Democratic Hegemony?: The March 2007 Finnish General Election." *West European Politics* 30: 1148–57.

Aubin, D., and K. Verhoest. 2014. *Multi-level Regulation in the Telecommunications Sector: Adaptive Regulatory Arrangements in Belgium, Ireland, the Netherlands and Switzerland.* Basingstoke, UK: Macmillan.

Australian Public Service Commission. 2005. *Connecting Government: Whole of Government Challenges to Australia's Priority Challenges.* Canberra: APSC.

Axelrod, R. M. 1997. *The Complexity of Cooperation: Agent-Based Models of Competition and Collaboration.* Princeton, NJ: Princeton University Press.

Bache, I., and M. Flinders. 2004. *Multi-level Governance.* Oxford: Oxford University Press.

Bäck, H., M. Debus, and P. Dumont. 2011. "Who Gets What in Coalition Governments?: Predictors of Portfolio Allocation in Coalition Governments." *European Journal of Political Research* 50: 441–78.

Bakvis, H., and M. Jarvis. 2012. *From the New Public Management to the New Public Governance: Essays in Honour of Peter C. Aucoin.* Montreal: McGill-Queen's University Press.

Bakvis, H., and L. Juillet. 2004. *The Horizontal Challenge: Line Departments, Central Agencies and Leadership.* Ottawa: Canadian Centre for Management Development.

Bamberger, K. A., and D. K. Mulligan. 2013. "Privacy in Europe: Initial Data on Governance Choices and Corporate Practices." *George Washington Law Review* 81: 1529–1611.

Banfield, E. C. 1970. *The Unheavenly City: The Nature and Future of Our Urban Crisis.* Boston: Little, Brown.

Bardach, E. 1996. "Turf Barriers to Interagency Collaboration." In *The State of Public Management,* edited by D. F. Kettl and H. B. Milward, 168–90. Baltimore, MD: Johns Hopkins University Press.

———. 1998. *Getting Agencies to Work Together: The Practice and Theory of Managerial Craftsmanship.* Washington, DC: The Brookings Institution.

Bardach, E., and C. Lesser. 1996. "Accountability in Human Services Collaboratives—For What? And To Whom?" *Journal of Public Administration Research and Theory* 6: 197–224.

Barkun, M., 2002. "Defending against the Apocalypse: The Limits of Homeland Security." In *Governance & Public Security,* Campbell Public Affairs Institute, 92–114. Syracuse, NY: Campbell Institute.

Barling, P. 1984. "Taxation + Means Test = Poverty Trap." *Australian Social Welfare Impact* 14: 15–22.

Barnard, C. I. 1938. *The Functions of the Executive.* Cambridge, MA: Harvard University Press.

Barnes, F. 2002. "The Hurdles Facing Homeland Defense." *Pentagon Report,* August, 8.

Barton, A., and P. Welbourne. 2005. "Context and Its Significance in Identifying 'What Works' in Child Protection." *Child Abuse Review* 14: 177–94.

Batty, D. 2003. "Government Unveils Children's Trusts." *Guardian,* July 10.

Béland, D., and R. H. Cox. 2011. *Ideas and Politics in Social Science Research.* Oxford: Oxford University Press.

Bender, B. 2003. "Intelligence Sharing Said Lacking Despite Agencies' Vow after 9/11." *Boston Globe,* April 25.

Bendor, J. B. 1985. *Parallel Systems: Redundancy in Government.* Berkeley: University of California Press.

Benson, J. K. 1975. "The Interorganizational Network as a Political Economy." *Administrative Science Quarterly* 20: 229–49.

Benton, J. C., and A. Bettelhelm. 2002. "New Homeland Security Duties Spotlight Service's Juggling Act." *CQ Weekly,* March 30, 860–5.

Bernstein, M. 1955. *Regulating Business by Independent Commission.* Princeton, NJ: Princeton University Press.

Bertelli, A. M., and L. E. Lynn. 2004. "Policymaking in the Parallelogram of Forces: Common Agency and Human Service Provision." *Policy Studies Journal* 32: 297–316.

Best, J. 1989. *Images of Issues: Typifying Contemporary Social Problems.* Chicago: Aldine DeGruyter.

———. 2012. "Constructionist Social Problems Theory." In *Communications Yearbook* 26, edited by C. T. Salmon, 244–76. London: Routledge.

Bettelhelm, A. 2002. "Homeland Security Revamp Hung Up on 'Dual Purpose' Agencies." *CQ Weekly,* July 6, 1809–10.

Bezes, P. 2012. "État, experts et savoir néo-managériaux." *Actes de recherches en sciences sociales* 193: 16–37.

Biermann, F., P. Pattberg, H. van Asselt, and F. Zelli. 2009. "The Fragmentation of Global Governance Architectures: A Framework for Analysis." *Global Environmental Politics* 9: 14–40.

Bignami, F. 2007. "Privacy and Law Enforcement in the European Union." *Chicago Journal of International Law* 8: 233–56.

Bijker, W. E., R. Bal, and R. Hendriks. 2009. *The Paradox of Scientific Authority: The Role of Scientific Advice in Democracies.* Cambridge, MA: MIT Press.

Blatter, J., and M. Haverland. 2012. *Designing Case Studies: Explanatory Approaches in Small-n Research.* Basingstoke, UK: Macmillan.

Blau, P. M. 1963. *The Dynamics of Bureaucracy,* 2nd ed. Chicago: University of Chicago Press.

Blick, A., and G. Jones. 2010. "The Centre of Central Government." *Public Policy Research* 17: 29–35.

Block, R., and C. Cooper. 2007. *Disaster: Hurricane Katrina and the Failure of Homeland Security.* New York: Henry Holt.

Bobbitt, P. 2004. *Terror and Consent: The Wars of the Twenty-First Century.* New York: Knopf.

Bobrow, D., and J. S. Dryzek. 1987. *Policy Analysis by Design.* Pittsburgh: University of Pittsburgh Press.

Bogdanor, V. 2005. *Joined-Up Government.* Oxford: Oxford University Press.

Boin, A., S. Kuipers, and M. Steenbergen. 2010. "The Life and Death of Public Organizations: A Question of Design." *Governance* 23: 385–410.

Boin, A., and P. Nieuwenburg. 2013. "The Moral Costs of Discretionary Decision-Making in Crisis." *Public Integrity* 15: 367–84.

Boisnier, A., and J. A. Chatman. 2002. *The Role of Subcultures in Agile Organizations.* Berkeley: Haas School of Business, University of California.

Bolleyer, N., and T. A. Börzel. 2010. "Non-hierarchical Coordination in Multilevel Systems." *European Political Science Review* 2: 157–85.

Borrás, S., and K. Jacobsson. 2004. "The Open Method of Coordination and New Governance Patterns in the EU." *European Journal of Public Policy* 11: 185–208.

Borrás, S., and B. G. Peters. 2011. "The Lisbon Strategy's Empowerment of Core Executives: Centralizing and Politicizing EU National Coordination." *Journal of European Public Policy* 18: 525–45.

Börzel, T. A. 2011. "Networks: Reified Metaphor or Governance Panacea?" *Public Administration* 89: 49–63.

Boston, J. 1992. "The Problem of Policy Coordination: The New Zealand Experience." *Governance* 5: 88–103.

Botterill, L.C. 2007. "Managing Intergovernmental Relations in Australia: The Case of Agricultural Policy Cooperation." *Australian Journal of Public Administration* 66: 186–197.

Bouckaert, G., and A. Halachmi. 1995. *Public Productivity through Quality and Strategic Management.* Amsterdam: IOS.

Bouckaert, G., D. Ormond, and B. G. Peters. 2000. *A Possible Governance Agenda for Finland.* Helsinki: Ministry of Finance.

Bouckaert, G., B. G. Peters, and K. Verhoest. 2010. *The Coordination of Public Sector Organizations: Shifting Patterns of Public Management.* Basingstoke, UK: Macmillan.

Bourgault, J. 2002. *Horizontalité et gestion publique.* Quebec: Presses Universitaires de Laval.

Bovens, M. A. P., and P. 't Hart. 1996. *Understanding Policy Fiascoes.* New Brunswick, NJ: Transaction Books.

Bovens, M. A. P., P. 't Hart, and B. G. Peters. 2000. *Success and Failure in Public Governance.* Cheltenham, UK: Edward Elgar.

Bradley, A. A. 2002. "Extremism in the Defense of Liberty?: The Foreign Intelligence Surveillance Act and the Significance of the USA PATRIOT ACT." *Tulane Law Review* 77: 465–502.

Briassoulis, H. 2005. *Policy Integration and Complex Environmental Problems: The Example of Mediterranean Desertification.* Aldershot, UK: Ashgate.

Brown, T. L., M. Potoski, and D. M. Van Slyke. 2006. "Managing Public Service Contracts: Aligning Values, Institutions and Markets." *Public Administration Review* 66: 323–31.

Bruel, J. D. 2007. "Three Bush Administration Management Reform Initiatives." *Public Administration Review* 67: 21–26.

Brunsson, N., and J. P. Olsen. 1993. *The Reforming Organization.* London: Routledge.

Bryson, A., and J. Jason. 1992. *Policing the Workshy: Benefit Controls, the Labour Market and the Unemployed.* Aldershot, UK: Avebury.

Bryson, J. M., and B. C. Crosby. 2006. "The Design and Implementation of Cross-Sector Collaborations: Propositions from the Literature." *Public Administration Review* 66: 44–55.

Buchanan, J. M., and G. Tullock. 1966. *The Calculus of Consent.* Ann Arbor: University of Michigan Press.

Buchs, M. 2007. *New Governance in European Social Policy: The Open Method of Coordination.* Basingstoke, UK: Macmillan.

Bungay, H. 2005. "Cancer and Health Policy: The Postcode Lottery for Care." *Social Policy and Administration* 39: 35–48.

Burgess, S., and M. Ratto. 2003. "The Role of Incentives in the Public Sector: Issues and Evidence." *Oxford Review of Economic Policy* 19: 285–300.

Cabinet Office. 2000. *Wiring It Up: Whitehall's Management of Cross-Cutting Policies and Services.* London: Performance and Innovation Unit.

Callaghan, K., and F. Schnell. 2005. *Framing American Politics.* Pittsburgh: University of Pittsburgh Press.

Campbell, C. E., and G. Szablowski. 1979. *The Superbureaucrats: Structure and Behaviour in Central Agencies.* Toronto: Macmillan.

Campbell, J. L. 2001. "Institutional Analysis and the Role of Ideas in Political Economy." *Theory and Society* 27: 377–409.

Carlson, A. C. 2005. *Fractured Generations: Crafting a Family Policy for Twenty-First Century America.* New Brunswick, NJ: Transaction.

Carlsson, L. 2000. "Policy Networks as Collective Action." *Policy Studies Journal* 28: 505–20.

Carpenter, D. A. 2001. *The Forging of Bureaucratic Autonomy: Reputations, Networks and Policy Innovation in Executive Agencies, 1862–1928.* Princeton, NJ: Princeton University Press.

Carter, A. B. 2006. "The Architecture of Government in the Face of Terrorism." *International Security* 26: 5–23.

Caruson, K., and S. A. MacManus. 2006. "Mandates and Management Challenges in the Trenches: An Intergovernmental Perspective on Homeland Security." *Public Administration Review* 66: 522–36.

Carvajal, D. 2013. "Europe's Rail Crashes Hint at System Gaps." *New York Times,* September 9.

Chaffin, J. 2004. "Tom Ridge: The Nice Watchman." *Financial Times,* August 7/8.

Challis, L., S. Fuller, M. Henwood, R. Klein, W. Plowden, A. Webb, P. Whittingham, and G. Wistow. 1988. *Joint Approaches to Social Policy: Rationality and Practice.* Cambridge: Cambridge University Press.

Chan, A., and S. Clegg. 2002. "History, Culture and Organization Studies." *Culture and Organization* 8: 259–73.

Chapman, J., and G. Duncan. 2007. "Is There Now a New 'New Zealand Model'?" *Public Management Review* 9: 1–25.

Chisholm, D. 1989. *Coordination without Hierarchy: Informal Structures in Multiorganizational Systems.* Berkeley: University of California Press.

Christensen, J.-G, and L. Jensen. 2009. "The Executive Core and Government Strategy in the Nordic Countries." Paper presented at the ECPR General Conference, Potsdam, Germany, September 9.

Christensen, T., and P. Laegreid. 2001. *New Public Management: The Transformation of Ideas and Practice.* Aldershot, UK: Ashgate.

———. 2007. "The Whole of Government Approach to Public Sector Reform." *Public Administration Review* 67: 1059–66.

Christensen, T., and S. Piattoni. 2003. *Informal Governance in the European Union.* Cheltenham, UK: Edward Elgar.

Clarke, H. D., M. C. Stewart, and P. F. Whiteley. 1998. "New Models for New Labour: The Political Economy of Labour Party Support." *American Political Science Review* 92: 559–74.

Clarke, R. A. 2004. *Against All Enemies: Inside America's War on Terror.* New York: Free Press.

Cohen, D. K., M. F. Cuellar, and B. R. Weingast. 2006. "Crisis Bureaucracy: Homeland Security and the Political Design of Legal Mandates." *Stanford Law Review* 59: 673–759.

Coleman, W. 2005. "Globality and Transnational Policy-Making in Agriculture: Complexity, Contradictions and Conflict." In *Complex Sovereignty,* edited by E. Grande and W. Pauley, 93–119. Toronto: University of Toronto Press.

Comanor, W. S. 2004. *The Law and Economics of Child Support Enforcement.* Northampton, MA: Edward Elgar.

Congressional Budget Office. 2004. *Federal Funding for Homeland Security.* April 30. Washington, DC: CBO.

Conklin, J. 2005. *Dialog Mapping: Developing Shared Understandings of Wicked Problems.* New York: John Wiley.

Conley, R. S. 2006. "Reform, Reorganization and the Renaissance of the Managerial Presidency: The Impact of 9/11 on the Executive Establishment." *Policy and Politics* 34: 304–42.

Considine, M. 2002. "The End of the Line? Accountable Governance in an Era of Networks, Partnerships and Joined-Up Services." *Governance* 15: 19–40.

Cooper, P. J. 2003. *Governing by Contract: Challenges and Opportunities for Public Managers.* Washington, DC: CQ Press.

Cooper, R. 1998 *Coordination Games.* Cambridge: Cambridge University Press.

Covarrubias Moreno, O. M. 2007. *Transversidalidad y coordinacion de las Politicas del Estado en el Federalismo.* Caracas: CLAD.

Cox, G. W., and S. Morgenstern. 2001. "Latin America's Reactive Assemblies and Proactive Presidents." *Comparative Politics* 32: 171–89.

Crozier, M. 1964. *The Bureaucratic Phenomenon.* Chicago: University of Chicago Press.

Daalder, I. H., and I. M. Destler. 2002a. "Behind America's Front Line: Organizing to Protect the Homeland." *Brookings Review* 20 (3): 17–19.

———. 2002b. "Advisors, Czars and Councils: Organizing for Homeland Security." *National Interest,* Summer.

Dahl, R. A., and C. E. Lindblom. 1953. *Politics, Economics and Welfare: Planning and Politico-economic Processes Resolved into Basic Processes.* New York: Harper and Row.

Dahlström, C., B. G. Peters, and J. Pierre. 2010. *Steering from the Centre: Strengthening Political Control in Western Democracies*. Toronto: University of Toronto Press.

Dahlström, C., and J. Pierre. 2010. "Studying the Swedish State: Politicization as a Control Strategy." In *Steering from the Centre: Strengthening Political Control in Western Democracies*, 148–66 edited by C. Dahlström, B. G. Peters, and J. Pierre. Toronto: University of Toronto Press.

Damaska, M. R. 1986. *The Faces of Justice and Authority: A Comparative Approach to the Legal Process*. New Haven, CT: Yale University Press.

Davies, J. S. 2009. "The Limits of Joined-Up Government: Toward a Political Analysis." *Public Administration* 87: 80–96.

Davis, G. 1996. *A Government of Routines: Executive Coordination in an Australian State*. Melbourne: Macmillan.

———. 1997. "Executive Coordination Mechanisms." In *The Hollow Crown: Countervailing Trends in Core Executives*, edited by P. Weller, H. Bakvis, and R. A. W. Rhodes, 143–66. London: Macmillan.

Dehejia, V. H., and P. Genschel. 1999. "Tax Competition in the European Union." *Politics and Society* 27: 403–30.

De Jong, A. 1996. "Interorganizational Collaboration in the Policy Preparation Process." In *Creating Collaborative Advantage*, edited by C. Huxham, 167–88. London: Sage.

Delone, G. J. 2009. "Organizational Cooperation: Law Enforcement Agencies Working Together." *Police Journal* 82: 34–49.

Denhardt, J. V., and R. B. Denhardt. 2011. *The New Public Service: Serving, Not Steering*. Armonk, NY: M. E. Sharpe.

Department of Health. 2000. *National Cancer Plan*. London: Department of Health.

Department of Homeland Security. 2007. *National Strategy for Homeland Security*. Washington, DC: Department of Homeland Security.

Derlien, H.-U. 1996. "Zum Logic und Politik des Ressortzuschnitts." *Verwaltungs Archiv* 87: 548–80.

———. 1999. "On the Selective Interpretation of Max Weber's Concept of Bureaucracy in Organization Theory and Administrative Science." In *Disembalming Max Weber*, edited by H.-U. Derlien, 56–70. Jyvaskala, Finland: SoPhi Press.

———. 2000. "Germany—Failing Successfully." In *The National Coordination of EU Policy— The Domestic Level*, edited by H. Kassim, B. G. Peters, and V. Wright, 54–78. Oxford: Oxford University Press.

Dery, D. 1998. "Policy by the Way: When Policy Is Incidental to Making Other Policies." *Journal of Public Policy* 18: 163–76.

Desage, F. 2013. "Les fonctionnaires intercommunaux ont il une âme?" In *La France et ses administrations: Un état des saviors*, edited by J.-M. Eymeri-Douzanes and G. Bouckaert, 461–95. Brussels: Bruylant.

Dewar, D. 2002. "Horizontal Budgeting, Results-Based Budgeting and the Coordination of Horizontal Policies in the United States and Canada." PhD dissertation, Department of Political Science, McMaster University, Hamilton, Ontario, Canada.

DfES. 2005a. *Area Protection Committees: Roles and Responsibilities*. London: Department for Education and Skills.

———. 2005b. *Integrated Children's Services*. London: Department for Education and Skills.

Di Francesco, M. 2001. "Process Not Outcomes in New Public Management?: 'Policy Coherence' in Australian Government." *The Drawing Board* 1: 103–16.

Dimaggio, P., and W. W. Powell. 1983. "The Iron Cage Revisited: Institutional Isomorphism and Collective Rationality in Organizational Fields." *American Sociological Review* 48: 147–60.

Dixit, A., G. M. Grossman, and E. Helpman. 1997. "Common Agency and Coordination: General Theory and Application to Government Policy Making." *Journal of Political Economy* 105: 752–69.

Doern, G. B. 1993. "From Sectoral to Macro Green Governance: The Canadian Department of the Environment as Aspiring Central Agency." *Governance* 6: 172–93.

Döring, H. 1995. *Parliaments and Majority Rule in Western Europe*. Frankfurt: Campus.

Downs, A. 1967. *Inside Bureaucracy*. Boston: Little, Brown.

Dubois, V. 2010. *La vie au guichet: Relation administrative et traitemente de la misère*. Paris: Economica.

Duit, A., and V. Galaz. 2008. "Governance and Complexity—New Issues in Governance Theory." *Governance* 21: 311–35.

Dunn, W. N. 1998. *The Experimenting Society*. New Brunswick, NJ: Transaction Press.

Duran, P. 1999. *Penser l'action sociale*. Paris: L. G. D. J.

Duran, P., and J.-C. Thoenig. 1996. "L'état et la gestion publique territoriale." *Revue française de science politique* 46: 580–623.

Dyckman, L. J. 2004. "Posthearing Questions Related to Fragmentation and Overlap in the Federal Food Safety System." Washington, DC: US General Accounting Office, May 26. GAO-04–832R.

Eckstein, H. 1975. "The Case Study." In *Strategies of Inquiry*, edited by F. I. Greenstein and N. W. Polsby. Reading, MA: Addison-Wesley.

Entman, R. M. 1993. "Framing: Toward Clarification of a Fractured Paradigm." *Journal of Communication* 43(4): 51–8.

Erkkilä, T. 2011. *Government Transparency: Impacts and Unintended Consequences*. Basingstoke, UK: Macmillan.

Evans, M., and C. Miller. 1996. *Joint Commissioning for Child Protection: A Future Role for Child Protection Committees*. London: Office of Public Management.

Every Child Matters. 2003. London: CM5860.

Falkner, G., O. Treib, M. Hartlapp, and S. Leiber. 2005. *Complying with Europe: EU Harmonisation and Soft Law in the Member Countries*. Cambridge: Cambridge University Press.

Fantacone, S., and L. Cotterli. 2003. "Stability and Growth Pact in Europe's Transition from Hard to Soft Coordination." *International Spectator* 38: 7–17.

Fauroux, R., and B. Spitz. 2002. *Notre État*. Paris: LaFont.

Fawcett, P., and R. A. W. Rhodes. 2007. "Central Government." In *Blair's Britain,* edited by A. Seldon, 79–103. Cambridge: Cambridge University Press.

Fewsmith, J. 2012. *The Logic and Limits of Political Reform in China*. Cambridge: Cambridge University Press.

Finer, S. E. 1997. *The History of Government from the Earliest Times*. Oxford: Oxford University Press.

"Finland Ex-Premier Goes on Trial." 2005. *New York Times,* April 3.

Fischer, F. 2003. *Reframing Public Policy: Discursive Politics and Deliberative Practices*. New York: Oxford University Press.

Flinders, M. 2004. "MPs and Icebergs: Parliament and Delegated Governance." *Parliamentary Affairs* 57: 767–84.

Flynn, M. E. 2005. "Military Leadership, Institutional Change and Priorities in Military Spending." *Foreign Policy Analysis* 10: 103–26.

Fournier, J. 1987. *Le travail gouvernemental.* Paris: Presses de la Fondation des Sciences Politiques.

Fox, E. M., and L. A. Sullivan. 1987. "Antitrust—Retrospective and Prospective—Where Are We Coming From, Where Are We Going?" *New York University Law Review* 62: 936–1010.

Frederickson, H. G. 2005. "Governance, Governance Everywhere: What Happened to Public Administration?" In *Oxford Handbook of Public Management,* edited by F. Ferlie, L. E. Lynn, and C. Pollitt, 79–99. Oxford: Oxford University Press.

Frederickson, H. G., and K. B. Smith. 2003. *The Public Administration Theory Primer.* Boulder, CO: Westview.

Freidson, E. 1986. *Professional Powers: A Study of the Institutionalization of Formal Knowledge.* Chicago: University of Chicago Press.

Garamone, J. 2010. *New National Strategy Takes a "Whole of Government" Approach.* Washington, DC: US Department of Defense, May 27.

Gargan, J. A. 1993. "Specifying Elements of Professionalism and the Process of Professionalization." *International Journal of Public Administration* 16: 1861–84.

Geddes, B. 2003. *Paradigms and Sand Castles: Theory Building and Research Design in Comparative Politics.* Ann Arbor: University of Michigan Press.

Gellman, B., and G. Miller. 2012. "U. S. Spy Network's Successes, Failures and Objectives Detailed in 'Black Budget' Summary." *Washington Post,* August 29.

Gilbert, N., and H. Specht. 1977. "Social Planning and Community Organization in *Encyclopedia of Social Work.*" Washington, DC: National Association of Social Workers.

Glor, E. D. 2011. "Patterns of Government Department Survival." *Canadian Public Administration* 54: 551–66.

Good, D. A. 2003. *The Politics of Public Management: The HRDC Audit of Grants and Contributions.* Toronto: University of Toronto Press.

Goodsell, C. T. 2010. *Mission Mystique: Belief Systems in Public Agencies.* Washington, DC: CQ Press.

Gorman, S. 2005. "Homeland Security Agency Narrows Intelligence Focus." *Baltimore Sun,* August 24.

Gouldner, A. W. 1954. *Patterns of Industrial Bureaucracy.* Glencoe, IL: Free Press.

Granastein, J. L. 1982. *The Ottawa Men: The Civil Service Mandarins, 1935–1957.* Toronto: University of Toronto Press.

Gregory, R. 2012. "Accountability in Modern Government." In *The Handbook of Public Administration,* 2nd ed., edited by B. G. Peters and J. Pierre, 681–97. London: Sage.

Gremion, P. 1976. *Pouvoir Péripherique: Bureaucrates et Notables dans le système politique Français.* Paris: Seuil.

Greve, M. 2001. "Laboratories of Democracy: Anatomy of a Metaphor." *AEI Federalist Outlook* (March).

Guild, E., S. Carrera, and A. F. Atger. 2009. *Challenges and Prospects for the EU's Area of Freedom, Security and Justice.* Brussels: Centre for European Policy Studies.

Gulick, L. H. 1937. "Notes on the Theory of Organization." In *Papers on the Science of Administration,* edited by L. H. Gulick and L. Urwick, 3–38. New York: Institute of Public Administration.

Gusentine, R. V. 2002. "Asymmetric Warfare—On Our Terms." *U.S. Naval Institute Proceedings* 128: 58–61.

Haas, M. 1992. "Introduction: Epistemic Communities and International Policy Coordination." *International Organization* 46: 1–35.

Hagen, M., and H. Kubicel. 2000. *One-Stop Government in Europe: Results of 11 National Surveys.* Bremen, Germany: University of Bremen.

Hall, P. A. 1986. *Governing the Economy: The Politics of State Intervention in Britain and France.* Cambridge: Polity.

———. 1989. *The Political Power of Economic Ideas: Keynesianism across Nations.* Princeton, NJ: Princeton University Press.

Hall, R. A., J. P. Clark, P. C. Giordano, P. V. Johnson, and M. Van Roekel. 1976. "Patterns of Interorganizational Relations." *Administrative Science Quarterly* 22: 457–74.

Hallerberg, M., and S. Basinger. 1998. "Internationalization and Changes in Tax Policy in OECD Countries." *Comparative Political Studies* 31: 321–52.

Halligan, J. A. 2004. *Civil Service Systems in Anglo-American Democracies.* Cheltenham, UK: Edward Elgar.

———. 2006. "The Reassertion of the Centre in a First Generation NPM System." In *Autonomy and Regulation: Coping with Agencies in a Modern State,* edited by T. Christensen and P. Laegreid, 45–67. Cheltenham, UK: Edward Elgar.

Halligan, J. A., and G. Bouckaert. 2007. *Managing Performance: International Comparisons.* London: Routledge.

Halligan, J. A., and J. Wills. 2008. *The Centrelink Experiment: Innovation in Service Delivery.* Canberra: ANU Press.

Halpert, B. P. 1982. "Antecedents." In *Interorganizational Coordination,* edited by D. L. Rogers and D. A. Whetten, 19–33. Ames: Iowa State University Press.

Hamburger, P., and P. Weller. 2012. "Policy Advice and a Central Agency: The Department of Prime Minister and Cabinet." *Australian Journal of Political Science* 47: 363–76.

Hammond, P. Y. 1960. "The National Security Council as a Device for Interdepartmental Coordination: An Interpretation and Appraisal." *American Political Science Review* 54: 899–910.

Hanley, D. 2007. *Beyond the Nation State: Parties in the Era of European Integration.* Basingstoke, UK: Macmillan.

Hansen, H. F. 2011. "NPM in Scandinavia." In *The Ashgate Research Companion to New Public Management,* edited by P. Laegreid and T. Christensen, 113–30. Aldershot, UK: Ashgate.

HAQ. 2013. *Budget 2013–14 and Children: A First Glance.* New Delhi: HAQ Centre for Child Rights.

Hardy, B., B. Hudson, and E. Waddington. 2000. *What Makes a Good Partnership? A Partnership Assessment Term.* London: Nuffield Institute.

Harkness, S., P. Gregg, and L. MacMillan. 2012. *Poverty: The Role of Institutions, Behaviours and Culture.* York, UK: Joseph Rowntree Foundation.

Harmon, M. M., and R. T. Mayer. 1986. *Organization Theory for Public Administration.* Glenview: Scott, Foresman.

Hart, J. 1998. "Central Agencies and Departments: Empowerment and Coordination." In *Taking Stock: Assessing Public Sector Reforms,* edited by B. G. Peters and D. J. Savoie, 285–309. Montreal: McGill-Queen's University Press.

Hay, C. 1995. "Structure and Agency." In *Theory and Methods in Political Science,* edited by D. Marsh and G. Stoker, 189–206. New York: St. Martin's.

———. 2004. "Theory, Stylized Heuristic, or Self-Fulfilling Prophecy?: The Status of Rational Choice Theory in Public Administration." *Public Administration* 82: 39–62.

———. 2011. "Ideas and the Construction of Interests." In *Ideas and Politics in Social Research,* edited by D. Béland and R. H. Cox, 65–82. Oxford: Oxford University Press.

Hayward, J. E. S., and V. Wright. 2002. *Governing from the Centre: Core Executive Coordination in France.* Oxford: Oxford University Press.

Heclo, H. 1974. *Modern Social Politics in Britain and Sweden.* New Haven, CT: Yale University Press.

———. 1978. "Issue Networks and the Executive Establishment." In *The New American Political System,* edited by A. King, 87–124. Washington, DC: American Enterprise Institute.

Heclo, H., and A. Wildavsky. 1974. *The Private Government of Public Money.* Berkeley: University of California Press.

Hedstrom, P., and R. Swedborg. 1998. *Social Mechanisms: An Analytic Approach to Social Theory.* Cambridge: Cambridge University Press.

Heinze, T., and C. Knill. 2008. "Analyzing the Differential Impact of the Bologna Process: Theoretical Considerations on National Conditions For International Policy Convergence." *Higher Education* 67: 493–510.

Helmke, G., and S. Levitsky. 2003. "Informal Institutions and Comparative Politics: A Research Agenda." *Perspectives on Politics* 4: 724–50.

Heritier, A., and D. Lehmkuhl. 2008. "The Shadow of Hierarchy and New Modes of Governance." *Journal of Public Policy* 28: 1–17.

Hertin, J., and F. Berkhout. 2003. "Analyzing Institutional Strategies for Environmental Policy Integration: The Case of EU Environmental Policy." *Journal of Environmental Policy & Planning* 5: 39–56.

Hisschemöller, M., and R. Hoppe. 1995. "Coping with Intractable Controversies: The Case of Problem Structuring in Policy Design and Analysis." *Knowledge and Policy* 8: 40–60.

Hjern, B., and D. O. Porter. 1981. "Implementation Structures: A New Unit of Administrative Analysis." *Organization Studies* 2: 211–27.

Hobbs, S., J. McKechnie, and M. Lavalette. 1999. *Child Labor: A World History Companion.* Santa Barbara, CA: ABC-CLIO.

Hogwood, B. W. 1995. "Whitehall Families, Core Departments and Agency Forms in Britain." *International Review of Administrative Sciences* 61: 511–30.

Hogwood, B. W., and B. G. Peters. 1986. *Policy Dynamics.* Brighton, UK: Wheatsheaf.

Holland, B. 2006. "Holistic Advocacy: An Important but Limited Institutional Role." *NYU Review of Law and Social Change* 30: 637–85.

Holman, K. 1999. *New Connections: Joined-Up Access to Public Services.* London: Community Development Foundation.

Home Office. 1991. *Working Together under the 1989 Children Act.* London: HMSO.

Hood, C. 1986. *The Tools of Government.* Chatham, NJ: Chatham House.

———. 2011. *Blame Game: Spin, Bureaucracy and Self-Preservation in Government.* Princeton, NJ: Princeton University Press.

Hood, C., O. James, C. Scott, and B. G. Peters. 2004. *Controlling Modern Government.* Cheltenham, UK: Edward Elgar.

Hood, C., and B. G. Peters. 2004. "Paradoxes of Public Management: The Middle-Aging of the New Public Management." *Journal of Public Administration Research and Theory* 14: 267–78.

Hoornbeek, J. A. 2004. "Runaway Bureaucracies or Congressional Control?: Water Pollution Policies in the American States." Unpublished PhD dissertation, Department of Political Science, University of Pittsburgh.

Howlett, M., and R. J. Lejano. 2013. "Tales from the Crypt: The Rise and Fall (and Rebirth?) of Policy Design." *Administration & Society* 45: 357–81.

Huber, J. D., and C. R. Shipan. 2002. *Deliberate Discretion?: The Institutional Foundations of Bureaucratic Autonomy*. Cambridge: Cambridge University Press.

Hueglin, T., and A. Fenna. 2006. *Comparative Federalism: A Systematic Inquiry*. Peterborough, Ontario: Broadview Press.

Hughes, J. A. 2002. *The Manhattan Project: Big Science and the Atomic Bomb*. New York: Columbia University Press.

Hult, K. M. 1987. *Agency Merger and Bureaucratic Redesign*. Pittsburgh: University of Pittsburgh Press.

Huxham, C. 2003. "Theorizing Collaborative Practice." *Public Management Review* 5: 401–23.

Huxham, C., and S. Vangen. 2003. "Leadership in the Shaping and Implementation of Collaboration Agendas: How Things Happen in a (Not Quite) Joined-up World." *Academy of Management Journal* 43: 1159–75.

Ingraham, P. W. 1993. "Of Pigs and Pokes and Policy Diffusion: Another Look at Pay for Performance." *Public Administration Review* 53: 348–56.

Innocenti Research Centre. 2003. *Children in Institutions: The Beginning of the End?* Florence: Innocenti Research Centre, UNICEF.

Itoh, H. 1992. "Cooperation in Hierarchical Organizations: An Incentive Perspective." *Journal of Law Economics and Organization* 8: 321–45.

Jacquet, P. 1998. "L'union monetaire et la coordination des politiques macroeconomiques." In *Coordination européenne des politiques economiques*, Conseil d'Analyse Economiquen, 27–36. Paris: La documentation francaise.

Jennings, E. T., and D. Krane. 1994. "Coordination and Welfare Reform: The Quest for the Philosopher's Stone." *Public Administration Review* 54: 341–348.

Jennings, E. T., and J. A. G. Ewalt. 1998. "Interorganizational Coordination, Administrative Consolidation, and Policy Performance." *Public Administration Review* 58: 417–28.

Jensen, L. 2003a. "Aiming for Centrality: The Politico-Administrative Strategies of the Danish Ministry of Finance." In *Controlling Public Expenditure: The Changing Roles of Central Budget Agencies—Better Guardians*, edited by J. Wanna, L. Jensen, and J. de Vries, 223–46. Cheltenham, UK: Edward Elgar.

———. 2003b. *Den Store Koordinator*. Copenhagen: Jurist og Økonomforlag.

Jerome-Forget, M., J. White, and J. M. Wiener. 1995. *Health Care Reform through Internal Markets*. Montreal: Institute for Research on Public Policy.

Johnson, G. 2013. *The Cancer Chronicles: Unlocking Medicine's Deepest Mystery*. New York: A. A. Knopf.

Johnson, R. A. 2003. *Whistleblowing: When It Works—and Why*. Boulder, CO: Lynne Reinner.

Johnston, D., and N. A. Lewis. 2002. "Whistle-Blower Recounts Faults with the FBI." *New York Times*, June 7.

Jordan, A., and A. Lenschow. 2010. "Environmental Policy Integration: A State of the Art Review." *Environmental Policy and Governance* 20: 147–58.

Kaiser, R., and H. Prange. 2005. "Missing the Lisbon Targets: Multi-level Innovation and EU Policy Coordination." *Journal of Public Policy* 25: 241–64.

Kall, W. M. 2010. *The Governance Gap: Central-Local Steering and Mental Health Reform in Britain and Sweden*. Uppsala: Acta Universitatis Upsaliensis.

Karre, P. M., M. Van der Steen, and M. Van Twist. 2013. "Joined-Up Government in the Netherlands, Experiences with Program Ministries." *International Journal of Public Administration* 36: 63–73.

Kassim, H., A. Menon, and B. G. Peters. 2005. *Coordination in the European Union: The EU Bureaucracy*. Lanham, MD: Rowman and Littlefield.

Kassim, H., B. G. Peters, and V. Wright. 1999. *Coordination in the European Union: The National Dimension*. Oxford: Oxford University Press.

Kavanagh, D., and D. Richards. 2001. "Departmentalism and Joined-Up Government." *Parliamentary Affairs* 54: 1–18.

Keast, R., and K. Brown. 2002. "The Government Service Delivery Project: A Case Study of the Push and Pull of Central Government Coordination." *Public Management Review* 4: 439–50.

Keiser, L. R., and K. J. Meier. 1996. "Policy Design, Bureaucratic Incentives and Public Management: The Case of Child Support Enforcement." *Journal of Public Administration Research and Theory* 6: 337–64.

Kekkonen, S., and T. Raunio. 2010. "Towards Stronger Political Steering: Program Management in Finnish Government." In *Steering from the Centre: Strengthening Political Control in Western Democracies,* edited by C. Dahlström, B. G. Peters, and J. Pierre, 241–62. Toronto: University of Toronto Press.

Kettl, D. F. 2002. *Transformation of Governance: Public Administration for Twenty-First Century America*. Baltimore, MD: Johns Hopkins University Press.

———. 2003. "Contingent Coordination: Practical and Theoretical Puzzles for Homeland Security." *American Review of Public Administration* 33: 253–77.

———. 2004a. *System under Stress: Homeland Security and American Politics*. Washington, DC: CQ Press.

———. 2004b. *The Department of Homeland Security's First Year*. New York: Century Foundation.

———. 2006. "Managing Boundaries in American Administration: The Collaboration Imperative." *Public Administration Review* 66: 10–19.

———. 2007. *System under Stress: Homeland Security and American Politics,* 2nd ed. Washington, DC: CQ Press.

Khademian, A. M. 1992. *The SEC and Capital Market Regulation: The Politics of Expertise*. Pittsburgh: University of Pittsburgh Press.

Kickert, W. J. M., E. H. Klijn, and J. F. M. Koopejan. 1997. *Managing Complex Networks*. London: Sage.

Kingdon, J. W. 2003 [1985]. *Agendas, Alternatives and Public Policies*. New York: Longman.

Klein, R. 1998. "Why Britain Is Reorganizing Its National Health Service—Again." *Health Affairs* 17: 111–25.

Klijn, E.-H. 1996. "Analyzing and Managing Policy Processes in Complex Networks." *Administration and Society* 28: 90–119.

Knill, C. 2001. *The Europeanization of National Administrative Systems*. Cambridge: Cambridge University Press.

Knudsen, T. 2000. *Regering og embedsmaend: Om magt og demokrati i staten*. Copenhagen: Sisteme.

Kooiman, J. 2003. *Governing as Governance*. London: Sage.

Krause, P. 2012. "Executive Politics and the Governance of Public Finance." In *Executive Politics in Times of Crisis,* edited by M. Lodge and K. Wegrich, 136–66. Basingstoke, UK: Macmillan.

Krauss, E. 2003. "Building a Bigger Bureaucracy: What the Department of Homeland Security Won't Do." *Public Manager* 32(1): 57–59.

Kriesi, H., S. Adam, and M. Jochum. 2006. "Comparative Analysis of Policy Networks in Western Europe." *Journal of European Public Policy* 13: 341–61.

Lafferty, W., and E. Hovden. 2003. "Environmental Policy Integration: Toward an Analytical Framework." *Environmental Politics* 12: 1–22.

Lam, W. F. 2005. "Coordinating the Government Bureaucracy in Hong Kong: An Institutional Analysis." *Governance* 18: 633–54.

Laming, Lord Herbert. 2009. *Protection of Children in England: A Progress Report.* HC 330. London: HMSO.

Landau, M. 1969. "Redundancy, Rationality and the Problem of Duplication and Overlap." *Public Administration Review* 29: 346–58.

Lane, J.-E. 1981. "The Concept of Implementation." *Statsvetenskapliga Tidskrift* 86: 17–40.

Lanzalco, L. 2011. "Bringing the Olympic Rationality Back In?: Coherence, Integration and Effectiveness of Public Policies." *World Political Science Review* 7 (1), Article 6.

Larkin, R. 2002. "Distributed Public Governance: Principles for Control and Accountability of Agencies, Authorities and other Government Bodies." In *Distributed Public Governance: Agencies, Authorities and Other Government Bodies,* Organization for Economic Cooperation and Development, 267–78. Paris: OECD.

Larsson, T. 1988. *Regierierung och des Kansli.* Stockholm: Student.

Lens, V. 2007. "Administrative Justice in Public Bureaucracies: When Citizens (Don't) Complain." *Administration & Society* 39: 382–408.

Lenschow, A. 2003. *Environmental Policy Integration: Greening Sectoral Policies in Europe.* London: Earthscan.

Lester, W., and D. Krejci. 2007. "Business Not as Usual: The National Incident Management System, Federalism and Leadership." *Public Administration Review* 67: 84–93.

Levin, K., B. Cashore, S. Bernstein, and G. Auld. 2010. "Paying It Forward: Path Dependence, Progressive Incrementalism, and the 'Super Wicked' Problem of Global Climate Change." Unpublished paper, World Resources Institute.

Lichtblau, E. 2002. "F.B.I. Attacks Firearms Agency in Draft Report." *New York Times,* November 12.

Lichtblau, E., and M. S. Schmidt. 2013. "Other Agencies Clamor for Data N.S.A. Compiles." *New York Times,* August 4.

Light, P. C. 1995. *Thickening Government: Federal Hierarchy and the Diffusion of Accountability.* Washington, DC: The Brookings Institution.

Lijphart, A. 2008. *Thinking about Democracy: Power Sharing and Majority Rule in Theory and Practice.* New York: Routledge.

Lindblom, C. E. 1965. *The Intelligence of Democracy: Decision Making through Mutual Adjustment.* New York: Free Press.

Lindblom, C. E. 1974. *The Policy-Making Process.* Englewood Cliffs, NJ: Prentice-Hall.

Linden, R. M. 2002. *Working across Boundaries: Making Collaboration Work in Government and Non-Profit Organizations.* San Francisco: Jossey-Bass.

Linder, S. H., and B. G. Peters. 1987. "A Design Perspective on Policy Implementation: The Fallacy of Misplaced Precision." *Policy Studies Review* 6: 459–75.

Ling, T. 2002. "Delivering Joined-Up Government in the UK: Dimensions, Issues and Problems." *Public Administration* 80: 614–42.

Litwak, E., and L. Hylton. 1962. "Interorganizational Analysis: A Hypothesis on Coordinating Agencies." *Administrative Science Quarterly* 6: 410–24.

London Borough of Brent. 1985. *A Child in Trust: Report of the Panel of Inquiry into the Circumstances Surrounding the Death of Jasmine Beckford*. London: Brent Health Authority.

Lundvall, B. A., and M. Tomlinson. 2001. "International Bench-marking as a Policy Learning Tool." In *The New Knowledge Economy in Europe*, edited by B. A. Lundvall and M. J. Rodrigues, 203–28. Cheltenham, UK: Edward Elgar.

Lynn, L. E, .C. J. Heinrich, and C. J. Hill. 2000. "Studying Governance and Public Management: Challenges and Prospects." *Journal of Public Administration Research and Theory* 3: 233–62.

Maas, A. 1951. *Muddy Waters: The Army Corps of Engineers and the Nation's Rivers*. Cambridge, MA: Harvard University Press.

McCabe, K. A. 2003. *Child Abuse and the Criminal Justice System*. New York: Peter Lang.

McHale, M. 2001. "Whitehall's Falling Czars." *Public Finance*, October 12–18, 18–20.

Mackie, T. T., and B. W. Hogwood. 1985. *Unlocking the Cabinet*. London: Sage.

Majone, G. 1994. *Independence vs. Accountability? Non-Majoritarian Institutions and Democratic Governance in Europe*. Florence: European University Institute.

Malkin, E. 2013. "Mexico: Soda-Tax Bill Moves Forward." *New York Times,* October 18.

Malloy, J. 2003. *Between Colliding Worlds: The Ambiguous Existence of Government Agencies for Aboriginal and Women's Policy*. Toronto: University of Toronto Press.

Maor, M. 1999. "The Paradox of Managerialism." *Public Administration Review* 59: 5–18.

March, J. G., and J. P. Olsen. 1984. "The New Institutionalism: Organizational Factors in Political Life." *American Political Science Review* 78: 734–49.

———. 1987. *Rediscovering Institutions*. New York: Free Press.

Marin, B., and R. Mayntz. 1991. *Policy Networks: Empirical Evidence and Theoretical Considerations*. Frankfurt: Campus Verlag.

Marinetto, M. 2011. "A Lipskian Analysis of Child Protection Failures from Victoria Climbié to 'Baby P': A Street-Level Re-evaluation of Joined-Up Governance." *Public Administration* 89: 1164–81.

Markon, J. 2008. "FBI, ATF Battle for Control of Cases." *Washington Post,* May 10.

Marks, G., L. Hooghe, and K. Blank.1996. "European Integration from the 1980s: State-Centric v. Multi-Level Governance." *Journal of Common Market Studies* 34: 343–77.

Marsh, D., and R. A. W. Rhodes. 1992. *Policy Networks in British Government*. Oxford: Clarendon Press.

Martin, L. W. 2004. "The Government Agenda in Parliamentary Democracies." *American Journal of Political Science* 48: 445–61.

Martinez-Gallardo, C. 2011. "Inside the Cabinet: The Influence of Ministers on the Policy Process." In *How Democracy Works: Political Institutions, Actors and Arenas in Latin America,* edited by C. Scartascini, E. Stein, and M. Tommasi, 119–46. Washington, DC: IADB.

Mastenbroek, E. 2003. "Surviving the Deadline: The Transposition of EU Directives in the Netherlands." *European Union Politics* 4: 371–95.

Matei, A., and T.-C. Gogaru. 2012. "Coordination of Public Policies in Romania: An Empirical Analysis." *Procedia: Social and Behavioral Sciences* 60: 2–6.

May, P. J., A. E. Jochim, and B. Pump. 2010. "Boundary-Spanning Policy Problems: Politics and Policymaking." Paper presented at Annual Meeting of the American Political Science Association, Washington, DC.

May, P. J., A. E. Jochim, and J. Sapotichne. 2009. "Constructing Homeland Security: An Anemic Policy Regime." *Policy Studies Journal* 39: 285–307.

May, P. J., B. D. Jones, B. E. Beem, E. A. Neff-Sharum, and M. K. Poague. 2005. "Policy

Coherence and Component-Driven Policymaking: Arctic Policy in Canada and the United States." *Policy Studies Journal* 33: 37–64.

May, P. J., J. Sapotichne, and S. Workman. 2006. "Policy Coherence and Policy Domains." *Policy Studies Journal* 34: 381–403.

May, P. J., S. Workman, and B. F. Jones. 2008. "Organizing Attention: Responses of the Bureaucracy to Agency Disruption." *Journal of Public Administration Research and Theory* 18: 517–41.

Mayntz, R. 2003. "Mechanisms in the Analysis of Social Macro-Phenomena." *Philosophy of the Social Sciences* 34: 237–59.

Meijers, E., and D. Stead. 2004. Paper presented at the Berlin Conference on the Human Dimension on Global Environmental Change.

Melkas, T. 2013. "Health in All Policies as a Priority in Finnish Health Policy." *Scandinavian Journal of Public Health* 41: 3–28.

Merton, R. K. 1957. *Social Theory and Social Structure*, 2nd ed. Glencoe, IL: Free Press.

Metcalfe, L. 1979. "Policy Making in Turbulent Environments." In *Interorganizational Policymaking: Limits to Coordination and Central Control*, edited by K. Hanf and F. W. Scharpf, 125–44. London: Sage.

———. 1994. "International Policy Co-ordination and Public Management Reform." *International Review of Administrative Sciences* 60: 271–90.

Meyerson, B., B.-C. Choi, and M. V. Mills. 2003. "State Agency Policy and Program Coordination in Response to the Co-occurrence of HIV, Chemical Dependency and Mental Illness." *Public Health Reports* 118: 408–14.

Mickwitz, P., and P. Kivimaa. 2007. "Evaluating Policy Integration. The Case of Policies for Environmentally Friendlier Technological Innovations." *Evaluation* 13: 68–86.

Miller, C. 2003. *The Organisational Implications of the Children's Services Green Paper*. London: Office of Personnel Management.

Miller, H. T., and C. J. Fox. 2001. "Epistemic Community." *Administration and Society* 32: 668–85.

Milward, H. B., and K. G. Provan. 1998. "Principles for Controlling Agents: The Political Economy of Network Structure." *Journal of Public Administration Research and Theory* 8: 3–21.

Ministry of Finance. 2002. *Final Report of the Ministerial Group*. Helsinki: Ministry of Finance.

Mintrom, M., and P. Norman. 2009. "Policy Entrepreneurship and Policy Change." *Policy Studies Journal* 37: 649–67.

Mitchell, K. D. 2003. "The Other Homeland Security Threat: Bureaucratic Haggling." *Public Manager* 32 (4): 40–41.

Moe, T. M. 1984. "The New Economics of Organizations." *American Journal of Political Science* 28: 739–77.

Mohr, L. B. 1982. *Explaining Organizational Behavior*. San Francisco: Jossey-Bass.

Mohr, M., and F. W. Scharpf. 1994. *Efficient Self-Coordination in Policy Networks: A Simulation Study*. Cologne: Max Planck Institute, Discussion Paper 94/1.

Moore, M. H. 1996. *Creating Public Value: Strategic Management in Government*. Cambridge, MA: Harvard University Press.

Morris, J. C., E. D. Morris, and D. M. Jones. 2007. "Reaching for the Philosopher's Stone: Contingent Coordination and the Military Response to Hurricane Katrina." *Public Administration Review* 67 (Special Issue): 94–106.

Morth, U. 2004. *Soft Law in the European Union*. Cheltenham, UK: Edward Elgar.

Mountfield, R. 2001. "Oral Evidence to Committee on Public Administration, House of Commons." London: House of Commons.

Mueller, W. 2000. "Austria." In *Administering the Summit,* edited by B. G. Peters, R. A. W. Rhodes, and V. Wright, 209–226. Oxford: Oxford University Press.

Mueller-Rommel, W. 2000. "Germany." In *Administering the Summit,* edited by B. G. Peters, R. A. W. Rhodes, and V. Wright, 81–100. Oxford: Oxford University Press.

Nathan, R. 1975. *The Plot That Failed: Richard Nixon and the Administrative Presidency.* New York: Wiley.

National Commission on Employment Policy. 1991. *17th Annual Report of the Commission.* Washington, DC: NCEP.

National Commission on Terrorist Attacks on the United States (9/11 Commission). 2004. *Final Report.* New York: Norton.

National Journal. 2001. "A Drama with Many Players." October 20, 42.

National Performance Review. 1996. *Reinventing the Department of Defense.* Washington, DC: National Performance Review.

Nealon, E. 1990. "A Chat with Trapeznikov, Russia's Cancer Czar." *Journal of the National Cancer Institute* 16: 815–16.

Nelson, R. 1967. *The Moon and the Ghetto.* New York: W. W. Norton.

Newmann, W. W. 2003. *Managing National Security Policy: The President and the Process.* Pittsburgh: University of Pittsburgh Press.

Nice, D. V. 1996. "Public or Private Operation of Publicly Owned Railways?" *Policy Studies Journal* 24: 567–77.

Nicholson-Crotty, S. 2005. "Bureaucratic Competition in the Policy Process." *Policy Studies Journal* 33: 341–61.

Nilsson, M., and Å. Persson. 2003. "Framework for Analyzing Environmental Policy Integration." *Journal of Environmental Policy and Planning* 5: 333–59.

Niskanen, W. 1971. *Bureaucracy and Representative Government.* Chicago: Aldine/Atherton.

Norman, R. 2008. "At the Centre or in Control? Central Agencies in Search of New Identities." *Policy Quarterly* 4: 33–38.

Norris, P. 2011. *Democratic Deficit: Critical Citizens Revisited.* Cambridge: Cambridge University Press.

Nousiainen, J. 1991. *Ministers, Parties and Coalition Policies.* Turku: Department of Political Science, University of Turku.

———. 1996. "Finland: Operational Cabinet Autonomy in a Party-Centred System." In *Party and Government,* edited by J. Blondel and M. Cotta, 216–37. Basingstoke, UK: Macmillan.

Nowlin, M. C. 2011. "Theories of the Policy Process: State of Research and Emerging Trends." *Policy Studies Journal* 39: 41–60.

Nurmi, H., and L Nurmi. 2012. "The Parliamentary Election in Finland, April 2011." *Electoral Studies* 31: 234–38.

O'Beirne, K. 2003. "Introducing Pork Barrel National Security." *National Review,* August 11.

Observatoire National de l'Enfance en Danger. 2005. *Report Annuel.* Paris: ONED.

O'Connor, A. 2001. *Poverty Knowledge: Social Science, Social Policy and the Poor in the Twentieth Century.* Princeton, NJ: Princeton University Press.

Office of Management and Budget. 2003. *Government-Wide Performance Indicators.* Washington, DC: OMB.

Office of National Drug Control Policy. 2004. *The President's National Drug Control Strategy 2004.* Washington, DC: Executive Office of the President.

Oleszek, W. 2007. *Congressional Procedures and the Policy Process.* Washington, DC: CQ Press.

Oliver, C. 1990. "Determinants of Interorganizational Relationships: Integration and Further Directions." *Academy of Management Review* 15: 241–65.

———. 1992. "The Antecedents of Deinstitutionalization." *Organization Studies* 13: 563–88.

Olsen, J. P. 2001. "Garbage Cans, New Institutionalism and the Study of Politics." *American Political Science Review* 95: 191–98.

O'Malley, E. 2007. "The Power of Prime Ministers: Results of an Expert Survey." *International Political Science Review* 28: 11–27.

Organization for Economic Cooperation and Development. 2005. *Policy Coherence for Development: Promoting Institutional Good Practice.* Paris: OECD.

Ostrom E. 1990. *Governing the Commons: The Evolution of Institutions of Collective Action.* Cambridge: Cambridge University Press.

Ostrom, E., R. B. Parks, and G. P. Whitaker. 1974. "Defining and Measuring Structural Arrangements in Interorganizational Arrangements." *Publius* 4: 87–108.

O'Toole, L. J. 1993. "Interorganizational Policy Studies: Lessons Drawn from Implementation Research." *Journal of Public Administration Research and Theory* 3: 232–51.

Oughton, C. 1997. "Competitiveness Policy in the 1990s." *Economic Journal* 107: 1486–503.

Page, E. C. 2012. *Policy without Politicians: Bureaucratic Influence in Comparative Perspective.* Oxford: Oxford University Press.

Page, S. 2003. "Entrepreneurial Strategies for Managing Interagency Collaboration." *Journal of Public Administration Research and Theory* 13: 311–40.

Paloheimo, H. 2003. "Finland: Let the Force Be with the Leader, But Who Is the Leader?" In *Presidentialization of Parliamentary Democracies,* edited by T. Poguntke and P. Webb, 236–81. Oxford: Oxford University Press.

Papadopolous, Y. 1998. *Démocratie directe.* Paris: Economica.

———. 1999. "Gouvernance, coordination et légitimité dans les politiques publiques." *EU Working Paper* 99/20. Florence: European University Institute.

Parker, M. 2000. *Organizational Culture and Identity.* London: Sage.

Payan, T. 2006. *Cops, Soldiers, Diplomats: Explaining Agency Behavior in the War on Drugs.* Lanham, MD: Lexington Books.

Pear, R. 2002. "Traces of Terror: The New Department; Lawmakers Asking If Plan on Terror Goes Far Enough." *New York Times,* June 7.

Pecora, P. J. 2000. *The Child Welfare Challenge: Policy, Practice and Research.* New Brunswick, NJ: Transaction Books.

Perry, J. L. 2000. "Bringing Society In: Toward a Theory of Public Service Motivation." *Journal of Public Administration Research and Theory* 10: 471–88.

Persson, Å. 2004. *Environmental Policy Integration: An Introduction.* Stockholm: Stockholm Environment Institute.

Peters, B. G. 1987. "Politicians and Bureaucrats in Comparative Perspective." In *Bureaucracy and Public Choice,* edited by J.-E. Lane, 255–82. London: Sage.

———. 1988. *Comparing Public Bureaucracies: Problems of Theory and Method.* Tuscaloosa: University of Alabama Press.

———. 1992. "Bureaucratic Politics in the European Community." In *Euro-Politics,* edited by A. M. Sbragia, 119–35. Washington, DC: The Brookings Institution.

———. 1999. *Institutional Theory in Political Science: The New Institutionalism.* London: Continuum.

———. 2003. "Governance and Public Bureaucracy: New Forms of Bureaucracy or New Forms of Control?" *Asia-Pacific Journal of Public Administration* 26: 3–15.

———. 2004a. "Back to the Centre: Rebuilding the State." *Political Quarterly* 75: 130–40.

———. 2004b. "Många mål och ännu fler alternativ: att utforma offentliga institutioner." In *Självstyrelse, likvärdlighet, effektivitet,* edited by P. Molander and K. Stigmark, 243–67. Stockholm: Gidlunds Forlag.

———. 2005. "The Garbage Can Model of Governance." In *Complex Sovereignty,* edited by E. Grande and L. Pauley, 68–92. Toronto: University of Toronto Press.

———. 2010. *Institutional Theory in Political Science: The New Institutionalism,* 3rd ed. London: Continuum.

———. 2013a. *Strategies for Comparative Political Research.* Basingstoke, UK: Macmillan.

———. 2013b. "Implementation Structures as Institutions." *Public Policy and Administration* 29: 131–44.

Peters, B. G., and J. A. Hoornbeek. 2004. "The Problem of Policy Problems." In *Designing Government,* edited by P. Eliasis, M. Hill, and M. Howlett, 223–45. Montreal: McGill-Queen's University Press.

Peters, B. G., and J. Pierre. 2001. *Politicians, Bureaucrats and Administrative Reform.* London: Routledge.

———. 2004. "Multi-Level Governance—A Faustian Bargain?" In *Multi-Level Governance,* edited by I. Bache and M. Flinders, 117–34. Oxford: Oxford University Press.

———. 2005. "Effective Governance as Good Governance: Steering Society and Creating Coherence." Paper presented at Annual Meeting of the American Political Science Association, Washington, DC.

———. 2014. "Food Policy as a Wicked Policy Problem." *World Food Policy Journal* 1: 3–17.

Peters, B. G., J. Pierre, and T. Randma-Liiv. 2011. "Global Financial Crisis, Public Administration and Governance: Do New Problems Require New Solutions?" *Public Organization Review* 11: 13–27.

Peters, B. G., R. A. W. Rhodes, and V. Wright. 2000. *Administering the Summit.* Oxford: Oxford University Press.

Peters, B. G., and D. J. Savoie. 1996. "Managing Incoherence: The Coordination and Empowerment Conundrum." *Public Administration Review* 56: 281–90.

Peters, B. G., L. Vass, and T. Verheijen. 2005. *Coalitions of the Unwilling?: Politicians and Bureaucrats in Coalition Governments.* Bratislava: NISPACee.

Pierre, J. 1998. *Partnerships in Urban Governance.* London: Macmillan.

Pierre, J., and B. G. Peters. 2000. *Governance, Politics and the State.* Basingstoke, UK: Macmillan.

Pierson, P. 2000. "Increasing Returns, Path Dependence and the Study of Politics." *American Political Science Review* 94: 251–67.

Pluvoise-Fenton, V., and J. Pionke. 2004. "Report Calls for End of Homeland Security Funding Logjam." *National Cities Weekly* 27 (June 21): 1–2.

Poguntke, T., and P. Webb. 2005. *Presidentialization of Politics: A Comparative Study of Modern Politics.* Oxford: Oxford University Press.

Polidano, C. 1999. "The Bureaucrat Who Fell under a Bus: Ministerial Responsibility, Executive Agencies, and the Derek Lewis Affair in Britain." *Governance* 12: 201–29.

Pollitt, C. 1984. *Manipulating the Machine: Changing Patterns of Ministerial Departments, 1960–1983.* London: Allen and Unwin.

———. 2003. "Joined-Up Government: A Survey." *Political Studies Review* 1: 34–49.

Pollitt, C., and G. Bouckaert. 2004. *Public Management Reform: A Comparative Perspective,* 2nd ed. Oxford: Oxford University Press.

Pollitt, C., and S. Dan. 2011. *The Impacts of New Public Management in Europe: A Meta-Analysis.* COCOPS Working Paper. Leuven, Belgium: Institute of Public Management, Catholic University of Leuven.

Pollitt, C., and C. Talbot. 2003. *Unbundled Government.* London: Routledge.

Pollitt, C., C. Talbot, J. Caulfield, and A. Smullen. 2004. *Agencies: How Governments Do Things through Semi-Autonomous Agencies.* Basingstoke, UK: Macmillan.

Posner, P. 2007. "The Politics of Coercive Federalism in the Bush Era." *Publius* 37: 390–412.

Pressman, J. L., and A. Wildavsky. 1974. *Implementation.* Berkeley: University of California Press.

Prime Minister's Office. 2007. *Program Management within the Finnish Government.* Helsinki: Prime Minister's Office.

———. 2011. *Policy Programmes: Parliamentary Term 2007–2011.* Helsinki: Prime Minister's Office.

Provan, K. G., and R. H. Lemaire. 2012. "Core Concepts and Key Ideas for Understanding Public Sector Interorganizational Networks: Using Research to Inform Scholarship and Practice." *Public Administration Review* 72: 638–48.

Provan, K. G., and J. Sydow. 2011. "Evaluating Interorganizational Relations." In *Handbook of Interorganizational Relations,* edited by S. Cooper, M. Ebers, C. Huxham, and P. S. Rings, 322–45. Oxford: Oxford University Press.

Qiu, M., and H. Li. 2008. "China's Environmental Super Ministry Reform: Background, Challenges and the Future." *Environmental Law Reporter* 13: 112–22.

Radaelli, C. 2003. "The Code of Conduct against Harmful Tax Competition: Open Method of Coordination in Disguise?" *Public Administration* 81: 513–31.

Radin, B. A. 1996. "Managing across Boundaries." In *The State of Public Management,* edited by D. F. Kettl and H. B. Milward, 145–67. Baltimore, MD: Johns Hopkins University Press.

———. 2002. *The Accountable Juggler: The Art of Leadership in a Federal Agency.* Washington, DC: CQ Press.

Randma-Liiv, T. 2014. "The Impact of the Fiscal Crisis on Public Administration." *Administrative Culture* 15, 4–9.

Raunio, T., and M. Wiberg. 2000. "Building Elite Consensus: Parliamentary Accountability in Finland." *Journal of Legislative Studies* 6: 59–80.

Remington, J. A. 1988. "Beyond Big Science in America: The Binding of Inquiry." *Social Studies of Science* 18: 45–72.

Renwu, T., and Z. Guoqin. 2012. *The Structural Logic of Holistic Governance and its Respond [sic] to Political Fragmentation.* Beijing: Atlantis Press.

Rettig, R. A. 2005. *Cancer Crusade: The Story of the National Cancer Act of 1971.* Princeton, NJ: Princeton University Press.

Rhinard, M., and B. Vaccari. 2005. "The Study of the European Commission." *Journal of European Public Policy* 12: 387–94.

Rhodes, R. A. W. 1997. *Understanding Governance: Policy Networks, Governance, Reflexivity and Accountability.* Buckingham, UK: Open University Press.

———. 2002. "Putting the People Back into Networks." *Australian Journal of Political Science* 37: 399–415.

Richardson, J. J. 2001. "Policy-making in the EU: Interests, Ideas and Garbage Cans of

Primeval Soup." In *European Union: Power and Policy-Making*, 2nd ed., edited by J. J. Richardson, 23–54. London: Routledge.

Ries, J. C. 1964. *The Management of Defense Organizations*. Baltimore, MD: Johns Hopkins University Press.

Rittel, H. W. J., and M. M. Webber. 1973. "Dilemmas in the General Theory of Planning." *Policy Sciences* 4: 155–69.

Robins, J. A. 1987. "Organizational Economics: Note on the Use of Transaction Cost Theory in the Study of Organizations." *Administrative Science Quarterly* 32: 68–86.

Rodrigues, M. J. 2009. *Europe, Globalization and the Lisbon Strategy*. Cheltenham, UK: Edward Elgar.

Rosacker, K. M., and D. L. Olson. 2008. "Public Sector Information Systems Critical Success Factors." In *Transforming Government: People, Process, Policy* 2, 60–70.

Rose, R. 1974. *The Problem of Party Government*. London: Macmillan.

Rouban, L. 2003. "Réformer ou recompser l'État?: Les enjeux sociopolitique d'une mutation annoncée." *Revue française d'administration publique* 63: 154–66.

Sabatier, P. A. 1986. "Top-Down and Bottom-Up Approaches to Implementation Research: A Critical Analysis and Suggested Synthesis." *Journal of Public Policy* 6: 21–48.

Sabatier, P. A., and H. Jenkins-Smith. 1993. *Policy Change and Learning: An Advocacy-Coalition Approach*. Boulder, CO: Westview.

Salamon, L. M. 1980. "The Goals of Reorganization." In *Federal Reorganization: What Have We Learned?*, edited by P. Szanton, 154–72. Chatham, NJ: Chatham House.

———. 2000. *Handbook of Policy Instruments*. New York: Oxford University Press.

Sartori, G. 1991. "Comparing and Miscomparing." *Journal of Theoretical Politics* 3: 243–57.

Savoie, D. J. 1999. *Governing from the Centre: The Concentration of Power in Canadian Politics*. Toronto: University of Toronto Press.

———. 2008. *Court Government and the Collapse of Accountability in Canada and the United Kingdom*. Toronto: University of Toronto Press.

Sayre, Wallace S. 1958. "Premises of Public Administration: Past and Emerging." *Public Administration Review* 18 (2): 102–105.

Scharpf, F. W. 1988. "The Joint Decision Trap: Lessons from German Federalism and European Integration." *Public Administration* 66: 239–78.

———. 1997. *Games Real Actors Play: Actor-Centered Institutionalism in Policy Research*. Boulder, CO: Westview.

Scharpf, F. W., B. Reissert, and F. Schnabel. 1976. *Politikverflechtung*. Konigsberg: Scriptor.

Schermerhorn, J. R. 1975. "Determinants of Interorganizational Cooperation." *Academy of Management Journal* 18: 846–56.

Schmidt, C. P. 2000. *Changing Bureaucratic Behavior: Acquisition Reform in the United States Army*. Santa Monica, CA: Rand.

Schön, D. A., and M. Rein. 1994. *Frame Reflection: Solving Intractable Policy Disputes*. Cambridge, MA: MIT Press.

Sciolino, E. 2004. "A Campaign to Drink Another Glass of Wine for France." *New York Times*, July 23.

Scott, I. 1988. *Specialists and Generalists*. Hong Kong: Oxford University Press.

Securities and Exchange Commission. 2009. "Report of Failure of the Securities and Exchange Commission to Uncover Bernard Madoff Ponzi Scheme." Washington, DC: Securities and Exchange Commission, Office of the Inspector General.

Seidman, H. 1998. *Politics, Power and Position: The Dynamics of Federal Organization*, 5th ed. New York: Oxford University Press.

Selznick, P. A. 1957. *Leadership in Administration*. New York: Harper and Row.

Shennon, P. 2004. "9/11 Report Is Said to Urge New Post for Intelligence." *New York Times*, July 17.

Sicurelli, D. 2008. "Framing Security and Development in the EU Pillar Structure: How the Views of the European Commission Affect EU African Policy." *European Integration* 30: 217–34.

Sieber, S. 1980. *Fatal Remedies*. New York: Plenum.

Simon, H. A. 1947. *Administrative Behavior*. New York: Free Press.

Simpson, C., R. Simpson, K. Power, A. Salter, and G. J. Williams. 1994. "GPs and Health Visitor Participation in Child Protection Case Conferences." *Child Abuse Review* 3: 211–30.

Skelcher, C. 2004. "Jurisdictional Integrity, Polycentrism and the Design of Democratic Governance." *Governance* 18: 89–110.

Skelcher, C., and H. Sullivan. 2008. "Theory-Driven Approaches to Analyzing Collaborative Performance." *Public Management Review* 10: 751–71.

Smith, A. 1997. "Studying Multi-Level Governance: Examples from French Translations of the Structural Funds." *Public Administration* 20: 711–29.

Smith, M. J. 1999. *The Core Executive in Britain*. Basingstoke, UK: Macmillan.

———. 2004. "Mad Cows and Mad Money: Problems of Risk in Making and Understanding Public Policy." *British Journal of Politics and International Affairs* 6: 312–32.

Smith, P. C. 2002. "Performance Management in British Health Care: Will It Deliver?" *Health Affairs* 21: 103–15.

Smith, S. R. 2012. "Street-Level Bureaucracy and Public Policy." In *The Handbook of Public Administration*, 2nd ed., edited by B. G. Peters and J. Pierre. London: Sage. 414–23.

Sofer, V. N. 1994. *Lysenko and the Tragedy of Soviet Science*. New Brunswick, NJ: Rutgers University Press.

Soss, J. 2000. *Unwanted Claims: The Politics of Participation in the US Welfare System*. Ann Arbor: University of Michigan Press.

Statsrådets Kansli. 2005. *Regeringens Strategidokument*. Helsinki: Statsråadet.

Stein, J. 2003. "Is Homeland Security Keeping America Safe?" *CQ Weekly*, June 14, 2–14.

Steinacker, A. 2010. "The Institutional Collective Action Perspective on Self-Organizing Mechanisms: Market Failures and Transaction Cost Problems." In *Self-organizing Federalism: Collaborative Mechanisms to Mitigate Institutional Collective Action Problems*, edited by R. C. Feiock and J. T. Scholz, 123–42. Cambridge: Cambridge University Press.

Stewart, J. 2004. "The Meaning of Strategy in the Public Sector." *Australian Journal of Public Administration* 63: 16–21.

Stinchcombe, A. L. 1990. *Information and Organizations*. Berkeley: University of California Press.

Stokman, F., and F. van Oosteen. 1994. "The Exchange of Voting Positions: An Object-Oriented Model of Policy Networks." In *European Community Decision-Making*, edited by B. Bueno de Mesquita and F. Stokman, 105–37. New Haven, CT: Yale University Press.

Stuart, D. and H. Starr. 1981. "The Inherent Bad Faith Model Reconsidered," *Political Psychology* 3: 1–33.

Sullivan, H. 2003. "New Forms of Local Accountability: Coming to Terms with 'Many Hands.'" *Policy & Politics* 31: 353–69.

Szanton, P. 1981. *Federal Reorganization: What Have We Learned?* Chatham, NJ: Chatham House.

Szczerski, K. 2005. "Multi-Level Governance in Post-Communist Conditions: Challenges to Governability for the New EU Member States." In *Institutional Requirements and Problem Solving in the Public Administrations of the Enlarged European Union and Its Neighbors,* edited by G. Jenei, A. Barabashev, and F. Van der Berg, 39–54. Bratislava: NISPACEE.

Tallberg, J. 2002. "Paths to Compliance: Enforcement, Management and the European Union." *International Organization* 56: 609–33.

Tanguy, G. 2013. "Des hauts fonctionnaires au service de l'État." In *La France et ses administrations: Un état des saviors,* edited by J.-M. Eymeri-Douzanes and G. Bouckaert, 103–32. Brussels: Bruylant.

Temkin, B. 1983. "State, Ecology and Independence: Policy Responses to Energy Crises in the United States." *British Journal of Political Science* 13: 441–62.

Thatcher, M. 2002. "Regulation after Delegation: Independent Regulatory Agencies in Europe." *Journal of European Public Policy* 9: 954–72.

Thelen, K. 2004. *How Institutions Evolve: The Political Economy of Skills in Germany, Britain, Japan and the United States.* Cambridge: Cambridge University Press.

Thelen, K., and S. Steinmo. 1992. "Historical Institutionalism in Comparative Politics." In *Structuring Politics: Historical Institutionalism in Comparative Analysis,* edited by S. Steinmo, K. Thelen, and F. Longstreth, 1–32. Cambridge: Cambridge University Press.

Thomas, C. 2002. "Office of Homeland Security." *Harvard Journal of Legislation* 39: 455–68.

Thomas, C. W. 1993. "Reorganizing Public Organizations: Alternatives, Objectives and Evidence." *Journal of Public Administration Research and Theory* 3: 457–86.

Thomas, N. 2011. "The Role and Impact of Independent Children's Rights Institutions in the UK and Europe." *Journal of Social Welfare and Family Law* 33: 279–88.

Thomas, P. C. 2012. "Introduction to Accountability Section." In *Handbook of Public Administration,* 2nd ed., edited by B. G. Peters and J. Pierre, 673–80. London: Sage.

Thompson, D. F. 1980. "Moral Responsibility of Public Officials: The Problem of Many Hands." *American Political Science Review* 74: 905–16.

Thompson, G., J. Frances, R. Levacic, and J. Mitchell. 1991. *Markets, Networks and Hierarchies.* London: Sage.

Thompson, V. A. 1961. *Modern Organizations.* New York: Knopf.

Thomson, R., F. Stockman, and R. Torenvlied. 2003. "Models of Collective Decision-Making: Introduction." *Rationality and Society* 15: 5–14.

Tiihonen, S. 2004. *From Governing to Governance.* Tampere, Finland: Tampere University Press.

Tiilikainen, T. 2005. "Finland: Any Lessons for Euro-Outsiders?" *Journal of European Integration* 27: 25–42.

Tilli, M. 2007. "Strategic Political Steering: Exploring the Qualitative Change in the Role of Ministers after NPM Reforms." *International Review of Administrative Sciences* 73: 81–94.

Tillin, L. 2007. "United in Diversity?: Asymmetry in Indian Federalism." *Publius* 37: 45–67.

Timsit, G. 1988. *Les autorités administratives independents.* Paris: Presses Universitaires de France.

Toke, D. 2000. "Policy Network Creation: The Case of Energy Efficiency." *Public Administration* 78: 835–54.

Tomlinson, I. J. 2010. "Acting Discursively: The Development of the UK Organic Food and Farming Policy Network." *Public Administration* 88: 1045–62.

Torfing, J., B. G. Peters, J. Pierre, and E. Sørensen. 2012. *Interactive Governance: Advancing the Paradigm.* Oxford: Oxford University Press.

Tsebelis, G. 1995. "Decision-Making in Political Systems: Veto Players in Presidentialism, Parliamentarism, Multicameralism and Multipartyism." *British Journal of Political Science* 25: 289–325.

Tsegaye, S., and Y. Mekonen. 2010. *Budgeting for Children in Africa: Concept and Framework for Analysis.* Addis Ababa: African Child Policy Forum.

Ugland, T. 2002. *Policy Re-Categorization and Integration.* Oslo: ARENA, University of Oslo.

Underdal, A. 1980. "Integrated Marine Policy: What? Why? How?" *Marine Policy* (July): 78–95.

UNICEF. 2012. *Child Maltreatment: Prevalence, Incidence and Consequences in the East Asia and Pacific Region.* Bangkok: UNICEF East Asia and Pacific Regional Office.

US General Accounting Office. 1999. *Observations on the Social Security Administration's 2000 Performance Plan.* Washington, DC: USGAO, July 21. GAO/HEHS-99-162R.

———. 2003a. *Information Technology: Terrorist Watch Lists Should Be Consolidated to Promote Better Integration and Sharing.* Washington, DC: USGAO, April 23. GAO-03-322.

———. 2003b. *Posthearing Questions from the September 17, 2003, Hearing on "Implications of Power Blackouts for Nation's Cybersecurity and Critical Infrastructure Protection."* Washington, DC: USGAO, December 8. GAO-04-330R.

———. 2003c. *Bioterrorism: A Threat to Agriculture and the Food Supply.* Washington, DC: USGAO, November 19. GAO-04-259T.

———. 2004a. *Guardianships: Collaboration Needed to Protect Incapacitated Elderly People.* Washington, DC: USGAO, July. GAO-04-655.

———. 2004b. *Homeland Security: DHS Needs a Strategy to Use DOE's Laboratories for Research on Nuclear, Biological and Chemical Detection and Response Technologies.* Washington, DC: USGAO, May. GAO-04-653.

———. 2004c. *Transformation Strategy Needed to Address Challenges Facing the Federal Protective Service.* Washington, DC: USGAO, July. GAO-04-537.

———. 2004d. *FBI Transformation: Data Inconclusive on Effects of Shift to Counterterrorism-Related Priorities on Traditional Crime Enforcement.* Washington, DC: USGAO, August. GAO-04-1036.

———. 2005. *Federal Housing Programs That Offer Assistance for the Elderly.* Washington, DC: USGAO, February. GAO-05-174.

———. 2007. *Numerous Federal Networks Used to Support Homeland Security Need to be Better Coordinated with Key State and Local Information-Sharing Initiatives.* Washington, DC: USGAO, April. GAO 07-455.

———. 2013a. *Information Sharing: Agencies Could Better Coordinate to Reduce Overlap in Field Based Activities.* Washington, DC: USGAO, GAO-13-471.

———. 2013b. *USAID Is Improving Coordination But Needs to Require Systematic Assessment of Country Risks.* Washington, DC: USGAO, GAO-13-809.

Van de Graaf, T. 2013. "Fragmentation in Global Energy Governance: Explaining the Creation of IRENA." *Global Environmental Politics* 13: 14–33.

Verhoest K., G. Bouckaert, and B. G. Peters. 2007. "Janus-Faced Reorganization: Specialization and Coordination in Four OECD Countries in the Period 1980–2005." *International Review of Administrative Sciences* 73: 325–348.

Verhoest, K., B. G. Peters, B. Verschuere, and G. Bouckaert. 2004. Controlling Autonomous Public Agencies as an Indicator of New Public Management." *Management International* 6: 25–36.

Viinamäki, P.-P. 2004. *A Theory of Coordination and Its Implications on EU Structural Policy.* Vaasa, Finland: Acta Wasaensia.

Walsh, K. 1995. *Public Services and Market Mechanisms: Competition, Contracting and the New Public Management.* Basingstoke, UK: Macmillan.

Warin, P. 2002. *Les dépanneurs de justice: Les "petits fonctionnaires" entre égalité et équité.* Paris: L. G. D. J.

Waugh, W. L., and G. Streib. 2006. "Collaboration and Leadership for Effective Emergency Management." *Public Administration Review* 66 (supplement issue): 131–40.

Weaver, R. K. 1986. "The Politics of Blame Avoidance." *Journal of Public Policy* 6: 371–90.

Webb, A. 1991. "Coordination: A Problem in Public Sector Management." *Policy and Politics* 19: 229–41.

Webb, E. T., D. T. Campbell, L. Sechrest, and R. D. Schwartz. 1981. *Unobtrusive Measures: Nonreactive Research in the Social Sciences.* Boston: Houghton Mifflin.

Weber, E. P., and A. M. Khademian. 2008. "Wicked Problems, Knowledge Challenges and Collaborative Capacity in Network Settings." *Public Administration Review* 68: 334–9.

Wechsler, W. 2002. "Law in Order: Reconstructing Homeland Security." *National Interest* 67 (Spring): 17–28.

Weil, A., and J. Holahan. 2002. *Health Insurance, Welfare and Work.* Washington, DC: The Brookings Institution.

Weimer, D. L., and W. T. Gormley. 1999. *Organizational Report Cards.* Cambridge, MA: Harvard University Press.

Weiss, J. 1989. "The Powers of Problem Definition: The Case of Government Paperwork." *Policy Sciences* 22: 97–121.

Weller, P. 2007. *Cabinet Government in Australia 1901–2006: Practice, Principles and Performance.* Sydney: University of New South Wales Press.

Whetten, D. A. 1982. "Objectives and Issues: Setting the Stage." In *Interorganizational Coordination,* edited by D. L. Rogers and D. A. Whetten, 3–22. Ames: Iowa State University Press.

White, M. 2008. "Squabble over Baby P Was Not the Commons at Its Best." *Guardian,* November 12.

Wiggins, K. 2013. "Ofsted Criticizes Children's Services 'Volatility.'" *Local Government Chronicle,* October 16.

Wildavsky, A. 1973. "If Planning Is Everything Then Maybe It's Nothing." *Policy Sciences* 4: 127–53.

Wilensky, H. L. 1967. *Organizational Intelligence.* New York: Basic Books.

Wilkinson, D., and E. Appelbee. 1999. *Implementing Holistic Government: Joined-Up Action on the Ground.* Bristol, UK: Policy Press.

Williamson, O. E. 1995. *Organization Theory: From Chester Barnard to the Present and Beyond.* New York: Oxford University Press.

Willumsen, E., and L. Hallberg. 2003. "Interprofessional Collaboration with Young People in Residential Care: Some Professional Perspectives." *Journal of Interprofessional Care* 17: 389–401.

Wilson, J. Q. 1989. *Bureaucracy: What Government Agencies Do and Why They Do It.* New York: Basic Books.

Winter, S. 2012. "The Implementation Perspective." In *The Handbook of Public Administration*, edited by B. G. Peters and J. Pierre, 265–78. London: Sage.

Wolf, C. 1993. *Markets or Governments: Choosing between Imperfect Alternatives.* Cambridge, MA: MIT Press.

Wolf, F. 2010. "Enlightened Eclecticism or Hazardous Hotchpotch? Mixed Methods and Triangulation Strategies in Comparative Public Policy Research." *Journal of Mixed Methods Research* 4: 144–67.

Woodside, K. 1986. "Policy Instruments and the Study of Public Policy." *Canadian Journal of Political Science* 19: 775–99.

Wright, V., and E. C. Page. 1999. *Bureaucratic Elites in West European Countries.* Oxford: Oxford University Press.

Yang, C. J., and M. Oppenheimer. 2007. "A 'Manhattan Project' for Climate Change?" *Climate Change* 80: 199–204.

Yesilkagit, K., and J.-G. Christensen. 2010. "Institutional Design and Formal Autonomy: Political versus Historical and Cultural Explanations." *Journal of Public Administration Research and Theory* 20: 53–74.

Yi, H. 2003. "Building a Department of Homeland Security: The Management Theory." *Public Manager* 32(1): 55–56.

Zito, A. R. 2001. "Epistemic Communities, Collective Entrepreneurship and European Integration." *Journal of European Public Policy* 10: 585–603.

Index

6, P., 2, 3, 7, 70, 96, 100

Accountability, 40–41, 137–138, 140–142
Adam, S., 24
Administrative reform, 47
Advocacy coalition framework, 158
Agranoff, R., 6, 97
Albert, S., 33
Alexander, E. R., 57
Allen, G., 78
Allen, M., 105
Allison, G. T., 26, 46
Althaus, R. R., 32
Amorim Neto, O, 76
Anderson, G., 2
Andeweg, R., 51, 82
Appelbee, E., 8
Arter, D., 161
Ashforth, B. E., 33
Atger, A. F., 123
Aubin, D., 131
Auditing, 130
Auld, G., 154
Australia
    Prime Minister and Cabinet Office, 77
Australian Public Service Commission, 146
Autonomy, of organizations, 28, 49, 131–
    132
Axelrod, R. M., 40

"Baby P.," 114
Bäck, H. M., 155
Bakvis, H., 31, 81, 93
Bal, R., 134
Bamberger, K. A., 137
Banfield, E. C., 158
Bardach, E., 6, 32, 66, 67, 68, 69, 71, 97, 98
Barling, P., 21
Béland, D., 144
Bendor, J. B., 130, 138
Benson, J. K., 58

Berkhout, F., 4
Bernstein, M., 131
Bernstein, S., 154
Bertelli, A. M., 61
Best, J., 68
Bettelhelm, A., 58
Bezes, P., 96
Biermann, F., 1
Bignami, F., 30
Bijker, W. E., 134
Blair, Tony, 7
Blame avoidance, 52
Blatter, J., 161
Blick, A., 50
Block, R., 29
Bobbitt, P., 161
Bogdanor, V., 3, 7, 100
Boin, A., 34, 116
Boisnier, A., 28
Bolleyer, N., 12, 13
Borrás, S., 121, 123
Börzel, T. A., 12, 13
Boston, J., 3
Bouckaert, G., 2, 7, 15, 26, 30, 33, 47, 75, 82,
    83, 96
Boundary spanning, 6, 28
Bovens, M. A. P., 43
Bradley, A. A., 161
Briassoulis, H., 23, 97
Brown, T. L., 55
Bruel, J. D., 36
Brunsson, N., 99
Bryson, A., 11
Bryson, J. M., 11
Buchanan, J. M., 159
Buchs, M., 13
Budgeting, 83
Bureaucracy, 14, 47–50
Bureaucratic politics, 17
Burgess, S., 31
Bush, George W., 105

Callaghan, K., 68
Campbell, C. E., 78
Campbell, D. T., 46
Campbell, J. L., 37
Canada, 83
    Canadian Food Inspection System, 20
    Human Resources and Skills Development
        Canada, 85, 146
    Treasury Board Secretariat, 78
Carlsson, L., 93
Carpenter, D. A., 28
Carrera, S., 123
Carter, A. B., 105
Carter, Jimmy, 33
Carvajal, D., 15
Cashore, B., 154
Catalonia, 12
Caulfield, J., 157
Central agencies, 31, 78–80, 157
Centrelink, 20, 31
Challis, L., 3
Chan, A., 37
Chapman, J., 101
Chatman, J. A., 28
Child abuse, 113–116, 124
Childrens' budgets, 18
Children's policy, xi, 14, 103, 112–117
Chisholm, D., 19, 24, 63
Choi, B.-C., 37
Christensen, J.-G., 28
Christensen, T., 8, 47, 101
Civil service, 63, 160
Clark, J. P., 160
Clarke, H. D., 160
Clientele groups, 16, 17, 28, 36, 48, 155
Climbié, Victoria, 114–116, 125, 136
Clinton, William, 36
Coalition government, 35–36, 158, 159, 160
Cohen, D. K., 107
Coleman, W., 39
Collaboration, 6–7, 16, 24, 65–69, 96–99
    Craftsmanship, 66, 98
    Public value, 66
Collective action problems, 26
Competitiveness policy, 87, 122
Complexity, 141
Conklin, J., 15

Conley, R. S., 77
Considine, M., 140
Constitutions, 159
Constructivism, 69
Contracting, 55–56
    Relational, 55, 92
Cooper, C., 29
Cooper, P. J., 29
Cooper, R., 54
Cooperation, 5–6
Coordination
    Definition, 3–5, 20–22
    Failure, 26
    Inside versus outside, 15
    Levels, 4
    Measurement, 22–24
    Policy-specific versus systemic goals, 17–18
    Policy versus administration, 13
    Political versus administration, 14–15
    Positive versus negative, 9–10
    Process versus outcomes, 10–11
    Short term versus long term, 18–19
    Similar versus complementary goals, 16–17
    Vertical versus horizontal, 11–13, 110–111
Cox, G. W., 75
Cox, R. H.
Crane, D., 2, 23
Crisis management, 19, 29, 89, 116
Crosby, B. C., 11
Crozier, M., 63
Cuellar, M. F., 107
Czars, 77, 106, 141, 160

Daalder, I. H., 105
Dahl, R. A., 52, 93
Dahlström, C., 15, 31, 77, 128
Dan, S., 119
Data privacy, 29–30
Davies, J. S., 6
Davis, G., 2
Debus, M., 155
Decentralization, 79–80
De Jong, A., 13
Delegation, 47, 51
Delone, G. J., 130
Denhardt, J. V., 61
Denhardt, R. B., 61

Derlien, H.-U., 47
Dery, D., 97
Desage, F., 11
Destler, I. M., 105
Dewar, D., 152
Di Francesco, M., 80
DiMaggio, P., 57
Diversity, 135–136
Dixit, A., 61
Doern, G. B., 17
Döring, H., 35
Downs, A., 27, 32
Dubois, V., 28
Duit, A., 133
Dumont, P., 155
Duncan, G., 101
Dunn, W. N., 132
Duran, P., 11, 65
Dutton, J., 33
Dyckman, L. J., 39

Eckstein, H., 149
Economic competitiveness, 9, 18
Egeberg, M., 151
Elder programs, 20, 161
Entman, R. M., 68
Environmental policy, 17–18
Epistemic communities, 12, 38, 59–60, 144
Erkkilä, T., 30, 41
Ethnicity, 18
European Union, 9, 12, 38, 91, 136
    Bologna Process, 123
    European Commission, 144, 157
    Euro Zone, 136
    Lisbon Strategy, 121
Every Child Matters, 115
Ewalt, J. A. G., 153
Expertise, 60–61

Fauroux, R., 12
Fawcett, P., 160
Federalism, 11–12, 35–36, 39–40, 132, 135
Fenna, A., 11
Fewsmith, J., 36
Finer, S. E., 157
Finland, 76, 101, 103–104, 117–121, 124
    Coalition governments, 120–121

Committee for the Future, 161
"Health in all Policies," 117
Ministry of Finance, 87
Prime Minister's Office, 118
Program Management, 117–118
Fischer, F., 69
Flynn, M. E., 86
Food regulation, 39–40, 136, 154
Fournier, J., 76, 90, 97
Fox, C. J., 59
Fox, E. M., 37
France, 76, 90
    Grand corps, 95
Frederickson, H. G., 59, 74
Freidson, E., 38

Galaz, V., 133
Garamone, J., 146
Gargan, J. A., 38
Geddes, B., 158
Gellman, B., 105
Gender, 17
Germany, 11, 137
    Bundeskanzlersamt, 77
Ghana, 1
Gilbert, N., 91
Globalization, 9
Gogaru, T.-C., 23
Good, D. A., 160
Goodsell, C. T., 5
Gormley, W. T., 138
Gouldner, A. W., 63
Governance, 7, 15, 16, 42–43, 128
Granastein, J. L., 160
Gregg, P., 21
Gregory, R., 140
Gremion, P., 36
Greve, M., 135
Grossman, G. M., 61
Guild, E., 123
Gulick, L. H., 47, 48

Haas, M., 59
Hagen, M., 20
Hall, P. A., 97
Hall, R. A., 4
Hallberg, L., 37

Halligan, J. A., 20, 33, 96
Halpert, B. P., 69
Hamburger, P., 77
Hammond, P. Y., 77
Hanley, D., 151
Hansen, H. F., 150
HAQ, 18
Harkness, S., 21
Harmon, M. M., 47
Haverland, M., 161
Hay, C., 26
Hayward, J. E. S., 75
Heclo, H., 95
Hedstrom, P., 45
Heinrich, C. J., 31
Heinze, T., 123
Helmke, G., 61
Helpman, E., 61
Hendriks, R., 134
Hertin, J., 4
Hierarchy, 46–52, 75–91, 150–151
    Advisory committees, 87–88
    Cabinet, 80–82
    Cabinet committees, 82–83
    Coordination agencies, 88–89
    Core executive, 75
    Executive staffs, 76–78
    Junior ministers, 84–85
    Lead agencies, 86–87
    Ministerial organizations, 85–86, 89–91
    Ministers without portfolio, 83
Hill, C. J., 31
Hisschemöller, M., 69
Historical institutionalism, 144
Hjern, B., 62
Hogwood, B. W., 12, 34, 82
Holistic governance, 7, 70, 100, 133, 145–146
Hong Kong, 54
Hood, C., 31, 52
Hoornbeek, J. A., 39
Hoppe, R., 69
Hovden, E., 4
Howlett, M., 66
Huber, J. D., 13, 47
Hueglin, T., 11
Hult, K. M., 86

Huxham, C., 27
Hybrid instruments, 99–101
Hylton, L., 53

Implementation, 13–14, 43, 58
Implementation structures, 58, 62
Information, 27–29
Ingraham, P. W., 96
Innovation, 133–135
Institutionalization, 19, 99
Institutional theory, 27, 68, 98–99
Intelligence, 106–107, 111, 157, 160–161
International politics, 1
Itoh, H., 55

Jacobssen, K., 121
Jarvis, M., 81
Jenkins-Smith, H., 158
Jennings, E. T., 2, 23
Jensen, L., 80
Jerome-Forget, M., 92
Jochim, A. E., 153
Jochum, M., 24
Johnson, P. V., 134
Joined-up government, xi, 7, 100, 103, 145
"Joint decision trap," 133
Jones, B. D., 50
Jones, D. M., 124
Jones, G., 50
Jordan, A., 69
Julliet, L., 31, 93

Kall, W. M., 38
Karre, P. M., 101
Kassim, H., 4
Kavanagh, D., 100
Kekkonen, S., 101, 117
Kettl, D. F., 16, 36, 105, 116
Khademian, A. M., 100
Kickert, W. J. M., 59, 61
Kingdon, J. W., 144
Kissinger, H., 69
Klijn, E.-H., 59, 61
Knill, C., 123
Knudsen, T., 35
Kooiman, J., 6–7, 59, 94

Koopenjan, J. F. M., 59, 61
Krause, P., 80
Krauss, E., 108
Krejci, D., 110
Kriesi, H., 24
Kubicel, H., 20
Kuipers, S., 34

Labor market policy, 2
Laegreid, P., 8, 47, 101
Lafferty, W., 4
Lam, W. F., 54
Laming, The Lord, 14, 114, 115
Landau, M., 129, 130, 162
Lane, J.-E., 13, 58
Lanzalco, L., 34, 67
Larsson, T., 77
Latin America, 75–76
Leadership, 15, 142–143
Legitimation, 8
Lejano, R. J., 66
Lemaire, R. H., 57
Lenschow, A., 69, 97
Lesser, C., 6
Lester, W., 110
Levin, K., 154
Levitsky, S., 61
Li, H., 85
Lichtblau, E., 33, 42
Lijphart, A., 151
Lindblom, C. E., 4, 6, 52, 69, 93
Linder, S. H., 13, 66
Ling, T., 91
Litwak, E., 53
"Logic of appropriateness," 68
Lynn, L. E., 31, 61

Maas, A., 17
Mackie, T. T., 82
MacMillan, L., 21
Madoff, Bernard, 2, 49
Malkin, E., 154
Malloy, J., 17, 89, 98
Maor, M., 95
March, J. G., 68
Marin, B., 93

Marinetto, M., 14, 116
Markets, for coordination, 52–57, 91–93
    Internal markets, 92
Markon, J., 33
Marsh, D., 57, 59
Martin, L. W., 82
Martinez-Gallardo, C., 76
Matei, A., 23
May, P. J., 5, 97
Mayer, R. T., 47
Mayntz, R., 45, 93
McGuire, M., 6, 97
Measurement, coordination, 152–153
Mekonen, Y., 18
Melkas, T., 117
Merton, R. K., 48
Metcalfe, L., 4, 22, 58
Meyerson, B., 37
Mile's law, 32
Miller, B., 105
Miller, C., 12, 115
Miller, G., 105
Miller, H. T., 59
Mills, M. V., 37
Milward, H. B., 59
Moe, T. M., 47
Mohr, L. B., 48
Mohr, M., 48
Moore, M. H., 159
Morgenstern, S., 75
Morris, E. D., 124
Morris, J. C., 124
Morth, U., 123
Mountfield, R., 3, 7
Mueller-Rommel, W., 77
Multi-level governance, 12

Nathan, R., 85
Nelson, R., 132
Netherlands, 83, 101
Network theory, 57–65, 93–96, 150
    Communications, 64
    Governance, 59
    Leadership, 94
    Measurement, 63–64
Newmann, W. W., 77

New Public Management, x–xi, 8, 30–31, 33, 49–50, 51–52, 63, 95, 101–102, 128, 138
    Agencies, 88
    Pay-for-performance, 96
    Virtual organizations, 90
New State Ice Company vs. Liebmann, 135
New Zealand, 158
Nicholson-Crotty, S., 53
Nieuwenburg, P., 116
Nilsson, M., 17
Niskanen, W., 130, 138, 158
Nowlin, M. C., 11
Nurmi, H., 120
Nurmi, L., 120

O'Beirne, K., 111
O'Connor, A., 132
Oleszek, W., 75
Oliver, C., 56, 57, 99
Olsen, J. P., 68, 99
Olson, D. L., 129
O'Malley, E., 78
One-stop shop, x, 15, 31, 162
Open method of coordination, 13, 17, 104, 121–123, 124–125
Oppenheimer, M., 134
Organizational costs, 34–35
Organizational culture, 28
Organizational ideologies, 37
Organizational report cards, 138
Organizational termination, 34–35
Organization for Economic Cooperation and Development, 23
Organization theory, 26, 45
    Competition, 130
    Informal organizations, 63
    Information processing, 129, 158
    Interdependence, 53–54
    Interorganizational relations, 58
    Line versus staff, 79
    Organizational fields, 57–58
    Process, 48
    Reflective organizations, 48
    Resource dependency, 56, 65
    Substructures, 49, 109, 143
    Uncertainty, 132–135
Ormond, D., 82

Ostrom, E., 23, 26
Oughton, C., 18

Page, E. C., 15, 47, 51
Papadopolous, Y., 42
Parks, R. B., 23
Partisan analysis, 69
Partisanship, 35–36
Party government, 50
Payan, T., 38
Pecora, P. J., 113
Performance management, x, 30–31
Perry, J. L., 34
Persson, Å., 5, 17
Peters, B. G., 2, 4, 13, 15, 16, 26, 31, 34, 42, 43, 46, 51, 52, 53, 58, 59, 66, 68, 71, 75, 76, 77, 79,82, 83, 89, 94, 97, 99, 123, 128
Pierre, J., 15, 16, 31, 51, 52, 59, 71, 89, 92, 128
Pierson, P., 27
Pionke, J., 110
Pluvoise-Fenton, V., 110
Poguntke, T., 76
Policy choices, 148–152
Policy coherence, 3, 4–5, 24
Policy communities, 59
Policy contingencies, 146–148
Policy domains, 7, 153
Policy entrepreneurs, 140, 144
Policy failure, 3
Policy framing, 6, 11, 38, 68–69, 143–145
Policy ideas, 97
Policy instruments, 149
Policy integration, 4, 24, 146
Policy networks, 24, 40
Policy problems, 149
Policy process, 127
Polidano, C., 162
Political culture, 158
Political parties, 151–152
Politics, 139–140, 145
Pollitt, C., 7, 15, 30, 47, 49, 75, 100, 119
Porter, D. O., 62
Posner, P., 29, 111
Potoski, M., 55
Poverty trap, ix, 21, 157
Powell, W. W., 57
Prefect, 157

Presidentialization, 76, 154
Pressman, J. L., 58, 62
"Primacy of politics," xi
Principal-agent theory, 61–62
Prisoner's Dilemma, 54
Privacy, 41–42, 136–137
Private sector organizations, 16
Professionalism, 36–38
Provan, K. G., 57, 59, 63
Public goods, 54
Public management, 30–31, 67, 108–110
    Administrative village, 94
    Internal controls, 137–139
    Scientific management, 74
Public value, 159
Pump, B., 153

Qiu, M., 85

Radin, B., 33
Randma-Liiv, T., 89, 96
Ratto, M., 31
Raunio, T., 101, 117
Recentering government, 128
Redundancy, 8, 20, 129–131, 162
Refsortsprinzip, 10
Rein, M., 6, 68, 69, 90
Reissert, B., 35
Remington, J. A., 135
Rettig, R. A., 134
Rhinard, M., 12
Rhodes, R. A. W., 57, 59, 65, 76, 94
Richards, D., 100
Ridge, Tom, 105, 162
Ries, J. C., 104
Risk, 31–32
Rittel, H. W. J., 154
Rodrigues, M. J., 121
Roosevelt, Franklin D., 138
Rosacker, K. M., 129
Rose, R., 50
Rouban, L., 96

Sabatier, P. A., 13
Salamon, L. M., 16
Sapotichne, J., 5
Sartori, G., 22

Savoie, D. J., 75, 78, 80, 81
Sayre, W. S., 108
Scandanavia, 87–88, 122
Scharpf, F. W., 10, 35, 52, 55, 56, 60, 70, 74, 93, 122
Schermerhorn, J. R., 5
Schmidt, C. P., 42
Schmidt, M. S., 42
Schnabel, F., 35
Schnell, F., 68
Schön, A. A., 6, 68, 69, 90
Schwartz, R. D., 46
Sciolino, E., 21
Scott, I., 131
Sechrest, L., 46
Secrecy, 29–30
Seidman, H., 2, 32
Selznick, P. A., 19, 98
Semi-presidentialism, 76
Services publics, 12
"Shadow of hierarchy," 52, 55, 70, 74, 93
Shipan, C. R., 13, 47
Sicurelli, D., 38
Sieber, S., 136
Simon, H. A., 53, 74, 127
Skelcher, C., 6, 67
Smith, K. B., 74
Smith, M. J., 75
Smith, S. R., 74
Social inclusion, 4, 91, 140, 161
Social mechanisms, 45
Social services, 42, 66
Sofer, V. N., 134
Soss, J., 132
Specht, H., 91
Specialization, ix, 5, 26, 47–48, 127, 131–132, 155
Spitz, B., 12
Standard operating procedures, 17
State and society linkage, 62
Steenbergen, M., 34
Stewart, J., 128
Stewart, M. C., 160
Stinchcombe, A. L., 129
Stokman, F., 10, 17
Street level bureaucrats, 141
Streib, G., 122

Structure-agency problems, 159
Sullivan, H., 6, 41, 67
Sullivan, L. A., 37
"Superministries," 85
Swedborg, R., 45
Sydow, J., 63
Szablowski, G., 78
Szczerski, K., 12

't Hart, P., 43
Talbot, C., 30, 49
Tanguy, G., 95
Task Force, 89
Tempkin, B., 68
Thatcher, M., 131
Thelen, K., 144
Thoenig, J.-C., 11
Thomas, C. W., 86
Thomas, N., 115
Thompson, D. F., 41
Thompson, G., 45, 72
Thomson, R., 10
Tiihonen, S., 16
Tilli, M., 119
Tillin, L., 135
Time, as barrier to coordination, 39–40
Timsit, G., 89
Tobacco policy, 20–21
Toke, D., 64
Tomlinson, I. J., 64
Torenvlied, R., 10
Torfing, J., 7, 59
Transaction cost analysis, 55
Triangulation, 46, 70–72
Tsebelis, G., 76
Tsegaye, S., 18
Tullock, G., 159
Turf battles, 32–34, 50, 78

Underdal, A., 4
Unfunded mandates, 111
UNICEF, 113
    Innocenti Research Center, 116
United Kingdom, 87
    Cabinet Office, 7, 9
    Children Act of 2004, 115
    Children's Commissioners, 115, 146
    Department of the Environment, 40
    DfES, 146
    HM Treasury, 40, 78
    Minister of Children, 115
    National Health Service, 93, 114
    Next Steps Agencies, 151, 157, 162
    Office of Standards in Education, 115
United Nations Convention on the Rights of
        Children, 115
United States
    9/11, 104, 129, 152
    Agency for International Development, 112
    Bureau of Alcohol, Tobacco and Firearms,
        33
    Central Intelligence Agency, 21, 54, 106
    Congress, 75
    Council of Economic Advisors, 77
    Customs and Border Protection, 105–106
    Department of Agriculture, 21, 48, 112, 159
    Department of Defense, 54, 86, 104
    Department of Education, 33
    Department of Energy, 134
    Department of Health and Human Ser-
        vices, 21, 33
    Department of Homeland Security, 86,
        103, 104–112, 124, 143, 148
    Department of Housing and Urban Devel-
        opment, 33
    Department of Justice, 33, 37
    Department of State, 54
    Department of Treasury, 109
    Environmental Protection Agency, 39
    Executive Office of the President, 77
    Federal Bureau of Investigation, 21, 33, 107
    Federal Emergency Management Agency,
        110, 133, 141
    Federal Trade Commission, 37
    General Accounting Office, 17, 20, 30, 108,
        111, 112
    Homeland Security Council, 107
    Immigration and Naturalization Service,
        21
    Model Cities, 91, 147
    National Aeronautics and Space Adminis-
        tration, 130, 132
    National Commission on Employment
        Policy, 2

National Commission on Terrorist Attacks on the United States, 104–105
National Institutes of Health, 38
National Security Agency, 21, 42, 54
National Security Council, 77, 160
Native American Health Service, 38
New Deal, 138
Office of Management and Budget, 158
Patriot Act, 162
Securities and Exchange Commission, 2, 49
Transportation Security Administration, 137
US Army, 138
Veterans Administration, 33
War on Cancer, 134
Unobtrusive measures, 46

Vaccari, B., 12
Van de Graaf, T., 1
Van der Steen, M., 101
Vangen, S., 27
van Oosteen, F., 16
Van Slyke, D. M., 55
Van Twist, M., 101
Verhoest, K., 2, 7, 26, 80, 83
Veto players, 76

Walsh, K., 93
Warin, P., 98
Waugh, W. L., 122
Webb, A., 2
Webb, E. T., 46
Webb, P., 76
Webber, M. M., 154
Weber, E. P., 100
Weber, Max, 47

Wechsler, W., 142
Weimer, D. L., 138
Weingast, B. R., 107
Weiss, J., 6
Weller, P., 77, 81
Whetten, D. A., 58
Whitaker, G. P., 23
White, J., 92
White, M., 114
Whiteley, P. F., 160
Whole client, 5, 37–38, 61
"Whole of government" (Australia), 146
Wicked problems, 100, 133, 154
Wiener, J. M., 92
Wiggins, K., 116
Wildavsky, A., ix, 19, 58, 62
Wilensky, H. L., 129
Wilkinson, D., 8
Williamson, O. E., 56, 91
Wills, J., 20
Willumsen, E., 37
Wilson, J. Q., 26
Winter, S., 13, 43
Wolf, C., 92
Wolf, F., 46
Woodside, K., 149
"Workfare," 132
Workman, S., 5
World Bank, 162
Wright, V., 4, 15, 75, 76

Yang, C. J., 134
Yarwood, D. L., 32
Yesilkagit, K., 28
Yi, H., 108

Zito, A. R., 38